# DON'T BELIEVE EVERYTHING YOU THINK

# Don't Believe Everything You Think

## Living with Wisdom and Compassion

Bhikshuni Thubten Chodron

SNOW LION

BOSTON & LONDON

2012

Snow Lion
An imprint of Shambhala Publications, Inc.
Horticultural Hall
300 Massachusetts Avenue
Boston, Massachusetts 02115
www.shambhala.com

9 8 7 6 5 4 3 2

Printed in the United States of America

∞ This edition is printed on acid-free paper that meets the
American National Standards Institute z39.48 Standard.
♻ This book is printed on 30% postconsumer recycled paper.
For more information please visit www.shambhala.com.

Distributed in the United States by Random House, Inc.,
and in Canada by Random House of Canada Ltd

Designed by Gopa & Ted2, Inc.

*Library of Congress Cataloging-in-Publication Data*
Thubten Chodron, 1950–
Don't believe everything you think: living with wisdom
and compassion / Bhikshuni Thubten Chodron.
pages cm
Includes bibliographical references.
ISBN 978-1-55939-396-6 (alk. paper)
1. Rgyal-sras Thogs-med Bzaṅ-po-dpal, 1295–1369. Rgyal-sras lag len so bdun ma.
2. Enlightenment (Buddhism)—Requisites. 3. Spiritual life—Buddhism.
I. Rgyal-sras Thogs-med Bzaṅ-po-dpal, 1295–1369. Rgyal-sras lag len so bdun ma.
English. II. Title.
BQ4399.T495 2012
94.3'420423—dc23
2012012415

# Table of Contents

# Appreciation

I AM GRATEFUL to the Buddha for teaching the Dharma—the path that ends all dukkha (unsatisfactory conditions)—and I am also grateful to all those who learned, practiced, and passed on these wonderful teachings to this present day. One of those people was Bodhisattva (Gyelsay) Togmay Zangpo, who composed *The Thirty-seven Practices of Bodhisattvas,* the root text on which this book is based. My gratitude and respect go to His Holiness the Dalai Lama and Khensur Jampa Tegchok Rinpoche for their kindness in teaching this text to me. I had the privilege of editing Khensur Jampa Tegchok's commentary on this text, which was published as *Transforming Adversity into Joy and Courage,* and I recommend this book to you as a more in-depth explanation of these verses. Geshe Sonam Rinchen, another of my teachers, also wrote a book about *The Thirty-seven Practices of Bodhisattvas,* which was translated into English by Ruth Sonam, who also translated the root verses as they appear here in this book. In a few places, I have replaced her translation of terms with alternative translations.

I have often used *The Thirty-seven Practices of Bodhisattvas* as the root text for Dharma talks. After the talks I gave in 2005 at a short course at Sravasti Abbey were transcribed, Esther Thien edited them with the help of Jo Simpson and Karri McKee. To illustrate the practical application of these teachings in our daily lives, I added the true stories that Dharma students recounted about applying these verses to their lives. One day we sat around the dining room table telling our personal stories, laughing and crying at how silly and how sad our thoughts and lives become when disturbing emotions run the show. Other people later contributed more stories from their own experiences. While the names of the authors and people and some minor details in the stories have been changed, all these tales are true. We can learn so much by sharing our experiences of making the Dharma applicable to our lives. As you read each verse in *The Thirty-seven Practices of Bodhisattvas*, contemplate its meaning and make some examples of how you could implement it in your life.

All errors are my own. I am trying to practice the teachings in this book; we are all on this path together. My hope is that you enjoy and benefit from this book and that it enhances the meaning and quality of your life and lives.

# Introduction:
## Don't Believe Everything You Think

IF SOMEONE told you to speak of the good qualities of a person who
has broadcast all sorts of critical remarks about you in your workplace,
you would probably tell them they were crazy. That person deserves not
our praise but our blame, and we're entitled to get even. In fact, we *should*
get even—it will teach that person a lesson and make sure he doesn't do it
again, at least not to us. Besides, we believe, saying a few choice scathing
remarks behind that person's back will make us feel better.

Or so we think.

But don't believe everything you think because, believe it or not, it is
often wrong. Even if all of our friends think it's a good way to think, when
we examine our own experience, we'll often discover that in fact that way
of thinking makes us more unhappy. For example, a friend of mine is a
public defender in federal court. She has attended at least twelve execu-
tions of men who have been tried and convicted of murder. During the
trial and sentencing, the victim's family firmly believes that executing the
murderer of their loved one will alleviate their grief. But my friend told
me that never once has she seen that happen. After the execution, people
remain angry and bitter. What they thought would bring them relief from
their suffering failed miserably.

In difficult situations, it is often the case that if we do the opposite of
what we think will resolve the problem, the outcome will be better. To
continue with the above example, I have another friend whose husband
was a police officer who was murdered on duty, leaving her widowed with
a young child. She told me that she begged the jury to give the murderer
the death sentence, and they did. But she continued to be miserable. A few

years later, she began to attend Buddhist teachings and started to meditate on love, compassion, and forgiveness. One day she realized that she no longer hated the man who killed her husband. Instead, she felt some compassion for his suffering and the confusion that made him do such a senseless act that ruined his own life as well. Her heart was now free because she stopped believing all those angry thoughts and changed her perspective on the situation.

The above example is an extreme situation, but it illustrates the point that it is our mind—our way of thinking—that creates our happiness or misery, our fulfillment or dissatisfaction. So instead of believing everything we think, we need to have some healthy doubt. In particular we need to doubt our disturbing emotions and the stories that lie behind them. For example, when we are furious, we never doubt the validity of our anger or our thoughts about and interpretation of the situation. In our mind, it is very clear: I am right and he is wrong. There is nothing to doubt about that, and anger is the only possible way I can feel in response to this situation.

But thinking like this puts us in a box—this is the proverbial prison of our own making—and it's all created by inappropriate attention and incorrect conceptualizations. Let's step back, have some creative doubt, and ask ourselves: Why do I need to get mad at this? Is anger really the only way anyone could possibly feel in this situation? Is the anger realistic? Is it benefiting me or anyone else? How else could I look at the situation that might be more realistic, not to mention beneficial, for my own mind?

This kind of questioning leads us to stretch our mind and to encompass new perspectives, and it is what the Tibetan monk and Bodhisattva Togmay Zangpo (1295-1369) encourages us to do in *The Thirty-seven Practices of Bodhisattvas*. The fact that this short text was written about eight hundred years ago doesn't limit its applicability. People were just as confused, greedy, angry, arrogant, and jealous then as now. Nowadays we may have a greater variety of external objects for these disturbing emotions to latch on to, but people in Tibet eight centuries ago also had to learn not to believe everything they thought.

*The Thirty-seven Practices of Bodhisattvas* is one of my favorite texts because it is both practical and concise. Each verse contains layers of meaning that can be explained in an expanded teaching. At the same time, the vast meaning may be condensed in a short verse that can be recited and recalled in a minute. At Sravasti Abbey, the monastery where I live in eastern Washington State, we chant a Buddhist text after lunch each day in order to direct our mind to the Dharma. *The Thirty-seven Practices of Bodhisattvas* is one of these texts, and memorizing it has benefited everyone in our community. Now when we find ourselves in a situation in which attachment, anger, conceit, or jealousy are getting revved up in our minds, the words of just the right verse will pop into our minds to help us counteract that disturbing emotion.

This book is for you. It doesn't matter if you are new to the Buddha's teachings or a longtime practitioner. In fact, you don't need to be a Buddhist at all. So many of the Buddha's teachings are common sense that is somehow uncommon enough that we never thought about it before. These teachings are applicable to everyone and can be applied by everyone. No dogma is required. (Thank goodness, or I would not have written this book!)

There are two ways to teach these practices. The first way helps us to solve our current problems and have more happiness in this life. The second way helps us to attain liberation and enlightenment. I'm going to teach the text in both ways, giving you tools that will help you in this life as well as describing methods that will lead you to liberation and enlightenment in the long term.

One of the distinguishing features of this book is the short vignettes that take the meaning of each verse and show examples of how it can be applied to our lives. Spirituality and religion should be practical. It's not about proving our particular doctrine is superior to those of others; it's not about looking holy at certain times or in particular places or situations. It's about transforming our heart and mind, accessing and expanding our inner human beauty, clearing away obstacles to doing this, and sharing who we are and what we know with others in ways that will benefit them. Spiritual practice is about how we live our daily lives. To live with wisdom and compassion, some quiet time alone to reflect and meditate is important. We will benefit the most if we spend some quiet time contemplating or meditating on what Togmay Zangpo teaches us and then trying it out in real life situations.

## Overview

The first chapter, "Helpful Background," sets the stage by presenting the Buddhist worldview and putting the thirty-seven practices into context. Here we review our present situation with its unsatisfactory conditions and learn that ignorance and its two cohorts—attachment and anger—lie at the root of these conditions. This ignorance can be eliminated because it misapprehends how things—including ourselves—actually exist. There is a path to practice that will accomplish this, and liberation or full enlightenment is the state of freedom and fulfillment that we will arrive at. This chapter, like the rest of the book, challenges some of our dearly held assumptions about ourselves, our bodies, and our lives, so get ready for an adventure!

In chapter 2, "Starting Out on the Path," we recognize the wonderful opportunity we have with our current precious human lives; see how to oppose attachment, anger, and confusion, which keep us locked into dysfunctional patterns of behavior; and learn how to seclude ourselves from what triggers our disturbing emotions and how to cultivate clarity of mind.

Chapter 3, "Transitioning," helps us to set good priorities about what is meaningful in our lives and what is not. We look at our current friendships to discern true from false friends, and see the importance of "virtuous friends"—spiritual mentors who understand our spiritual longing and who can guide us appropriately. Through their influence, we are connected to the Three Jewels: the Buddha—the supreme spiritual teacher, the Dharma—the freedom we seek and the path to it, and the Sangha—those who have realized reality and who can aid us on the path.

Chapter 4 is "The Next Step," which is to realize that our actions have an ethical dimension and that what we think, say, and do has effects not only on others, but also on our own future circumstances. Following that, we take the step of aspiring for true liberation from ignorance, anger, and clinging attachment.

Chapter 5, "Cultivating Love, Compassion, and Altruism," shows us how to open our heart to others. This isn't a matter of telling ourselves what we "should" feel, but taking concrete steps to change the way we view others so that we can see them in beauty. Also involved in this process is seeing that everyone wants happiness and freedom from suffering as much as we do and diminishing our self-centered thoughts so that we can sincerely work for their benefit.

Chapters 6, 7, and 8 are the nitty-gritty practices that transform our thoughts and thus transform the external situations we encounter in life. These situations include facing loss, illness and suffering, undeserved blame, criticism, betrayal of trust, derision, and lacking what we need. We also learn how not to let success and wealth go to our head and how to work with anger and unstick ourselves from attractive objects.

In chapter 9 we look at the true nature of reality—how things actually exist—and learn how to apply that view to daily life difficulties. Chapter 10 speaks of practices to cultivate throughout our life—generosity, ethical conduct, fortitude, joyous effort, meditation, and wisdom. Then we look at important practices to do in order to stay on the path once we're on it. Hypocrisy, judgmental attitude, jealousy, harsh words, and disturbing emotions hijack our practice, so we want to be aware of them. Mindfulness and introspective awareness enable us to do that. To complete all virtuous actions, we then dedicate the positive energy, merit, and goodness for the welfare and enlightenment of all sentient beings.

The root text of *The Thirty-seven Practices of Bodhisattvas* and the outline of the topics of its verses are in the appendix. We regularly chant this text at Sravasti Abbey; you can learn it at www.thubtenchodron.org/Prayers AndPractices/37_practices_of_bodhisattvas.html.

In Buddhist terminology, no difference is made between heart and mind, one word being used for both. For convenience sake, "mind" is used here, although this term doesn't refer to our brain or to our intellect only. Our mind is what perceives and experiences our external and internal worlds. It's formless, and includes our sense consciousness, mental consciousness, emotions, intelligence, and so on. Each of us has our own mind, so the phrase in this book "our mind" refers to each person's individual consciousness.

A glossary is included so that you can look up technical terms, along with a list of further reading. Enjoy not believing everything you think!

# 1. Helpful Background

"DON'T BELIEVE everything you think" is a call to let go of feelings of hopelessness, self-deprecating thoughts, and useless conceptualizations and to reenvision our lives. In the depths of our hearts all of us want to live meaningful lives and make a positive contribution to the world, but some of our unexamined assumptions about life encumber us.

For example, we may believe that the purpose of life is to be as successful as we can according to society's standards. But in pursuing this goal, we're dissatisfied. Nothing ever goes exactly the way we want; we face so many unwanted obstacles, and although we work hard to achieve certain goals, we perpetually seem to fall short. Or if we do achieve them, either the success brings new problems with it or we're not as happy as we expected.

Meanwhile, from a Buddhist point of view, we have something much more precious than material success: we have the Buddha nature, or Buddha potential—the fundamental nature of our mind which is pure. This pure nature of our mind is always with us and can never be removed, thus it is a firm basis upon which to establish self-confidence. By cultivating our Buddha nature we have the potential to become completely enlightened Buddhas.

Our Buddha nature has two aspects: the natural Buddha nature and the transforming Buddha nature. The transforming Buddha nature includes the love, compassion, and other virtuous qualities we already have now. These can be cultivated limitlessly. The natural Buddha nature is more subtle; it refers to the ultimate nature of our mind, its lack of existing inherently, independent of any other factors. This very lack of inherent existence makes enlightenment possible. By cultivating our good qualities and clearing away the clouds that prevent us from seeing the beautiful skylike empty nature of our mind, we will be able to become a fully enlightened being, a Buddha.

Buddhas are forever free from all causes of dukkha—a Pali term that is often translated as "suffering," but actually means "unsatisfactory in nature." In addition, Buddhas have impartial love and compassion that joyfully extend to all sentient beings. Furthermore, they have the skill, wisdom, and ability to be of the greatest benefit to all other sentient beings. When we compare these qualities of a Buddha with what we now believe we are capable of being and doing, it becomes clear why we shouldn't believe everything we think: our uninformed way of thinking puts unnecessary restrictions on our ability to be peaceful, satisfied, and happy and to help others be so as well.

## Cyclic Existence

Cyclic existence, or samsara, is our unsatisfactory situation of being subject to birth, aging, sickness, death, and the other difficulties and stress mentioned above. Cyclic existence is also the five psychophysical aggregates that we live with right now—our 1) body; 2) feelings of happiness, unhappiness, and indifference; 3) discriminations of objects and their attributes; 4) emotions, attitudes, and other mental factors; and 5) consciousnesses—the five sense consciousnesses, which know sights, sounds, smells, tastes, and tactile sensations, and the mental consciousness, which thinks, meditates, and so forth.

In short, cyclic existence is our body and mind under the influence of ignorance. Often people think cyclic existence refers to the outer world, but this is not the case. If it were, renouncing cyclic existence would mean escaping from the world and going to "Lala Land." However, according to the Buddha, true renunciation is the determination to be free of cyclic existence: it's about renouncing suffering, unsatisfactory circumstances, and their causes.

Cyclic existence is rooted in ignorance: we don't know how things really exist and instead grasp false appearances to be true. Based on ignorance, wrong conceptions and disturbing emotions arise in our mind, and these motivate us to act. Our actions are called "karma" and they propel us to take rebirth in cyclic existence. Our actions also influence the conditions we are born into and what we experience in our lives.

Ignorance is the mental factor that misunderstands how things exist. It not only obscures the ultimate nature of things, but it also actively misapprehends the ultimate mode of existence. While persons and phenomena exist dependently, ignorance doesn't see things this way. It grasps phenomena as having their own inherent essence, existing from their own side and under their own power. Due to beginningless latencies of ignorance, persons and phenomena appear inherently existent to us, and ignorance actively grasps this mistaken appearance to be true.

By grasping at inherent existence, ignorance misapprehends how phenomena actually exist. Wisdom, on the other hand, realizes the opposite of ignorance; it directly perceives the emptiness of inherent existence of phenomena. By learning about emptiness and meditating on it, our wisdom will grow. When we generate the wisdom that directly and nonconceptually realizes reality—the emptiness of inherent existence—the ignorance that grasps the opposite of reality is automatically overpowered and will eventually be eliminated completely. When ignorance ceases, the mental afflictions that are born from it also cease. Thus our actions produced by the afflictions cease and, as a result, the dukkha of cyclic existence stops. Therefore, the wisdom realizing emptiness is the true path that leads us out of dukkha, out of cyclic existence and to the bliss of liberation, or nirvana, and to Buddhahood.

If we want to generate the energy to practice the path leading to nirvana we must first develop the awareness of the unsatisfactory nature of cyclic existence. The Buddha didn't talk about suffering so that we would get depressed. Feeling depressed is useless. We think about cyclic existence and its causes so that we will act to free ourselves from it. If we're not aware of what it means to be under the influence of afflictions and karma, we will remain indifferent and won't do anything to improve our situation while we have the opportunity. The tragedy of such indifference is that suffering does not stop at death. Cyclic existence continues into our future lives. We need to pay attention to what the Buddha said so that we don't find ourselves in an unfortunate rebirth in the next life, a life in which there's no opportunity to learn and practice the Dharma.

## Rebirth

The basis upon which we label "I" is our body and mind. While the body is material in nature, the mind is not. Its nature is clarity and cognizance and it is formless. The mind includes all conscious aspects of ourselves. The presence or absence of consciousness is what differentiates a corpse from a living being. The mind isn't the brain—the brain is part of the body and is made of matter.

Our body is material in nature and its causes—the sperm and egg of our parents and all the food we've ingested—are also matter. When the body and mind separate at the time of death, the continuity of the body is a corpse, which decomposes and is recycled in nature.

However, being formless, the mind's causes are previous moments of clarity and cognizance. There is a continuity of mind that existed before our birth into this body. The continuity of our mind has existed beginninglessly and will continue to exist endlessly. Thus, we need to be concerned about the course that this continuum takes. Our happiness depends on what is going on in our mind. If our mind is contaminated by ignorance, the result is cyclic existence. If the mind is imbued with wisdom and compassion, the result is enlightenment.

## Getting Clear

From what we have discussed so far, we can see that it is crucial to think about our situation in cyclic existence. The appearance of this life is so strong. That's one of the things that makes it so difficult for us to clearly see our situation. What appears to our senses seems so real, so urgent and concrete that we can't imagine anything else. Yet, everything that appears to exist with its own, true, and inherent nature does not exist in the way it appears. Things appear unchanging, whereas they are in continual flux. What is in fact unsatisfactory by nature seems to be happiness. Things appear as independent entities, whereas they are dependent. Our mind is tricked and deceived by appearances. Believing false appearances to be true obscures us from seeing what cyclic existence really is and prevents us from cultivating the wisdom that frees us from it.

We have amazing human potential that can be used to bring about peace and happiness for ourselves and others. To do that we need to question our assumptions about life and get in touch with our heart. When we do, we'll see that true fulfillment comes from having a peaceful heart and a mind imbued with love, compassion, and wisdom. When we are clear on this, then we'll seek a method that will help us develop these inner qualities. In short, we'll seek a path that will take us out of cyclic existence and to liberation or full enlightenment. As fully enlightened beings, all our faults will have been completely abandoned and our excellent qualities completely realized. With full wisdom, compassion, and skillful means, we'll be able to manifest many forms that work for the benefit of all sentient beings.

### An Alternative Path

How do we get from where we are now to the fully enlightened state? By engaging in the thirty-seven practices of bodhisattvas, which are the topic of this book. They describe the antidotes to this cycle of constantly recurring problems into which we are born again and again under the influence of ignorance, afflictions, and karma. These also present a way to live a meaningful life right now, free from the stress and frenzy our disturbing emotions bring.

The thirty-seven practices show us the way to examine our thoughts and to see if they are accurate or not. Doing this is crucial for our well-being and the well-being of those around us. Otherwise, unquestioned thoughts, assumptions, and emotions that are potentially erroneous run our lives. When we examine our thoughts, being kind and truthful with ourselves is important. But let's not scold ourselves for having negative thoughts and disturbing emotions.

It's important to differentiate a thought from an emotion. We say things such as, "I feel like they don't accept me." Actually, that is a thought. We may *feel* hurt or frustrated, and it's because we're *thinking* that others don't accept us. How do we know they don't accept us? We don't. We haven't asked them. Instead, on the basis of how they looked at us or a comment they made, our mind constructs a story that we believe.

Similarly, we say, "I feel rejected." Actually, rejected isn't a feeling; it's a thought—we're thinking someone is rejecting us, but we don't really know that for sure because we haven't asked them.

As soon as you hear yourself saying, "I feel like . . .," stop and recognize that you can't "feel like" something. You are thinking. After you have identified the thought, ask yourself, "Is that true? How do I know it's true? What evidence do I have to prove the validity of that thought?" It's really startling to see how often we assume our interpretation of a situation is true when in fact it is based on flimsy evidence.

Some of the thoughts that we often get stuck on are, "I'm a bad person," "I'm a failure," "I'm not good enough," "I'm unlovable." These self-deprecating thoughts are some of the most ingrained and harmful ones we have. When we think them, depression, despair, and anger overwhelm us and it's hard to see clearly. These kinds of thoughts impact all aspects of our lives—our health, our relationships, our work, and our spiritual practice. Sometimes it's hard to discern that these thoughts are present; we're so habituated to thinking them that they form the stage on which the drama of our life takes place.

### Is What We Think True?

When we notice these thoughts underneath our unpleasant emotions, let's stop and question them: "Is it true that I'm a bad person? Prove it to me!" We may start listing all sorts of mistakes we have made, but we keep questioning, "Does that mistake make me a bad person?"

In Tibetan Buddhism we learn debating, and we can use this same technique to test the validity of the thoughts that lie behind our low self-esteem. In debate we use syllogisms that consist of a subject, a predicate, and a reason. For example, in the syllogism "sound is impermanent because it's a product of causes," "sound" is the subject (A), "impermanent" is the predicate (B), and "because it's a product of causes" is the reason (C). For this syllogism to be true, three criteria need to be true. First, the subject is present in the reason; in other words, sound is a product of causes. Second, if it's the reason, it has to be the predicate. That is, if something is a product of causes, it must be impermanent. Third, if it's not the predicate, it isn't the reason. If it's not impermanent, it isn't a product of causes. To put it more simply:

A is C.
If it's C, it must be B.
If it's not B, it can't be C.

Now let's apply it to the syllogism "I'm a bad person because I lied." "I" is the subject, "bad person" is the predicate, and "because I lied" is the reason. Then we examine: It is true that I lied. But is it true that everyone who lies is a bad person? Does one action make someone a bad person? Do thousands of harmful actions make someone a bad person? There is a difference between a harmful action and the person who did it. While the action can be harmful, we can't say that the person who did it is bad. Since everyone has the potential to become a Buddha, how can anyone be a bad person? Here we see that our belief doesn't hold up under analysis.

What about the thought "I'm a bad person because this person doesn't like me"? Does someone not liking us make us a bad person? Does someone not loving us mean we are defective? Someone not liking or loving us has nothing to do with us. It is a thought in another person's mind and, as we know, thoughts are not so reliable and they change frequently.

I find it extremely helpful to challenge my thoughts in this way. It shows me very clearly that my way of thinking is erroneous. If a thought is incorrect, I drop it. It doesn't make any sense to continue to believe something we have just proven is incorrect.

It's helpful to question our emotions in a similar way. For example, let's say we're upset because someone criticized us. Here the syllogism is "I am mad because he criticized me." Yes, he criticized me, but do I have to be mad because someone criticized me? No, I have a choice of how to feel. I don't *have* to be mad.

When I'm really mad, I keep asking myself, "Why am I mad?" My mind answers, "Because he criticized me." I reply to myself, "Yes, he said those words, but why are you mad?" My mind says, "Because he said I'm stupid." I reply, "Yes, he said that, but why are you mad?" In other words, to all the reasons my mind uses to justify why I should be mad I question, "But why do I need to be mad at that?" When I do this long enough, I see that I'm mad because I want something. Behind the anger I may discover that I want love, safety, acknowledgment, encouragement, understanding, space, creativity, peace, or something else. Instead of pinning what I want or need on that person, I give myself some understanding and compassion and then consider other ways to meet that need. If I get stuck, I ask a friend to help me see the situation more clearly.

In this process of questioning our thoughts and feelings, it's very important to be kind to ourselves. Criticizing ourselves for being upset isn't productive. Many people find it much easier to be kind to others than to themselves. Being kind to ourselves, forgiving ourselves, and extending compassion to ourselves is a skill we need to learn. Then we need to practice it repeatedly. It's not selfish to be kind to ourselves; this is very different from being self-indulgent. We are a sentient being, and in Buddhism we want to have love and compassion for *all* sentient beings and to work for the benefit of *all* sentient beings. We can't leave one sentient being out, saying, "I'll extend kindness to all sentient beings except myself!"

### Our Human Potential

Each of us has great potential within us. Since we are not inherently this or that, we don't need to be locked into any rigid conceptualizations of ourselves or of the world. Instead, we can access our love, compassion, friendliness, joy, concentration, and wisdom and expand them limitlessly. When we eliminate ignorance completely from our mindstream and attain liberation (nirvana), we are truly free. Our good qualities will function without being impeded by fear, conceit, and other disturbing emotions.

But our real goal is not simply our own personal liberation: it is to be of the greatest benefit to everyone. Think about it—if you were drowning, your immediate goal would be to save yourself, but you would also want to rescue others as well. You wouldn't feel right about swimming to shore yourself and then relaxing while others drowned. We feel too connected to others to do this, and so, too, in our spiritual path, while accomplishing our own liberation would be wonderful, it wouldn't be totally fulfilling.

Thus we want to attain the full enlightenment of a Buddha so that we can be of the greatest benefit to ourselves and all others. While a description of Buddhahood contains many lofty and marvelous qualities, a good way to begin to get a sense of the state of a Buddha is to imagine what it would be like never to get angry at anyone, no matter what they said or did to you. Imagine this for a while: wouldn't it be wonderful to be totally free from fear, anger, defensiveness, arrogance, the need to be right or to win? People could say or do whatever they wished, and our mind would remain peaceful and undisturbed. There would be no anger to repress; it all would have evaporated.

Similarly, what would it be like to look upon any living being and spontaneously feel affection and wish the best for them? Wouldn't it be wonderful to feel connected to everyone and to wish them well?

These are some simple things to imagine in order to get an idea of where we are going on the path. It is possible for us to actually become like that. While we don't want to believe everything our self-centered thought thinks, we do want to believe in our human potential. And we *can* believe it because many other people have attained enlightenment before us, and they can show us the path.

# 2. Starting Out on the Path

## PAYING HOMAGE

*Homage to Lokeshvara.*

*I pay constant homage through my three doors*
*To my supreme teacher and protector Chenrezig,*
*Who while seeing all phenomena lack coming and going,*
*Makes single-minded effort for the good of living beings.*

*Perfect Buddhas, source of all well-being and happiness,*
*Arise from accomplishing the excellent teachings,*
*And this depends on knowing the practices.*
*So I will explain the practices of bodhisattvas.*

THESE ARE THE opening verses of *The Thirty-seven Practices of Bodhisattvas*, a text composed in the fourteenth century by a Tibetan monk, Gyelsay Togmay Zangpo. He was from the Kadam tradition, which began with Lama Atisha, a great Indian master who came to Tibet in the eleventh century. Togmay Zangpo received the precious teachings on bodhicitta—the aspiration to attain full enlightenment for the benefit of all sentient beings—from his spiritual mentor, Sonam Drakpa. A great practitioner who implemented what he taught in his own life, Togmay Zangpo was regarded as an emanation of Avalokiteshvara, the Buddha known as the Great Compassionate One. It is said that Togmay Zangpo's fortunate disciples who had pure vision perceived him as Avalokiteshvara.

Due to Togmay Zangpo's close connection with the Great Compassionate One, the text begins by paying homage to Avalokiteshvara (Lokeshvara). Avalokiteshvara is called Chenrezig in Tibetan, Kuan Yin in Chinese, and Kannon in Japanese. *Paying homage through three doors* means showing respect physically, verbally, and mentally. Chenrezig simultaneously sees that *all phenomena lack coming and going*. That is, that all phenomena are empty of inherent existence in that they do not inherently arise or inherently cease. *Makes single-minded effort for the good of living beings* indicates that Avalokiteshvara acts with love, compassion, and bodhicitta to liberate all sentient beings and lead them to full enlightenment.

A Buddha is a being who has completely eliminated all defilements from the mind and developed all good qualities limitlessly. Buddhas are sources of all well-being and happiness because they teach us the Dharma—the path to true freedom. By practicing the Dharma, we too will eliminate all misery and create the causes for all happiness and peace. However, to accomplish this noble spiritual goal, we must know what to practice. For this reason, Bodhisattva Togmay Zangpo will explain the practices of bodhisattvas—those beings who have a strong, sincere motivation to attain Buddhahood for the benefit of all living beings. Because they are following in the Buddha's footsteps, bodhisattvas are often referred to as "Buddha's children." By transforming our minds by engaging in these bodhisattva practices, we will become bodhisattvas and advance on the bodhisattva path. Eventually, we too will become fully enlightened Buddhas, like Avalokiteshvara.

## VERSE 1: PRECIOUS HUMAN LIFE AND HOW TO USE IT WISELY

*Having gained this rare ship of freedom and fortune,*
*Hear, think, and meditate unwaveringly night and day*
*In order to free yourself and others*
*From the ocean of cyclic existence—*
    *This is the practice of bodhisattvas.*

## An Amazing Opportunity

This initial verse is a summary of the entire path to enlightenment. The first step of this path is to recognize the unique opportunity we have in this life to learn, think about, and meditate on the Dharma, the Buddha's teachings. *Having gained this rare ship of freedom and fortune,* refers to a precious human life, which isn't just any human life. It's a human life that has some specific features.

Our current lives are free in the sense that we are free from being born in the realms of great suffering or great happiness. If we are born in realms of great suffering—the hellish realms, the hungry ghost realm, the animal realm—the mind is too distracted by either ignorance or physical suffering to be able to do spiritual practice. Conversely, if we are born in the god realms—where beings have incredible sensory and mental pleasure—we are too engrossed in pleasure to focus on freeing ourselves by practicing the path. If we are born impoverished or in a country that lacks religious freedom or one where the Buddha's teachings do not exist, we will lack the opportunity to progress on the path.

Not every human life is a precious human life. In addition to having human aggregates—the body and mind—we must be physically and mentally healthy, have interest in the Dharma, and the aspiration to practice it. We must encounter Buddhist teachings, meet and study under the guidance of qualified Mahayana spiritual mentors, know the sangha (monastic community), and have Dharma friends. The four requisites—food, clothing, shelter, and medicine—must be readily available. Looking at it this way, we see that the vast majority of human beings don't have a precious human life.

A precious human life is rare because it is not easy to create the causes to receive it and comparatively few sentient beings have such a life. The causes for a precious human life include good ethical conduct, generosity, cultivating tolerance, fortitude, and joyous effort for spiritual practice. In addition, the merit from engaging in such practices must be dedicated to attain a precious human life. Just take a look around. Numerically, how many living beings on this planet have a precious human life? Compared to animals and insects, human beings are vastly out-numbered. Among human beings, the number of people who have all the circumstances required for a precious human life is small.

A precious human life is meaningful because with it we have the opportunity to create the causes for a fortunate rebirth and even to attain liberation and enlightenment. It acts like a ship, in that if we use this life properly, we can cross the ocean of cyclic existence to arrive at the other shore of lasting peace—liberation and enlightenment. It is a life of freedom because we are unhindered by obstacles that impede learning and practicing the Dharma. It is a life of fortune in which we have conducive circumstances to learn and practice the Dharma.

A precious human life has exactly the right combination of suffering and happiness and thus is a good life to engage in spiritual practice. We are not constantly overwhelmed by pain, but there is enough suffering to remind us that we're not liberated yet. Having attained this fortunate state, we need to make effort to use it wisely and not to waste our time.

Our present opportunity is quite extraordinary—almost like a miracle. However, unless someone points out our fortune to us—unless we recognize and appreciate this opportunity—we will spend our lives complaining about everything that is wrong. But when we are interested in spiritual practice, we realize how incredibly fortunate our life is and discover that there's not much to complain about at all. Contemplating our precious human life is a great antidote to depression.

If you're interested in spiritual practice and meditate on your precious human life, your heart will be filled with joy. You will feel so fortunate and will find nothing to complain about. You will realize that you have the freedom to do what is most important—to practice Dharma in order to free yourself and others from cyclic existence.

How do we free ourselves and others? *Hear, think, and meditate unwaveringly night and day* on the Buddha's teachings. Here the emphasis is both the formal practice of studying, reflecting, and meditating and the informal practice of integrating the teachings in the activities of our daily life. Dharma practice is not just to be done on the meditation cushion, in a temple, or in a Dharma center, but everywhere and all the time.

To do this, first we have to hear the Dharma. "Hear" means not just hearing with our ears, but includes all methods of learning the teachings. That is, we want to hear teachings orally, read Dharma texts, and study what we have heard and read. Hearing is mentioned specifically because in previous times, books were rare. Certainly, at the time of the Buddha, and for centuries after that, printed material was scarce. The teachings were transmitted orally and learning centered on listening to the teachings. Learning the teachings is essential if we want to know what to practice and what to abandon on the path. If we don't hear teachings, then we basically make up our own path to enlightenment.

In addition, we receive something special when we hear the teachings directly from a teacher that we don't receive when we read them. We receive the oral transmission. We receive the teachings from someone who practices the Dharma and who tells us in person how to practice. We make a connection with an experienced practitioner who will inspire us to practice. In-person instruction is very different from listening to a tape at home, reading a book, or watching a video of a Dharma teaching. A book can be very inspiring, and by reading it we gain useful information. Supplementing listening to teachings with reading Dharma books is excellent. However, if all we do is read and study through printed material without receiving oral teachings from someone who practices them, something is lacking.

I say this based on personal experience. Nothing can take the place of having a real, live human teacher. A living teacher is a role model of what we can become. He or she provides a vision that inspires us to practice and become like him or her. Our teacher can correct our faults and guide us by giving personal advice that fits our specific situation. A spiritual mentor shows by his or her example how to live the teachings. That's quite precious. A book doesn't show us how to live the teachings in day-to-day life. However, when we watch how our spiritual mentors act in their daily lives—how they relate to the people and events happening around them—it gives us a living example of Dharma in action.

Hearing the teachings live is also precious. In this day of the Internet, you can listen to valuable teachings online, which is very helpful. However, it's different than sitting in a room with your spiritual mentor who is speaking directly to you. Even if you're there with thousands of other students—as is the case when His Holiness the Dalai Lama teaches—he is talking directly to you in real time.

You may ask, "Why do I need to leave the comfort of my own home and go somewhere to hear teachings? Can't I just lie down, relax, and have a Pepsi while I listen to the MP3 recording? It's so much more comfortable to sit in my easy chair and watch a streamed teaching on my computer. What's wrong with listening to a tape while I drive to work? My life is very busy and at least this way I can learn the Dharma."

All of that is true, and certainly if you live in a place where there are no Dharma centers, monasteries, or temples, learning the Dharma through the Internet, books, videos, and audio recordings is good. But if you have a choice, which mode of learning the teachings will make the most impact on your mind? What do you get from attending a teaching live that you don't get from listening to a recording? First, there is the effect of the effort that you make to be there. That makes a big difference. When we have to put in effort to be somewhere, we pay more attention to what we learn. We cherish it more. In addition, when you go to a center, temple, or monastery to listen to teachings, you have to sit up straight. You're not lying in your bed drinking a cup of tea, relaxing. Thus, your body and mind are both more attentive. Your physical posture is one of respect towards the teacher and teachings. This, too, influences your mind. It's very different than lying down or leaning back on your sofa.

Furthermore, by attending teachings, you have to travel to where the teacher is. In other words, you have to go outside the comfort of your own home to receive something of great value to you. Unlike listening to teachings while you're driving, in the presence of your teacher you're able to pay closer attention; you do not have to look out for red lights or check your speedometer. Your teacher will look at you—that inspires you to listen closely instead of letting your mind wander. This is especially true if your spiritual mentor occasionally stops and questions the students in the middle of a teaching. Also, sitting in a room with other people reminds you that you're connected to other living beings. You're not sitting there with headphones on in your own little world. You're practicing with other people.

Making the effort to listen to teachings with a group of people who have gathered with a virtuous intention makes a big difference. We are in a room used especially for teaching and meditation; not for sleeping, calculating our insurance, or playing with the kids. Most of all, we're listening to someone we respect and trust tell us about how he or she practices, which is how an entire lineage of practitioners going back to the time of the Buddha also practiced.

## Reflecting and Meditating

After learning teachings from a reliable guide, we have to think about them. Learning about the teachings is the first step, but it's not sufficient for gaining realizations. We need to think about what we heard to cultivate a correct understanding. In other words, we activate our reasoning capabilities to see if the teachings hold up to intelligent scrutiny, and we apply the teachings to our lives to see if they explain the world around us. In this context, reflecting includes pondering the teachings ourselves as well as discussing them with other people. If we don't discuss the teachings with others, we may think that we understand them, but when somebody asks us a question, we realize we don't understand the meaning well enough to give a clear response. Our wisdom increases when we discuss the teachings with other people, listen to their questions, consider their interpretations of the teachings, and debate the validity of our own and their thoughts. Each of these activities causes us to think more deeply about the teachings and to develop a more comprehensive understanding of their meaning.

However, thinking and discussing the teachings alone doesn't bring in-depth realizations. Although such activities have a strong impact on our mind, meditating and putting the teachings into practice in our daily life is essential. We must integrate the teachings with our minds. Towards this end, it's good to have a consistent daily practice during which we meditate on the teachings in a more concentrated way. During meditation sessions we apply what we have learned and thought about to our lives in order to gain an in-depth realization of their meaning. The teachings are not something outside of us. Rather, they become something inside, the actual way our mind thinks, the way we regard life. Integrating the teachings into our thoughts takes both practice and time. It doesn't happen quickly or easily. There's no shortcut to get around this process.

Our daily practice may include learning, reflecting, and meditating. It is not the case that we have to learn everything before thinking about any of it or meditating on it. However, when engaging with a particular Dharma topic, the great masters recommend we engage in learning, reflecting, and meditating and in that order. Why? In order to meditate, we need to have a correct conceptual understanding of the teachings gained by thinking about them. In order to think about the teachings, we have to learn them first. So, we start out by hearing and learning, add critical reflecting, and finally, meditate.

This is important because many people think that just sitting with closed eyes is meditating. That's not meditating. Sitting still with closed eyes is what the body is doing. Meditating is done with our mind. We can sit still and look serene and at the same time daydream about a wonderful person we met or plan our revenge against someone who hurt us. Rather than being meditation, that is encouraging afflictions.

Thus, we have to learn exactly what meditation is and how to do it. If we don't, we'll invent our own "meditation," in which case we'll get the result of inventing our own meditation. That result will be different from following the meditation method taught by a fully enlightened being who describes what he or she did to become enlightened. There's a big difference between making up our own style of meditation, where we don't really have a clue what we're doing, and following a tried-and-tested method that others have practiced and actualized the result of for 2550 years.

Many people don't really understand what meditation is. I get e-mails from people saying, "I listen to music when I meditate. What kind of music do you think is best for meditation?" It's clear these people have not listened to teachings because the great masters do not recommend listening to music when you meditate. When you listen to music, you're listening to music. You're not thinking about the teachings and integrating them.

Recently someone told me she meditates best when she's swimming.

I wasn't sure what she meant by meditation. Did she mean relax and feel calm? Yes, swimming can accomplish that, but meditation isn't a relaxation technique, although it makes the mind calm and relaxed. The full purpose of meditation is to understand both conventional and ultimate reality so that we can liberate ourselves and others from cyclic existence.

The verse advises us to *hear, think, and meditate unwaveringly night and day.* Does that mean we never sleep? No, our body needs rest. However, we can transform sleep into a virtuous activity by taking refuge, remembering the qualities of the Three Jewels, generating bodhicitta, or contemplating emptiness before falling asleep. Instead of collapsing in bed with a groan and a lot of attachment to lying down on a comfortable bed, think, "I'm going to sleep to rest my body and mind so I can continue practicing tomorrow." Then sleep for an appropriate amount of time to maintain the health of both body and mind.

Why do we practice hearing, thinking, and meditating as much as possible? *In order to free yourself and others from the ocean of cyclic existence.* In other words, we're not meditating because we want to be great yogis and famous spiritual practitioners. We're not meditating because we want to liberate ourselves alone. We're not doing it for who knows what other kind of motivation. Instead, within ourselves, we're cultivating the motivation to free ourselves from cyclic existence and to attain full Buddhahood so that we can lead others on the path to enlightenment. Our underlying motivation is bodhicitta, the aspiration to benefit all sentient beings and to attain full enlightenment in order to do so most effectively.

These verses present an effective way to practice the Buddha's teachings. Bodhisattva Togmay Zangpo doesn't expect us to be able to actualize these instructions instantaneously. Rather, he points the direction for us to go. From our side, we begin where we are and progress gradually. Don't feel pressured to do it "right" and don't criticize yourself for not being able to live each verse exactly as it is written. Remember, we are *training* our minds, and this entails repeated practice over time. Have an expansive approach, thinking that your practice will benefit yourself and others in the long term, not just the short term. Of course, if we practice with a mind dedicated to benefiting all sentient beings in the long term, our immediate feeling of well-being will increase as a by-product. However, we're not practicing simply for our own immediate pleasure. In fact, the mind seeking a quick "spiritual high" is a hindrance to genuine spiritual practice. Be joyful when you practice, confident that you will be able to actualize and integrate each verse in time.

## Pat: Renewed Appreciation for Life

One summer, my sister Jen and her daughter Karen came to visit me in Idaho. My friend Sue had a small fishing boat—one of those silver ones that run on an outboard motor. One beautiful summer day, we headed out of Garfield Bay in Sagle with a plan to take a leisurely cruise on Lake Pend Oreille. The boat didn't go very fast but we didn't mind. That is, until halfway across the lake when the wind picked up and the clouds moved in. The little boat got tossed here and there. At one point, the waves were so high that they were coming into the boat and we started taking on water. We were all quite frightened, particularly Karen who was only four years old. Sue headed the dinghy to a group of islands. Just as the storm broke, we pulled the water-laden boat onto the shore and headed for cover. We were relieved to be on solid ground. We had no food, drink, or raingear, so we sat it out, hungry and cold.

The storm went as fast as it came. We returned to the boat to find it half full of water and started bailing it out with a small bucket and cups. Amazingly, the engine started and we gingerly headed back across the lake. The wind was still brisk and we were heading into it, which made the trip twice as long as going out. It was an adventure and is a fit analogy for the meaning of this verse. This life, with a human body and mind, is like a boat that can take us across the ocean of samsaric suffering. The unpredictability of the winds of karma arises like storms in our lives. If we are not prepared—as we were not that day—we can get tossed around by our karma, as well as our afflictions, to the point where we may feel like we're sinking with no land in sight. So it is crucial that we build a body and mind that are sturdy and able to sail across the ocean of cyclic existence to the other shore. Just as we did that day, we must be strong and creative to deal with the storms of afflictions and karma we experience in cyclic existence. If we just throw up our hands and let feelings of helplessness and hopelessness overtake us, we will do nothing to improve our situation and will surely sink. Furthermore, just as taking good weather for granted is ill advised, let's not take the good circumstances in our lives for granted. Instead, let's use them to hear, think, and meditate on the Dharma as much as we can.

### Roy: No Dogma for Me

The Buddha encouraged us to hear, think, and meditate on his teachings and to avoid forming hard and fast opinions that we then assert as objective absolutes. Thus, the only time I can honestly say that I'm absolutely right is when I'm saying, "I'm not sure I know." If I have learned nothing else from my Dharma study, I did learn never to be absolutely certain of anything I don't fully understand. Or, to put it another way, I'm not a Buddha; I'm not even an arya for that matter. I haven't seen ultimate reality even once, as it truly is. So, how can I possibly be dogmatically certain about anything? This isn't to say I can't believe things. For example, I know through examining my own experience that the ten nonvirtues lead to suffering and the ten virtues, to happiness in this very life. As far as the more complex tenets, I can have a working hypothesis and go from there, continuing to learn, think, and meditate as much as I can until I have direct experience.

## VERSE 2: THE POISONS OF ATTACHMENT, ANGER, AND IGNORANCE

> Attached to your loved ones, you're stirred up like water.
> Hating your enemies, you burn like fire.
> In the darkness of confusion you forget what to adopt and discard.
> Give up your homeland—
>     This is the practice of bodhisattvas.

## The Three Poisons

The second verse is very powerful. It begins, *Attached to your loved ones, you're stirred up like water.* Is that true or not? We're attached to our friends. We're attached to our family. We want to be with certain people. We don't want to be separated from them. We think they're going to make us everlastingly happy. When we're not with them, we long to be with them. We miss them. When we are attached to people, we cling to them: "I love you so much. I can't be separated from you." Is our mind peaceful at that time? No. We're stirred up like churning water. We worry that something will happen to them. We're afraid they will stop loving us. We're anxious about not pleasing them. We daydream about how wonderful they are and long to be with them. Our mind is not peaceful because it is overwhelmed by attachment.

Attachment and love are similar in that both of them draw us to the other person. But in fact, these two emotions are quite different. When we're attached, we're drawn to someone because he or she meets our needs. In addition, there are lots of strings attached to our affection that we may or may not realize are there. For example, I "love" you because you make me feel good. I "love" you as long as you do things that I approve of. I "love" you because you're mine. You're my spouse or my child or my parent or my friend. With attachment, we go up and down like a yo-yo, depending on how the other person treats us. We obsess, "What do they think of me? Do they love me? Have I offended them? How can I become what they want me to be so that they love me even more?" It's not very peaceful, is it? We're definitely stirred up.

On the other hand, the love we're generating on the Dharma path is unconditional. We simply want others to have happiness and the causes of happiness without any strings attached, without any expectations of what these people will do for us or how good they'll make us feel.

*Hating your enemies, you burn like fire.* True or not true? Here, the word "enemies" doesn't necessarily mean Saddam Hussein. It means anybody we don't like. It could be the guy that cuts you off when you're driving on the highway. It could be the colleague that you're jealous of because she got a promotion and you didn't. It could be the neighbor next door who lied to you. It could be the thief who stole your valuables. It could be the person who scratched your car. It could be the kid who took the battery out of your car when you had to go to work. The people who don't give us what we want, the people who don't respect us, who don't approve of us, who get in the way of our getting what we want, who criticize us, who forget our birthday, who tell bad things about us behind our back, who hit us, who harm those we're attached to, those people we can't stand and we just hate them. Whoever we happen to be upset with at that moment becomes our enemy. We burn with anger towards the people who disturb our peace and interfere with our getting what we want. We won't listen to anything they have to say. We just want to quarrel and beat them up either verbally, physically, or mentally. Some people express their anger; others stuff it inside and become cold. Whether we explode or implode, it's not a state of good mental health.

*In the darkness of confusion you forget what to adopt and discard.* When we're confused or spaced out, when we're intoxicating ourselves with television and media, we can't think straight, and so we forget what the causes of happiness are that we need to adopt on the path. "Adopt and discard" and "realize and abandon" are terms that come often in Dharma studies. "Adopting" means the practices that you want to engage in such as keeping your precepts well, training your mind in bodhicitta, and cultivating an understanding of the Four Noble Truths. "Discarding" involves counteracting undesirable elements—afflictions such as ignorance, anger, and attachment, and purifying destructive karma we have created.

Knowing what to adopt and what to discard is very important in order for our spiritual practice to bear the results we seek. However, when our mind is clouded by ignorance and confusion, we're unable to differentiate what to abandon and discard and, as a result, our ethical conduct becomes nebulous, our concentration is foggy, and our wisdom is distorted. We practice the path incorrectly and then wonder why we're not progressing. We begin to think that drinking and using drugs bring happiness and that getting up early in the morning and meditating bring suffering. The mind is befuddled in the darkness of confusion, and although our wish is to be happy, we create the karmic causes for suffering instead. We don't know how to live our lives. This is what is called being in cyclic existence.

The first three lines—indicating attachment, anger, and confusion, respectively—point out what are called "the three poisons." These disturbing emotions and negative attitudes poison our happiness because when they are active in our mind they make us create destructive karma.

What is the solution to these three poisons? The ultimate remedy is to realize reality, the emptiness of inherent existence. The temporary solution is to *Give up your homeland.* What does that mean? The deeper meaning is to remove from our mind the views, attitudes, and emotions that form the familiar "homeland" of cyclic existence, all our recurring thoughts, ideas, attachments, aversions, and repeated harmful habits. This "homeland" is all the conditioning that we grew up with. As children we didn't know we were getting conditioned. We didn't have any wisdom to be able to discriminate about these things. It just happened to us. Now that we're adults, we have to go back and review all that conditioning that we had as children—everything we learned—and figure out what is and isn't useful in life. As adults we now have the ability to discern what encourages attachment and what encourages aversion and hatred; we have the capacity to learn how to subdue these destructive emotions and how to cultivate beneficial ones. In short, we do some remodeling on our own internal "homeland."

It also means to remove ourselves from situations in which everything and everyone is so familiar to us that we keep on acting out our habitual, dysfunctional emotional and behavioral patterns again and again. It doesn't necessarily mean our childhood place. It could also refer to the situation we're in as adults, where we have a certain social role. We're with our friends and "all my friends are drinking, so I'll just go along. All my friends are using drugs, so I'll join in. All my friends are going out to movies and watching sex and violence, so I'll do that too."

Some families have what almost resembles a script with the roles that each member plays. Every family dinner, the brother and sister compete, the son argues with his father, the daughter succumbs to the mother's will, the husband and wife pick at each other. In such situations, we find ourselves acting just as we did when we were ten years old because the family dynamic is the same as in the past. Because the situation is so familiar and we've played a certain role for so many years, we and the others keep acting in the same way even though no one is happy in their role.

Every family dynamic is a little bit different, but often this is what we get into when we know people too well. We just play out the same thing. For example, Mom continually asks when you are going to get married and have a family. Or, if you are already married, when you are going to have kids. If you already have kids, why don't you raise your children a certain way? Your sister competes with you. Your brother plays the joker. You get into the same old interactions again and again, just like you did when you were children.

The meaning of *Give up your homeland* is to give up these situations. This doesn't mean you stop going to family dinners. It means that when you are at a family dinner you don't act on automatic, playing your old role. Be the adult that you are. Be a wise adult with a helpful and kind attitude. If you don't play your role, others can't play theirs. If Dad asks you, as he does every year, "Isn't it time you figured out what you're going to do with your life and get a high paying job?" instead of becoming defensive or rebellious like you did when you were a teenager, say truthfully, "Yes, maybe it is, Dad. I'm doing the best I can. I enjoy the work I do even though you would like to see me get paid more and have more prestige." Give up being defensive and be comfortable with who you are.

"Homeland" could also refer to the society around us and how we relate to people at work and school. For example, we tend to have a lot of authority issues that we reenact with our boss, our Dharma teacher, and whoever else we see as being in a position of authority. Playing out our authority issues again and again keeps us mentally imprisoned. Dharma practice involves liberating ourselves mentally from these habitual emotional, verbal, and physical behaviors and thinking more creatively about how we relate to others. This is giving up our homeland. We investigate these situations and our habitual reactions to them with wisdom in order to understand their causes and their effects. Then, realizing that it is painful and not at all beneficial to hold on to all the conceptualizations that create authority issues, we give them up.

If you choose a monastic way of life, practicing in a monastery is recommended. If you stay with your family and old friends, you will tend to think, speak, and behave as you always have with them. Transforming your body, speech, and mind will be more difficult due to the force of habit that comes into play in a familiar environment with familiar people. In Dharma practice we are trying to uproot the wrong views and ways of thinking that we've had since beginningless time. We're trying to let go of emotions and attitudes that society assumes are real and beneficial. Staying with a group of like-minded people who are all trying to do the same thing is much easier. If we live with the people we're attached to, practice will be difficult because our attachment will distract us. If we stay in the same hostile environment when we are a beginner, our anger will increase and applying antidotes to it will be difficult. When we associate with people who act in confused ways—such as our old friends who drink and use drugs—we'll do the same. Thus, it's wise to avoid situations in which our mental afflictions get stirred up. We do this not because those people are bad or wrong—we are not judging them—but because our own mind isn't strong enough to deal with that social pressure. Creating some distance helps us build up our internal wisdom and antidotes to afflictions.

We established Sravasti Abbey so that people who want to lead a monastic life can leave their homeland and come live here. Here our days are structured around Dharma practice. We're doing Dharma activities frequently throughout the day so it's easier to learn, think, and meditate. We practice acknowledging our mental afflictions, so resolving conflicts is done in a different manner than is usually found in the world. Living in a monastery provides a way to practice that isn't available in the city or when we have a very busy work life.

This is not a prescription for everybody to move out of their house tomorrow. The advice is more about giving up the preconceptions that form the homeland of our mind. This idea is powerful. *Give up your homeland* is a call for us to change, whether we make this internal change while having the lifestyle of a lay person or of a monastic.

### Chris: Caught in the Current of Clinging

This verse makes me think of my relationship with my family. When I first learned this verse, I used to say it incorrectly, "Attached to your loved ones, you're stirred up like fire." Then I realized, it's "stirred up like water." The image of the weight and force of water accurately describes situations of attachment.

On a camping trip my friends and I were filling our water bottles at a stream. We kept losing the bottles due to the powerful force of the water in the stream. One person wanted to go in the water and walk across the stream. However, the water was up to the middle of our thighs, and we could have easily been thrown by the force of the water currents and been severely injured. This is exactly what happens with attachment to family: we are helplessly carried away by the force of attachment and are battered on the rocks as the water tosses us downstream. If we are wise, we will see the danger and won't put ourselves in that situation. Similarly, when we see the uncontrollable nature of attachment and its outcomes in our lives, we remain friendly and kind to others, but don't let our mind get hopelessly caught in the current of clinging.

### Don: More Attachment Means More Anger

When I reflect on the experiences in my life that brought me to the Dharma and my spiritual mentor, I often find myself contemplating the immense attachment that I experienced for a coworker. I had just finished graduate school and began working in Child Protective Services. I can still vividly recall meeting Ruby. It really felt like love at first sight—I know this phrase is overused and a cliché but that's really how it felt. I thought she was absolutely beautiful, so it will come as no surprise that I was physically attracted to her. However, it was also more than mere attraction to her good looks; when we talked, she seemed to always know the right things to say that would deeply resonate with me. It seemed we shared a powerful connection. When I would see her and talk with her, it felt like time stopped. She once asked me if I had ever been so in love with someone that after we broke up I just wanted to die. With heartfelt emotion, I replied in the affirmative. At that time I was convinced that she was the key to my happiness.

Led by the conviction that true and everlasting happiness could be found in another person, I quickly found myself enslaved by intense attachment to Ruby. As a result, any person I perceived as a threat or obstacle preventing ME from MY happiness soon became an enemy. What started out as a feeling of happiness, joy, and love quickly transformed into something quite opposite—twisted and insidious. When I saw Ruby talking with another man, I would become uncontrollably consumed by anger, rage, hatred, and jealousy. I had not experienced such overwhelmingly intense negative emotions due to attachment to another person since high school. I had foolishly convinced myself that I had matured over the years and had finally overcome the anger and jealousy that had plagued me in my youth. During this new adventure with attachment, I was rudely awakened from my false sense of security as these dormant emotions arose and pounced at the opportunity.

My mind was so confused. I simultaneously experienced the desire of wanting to be with the person that I perceived had the ability to grant happiness and the aversion of fearing the pain, hurt, and anger that were like loyal companions on the arduous journey for happiness. I was drowning in a sea of confusion and negative emotions and couldn't see a life raft.

During that time I was blind, deaf, and dumb to the Dharma. Consumed by anger and jealousy that blazed inside me like an inferno and erupted like a volcano spewing its lava in all directions, I forgot all of the Dharma teachings I had ever read. It was as if the flames of anger incinerated all the Dharma teachings that were at one time in my heart and mind, and jealousy's destructive lava melted away any love that was in its path. I had lost my mind—it was obliterated and possessed by negative emotions. It was as if I had never read one word of the Dharma.

In my ignorance, I felt compelled to grasp on to the elusive fantasy of ultimate happiness with Ruby. She recognized my jealousy and once wisely told me that I had to "let go." As difficult and challenging as it was, I tried my best to follow her wise advice.

The next year Ruby resigned from work to attend graduate school in another state and we broke up. During the aftermath—as the anger subsided, the jealousy dissipated, and I was able to think more clearly again—I came to the realization that my deluded mind had intellectualized all the Dharma I had read. My experience with Ruby showed me that I wasn't actually practicing Dharma. I had attempted to independently transform my mind all by myself, without any guidance. With this realization came the sobering understanding that I needed to seek the guidance of a spiritual teacher who could show me how to travel the spiritual path. Due to good karma, I was able to meet a qualified spiritual mentor to guide me.

Now, when my mind flies off in fantasies with the allure and temptation of finding happiness from another person, I contemplate my experiences with Ruby. In doing so, my heart fills with gratitude at the realizations that came and the lessons that were learned. When I read the second verse of *The Thirty-seven Practices of Bodhisattvas* I'm also reminded of the experiences that served as catalysts for my journey on the spiritual path. I hope never to forget the lessons that I learned from Ruby and the realizations that led me to my spiritual mentor.

## VERSE 3: CALMING THE MIND, SIMPLIFYING OUR LIVES

*By avoiding bad objects, disturbing emotions gradually decrease.*
*Without distraction, virtuous activities naturally increase.*
*With clarity of mind, conviction in the teaching arises.*
*Cultivate seclusion—*
     *This is the practice of bodhisattvas.*

### Seclusion

Disturbing emotions—such as attachment, anger, resentment, vengeance, belligerence, laziness, concealment, deceit, and pretension—gradually subside when you are not surrounded by the objects that provoke them. When we look at what triggers the arising of disturbing emotions, we see that it's usually because we have encountered some kind of "bad object" that triggers our habitual emotional reactions. The designation "bad object" doesn't mean the objects are bad in and of themselves. Rather, it indicates that our mind is very reactive when we're in the proximity of certain people, situations, or things. In such cases, our old habits come up strongly and our mind becomes uncontrolled. We might be going along very smoothly, and then we encounter someone that we had a quarrel with five years ago. Just seeing or thinking of that person brings the unpleasant experience flooding back and we become upset, depressed, and angry. Although nothing happened at this present moment, we get angry.

Our response is not the fault of the object. This point is important to understand so that we do not blame the people or things that we react to. Although we often say, "You made me angry," in fact, no one makes us angry. The anger comes from within ourselves. Yet, because we are beginners and our mind is uncontrolled, when we're around certain people or objects or in particular situations, our destructive emotions can arise easily. Knowing this, we choose to put ourselves in a different situation. If we don't put ourselves in situations where the objects of attachment or anger are, or where we are around people who are a bad influence on us, then certain afflictions will not arise so much in our minds. This is not running away from the situation. Rather, we're giving our minds some space from the objects or people that act as triggers for our disturbing emotions. We do this so that we can investigate how these emotions arise and practice the antidotes to them. Having developed the antidotes to those mental afflictions, later, when we face the same situation again, we will be less reactive and more balanced in our response.

For example, if you're attached to ice cream, you understand it's bad for your health, and know you don't feel good about yourself when you eat it, then don't go to an ice cream parlor to meet your friends. This doesn't mean the ice cream or the ice cream parlor is bad. It just means your mind is uncontrolled. Initially we stay away from those things that provoke attachment in our mind. If we avoid the objects that incite our ignorance, anger, attachment, resentment, and laziness, our disturbing emotions will gradually decrease. This happens because we are now actively hearing, thinking, and meditating on the Dharma to cultivate the antidotes to those disturbing emotions.

Similarly, let's say we are so attached to someone that every time we're near him or her, our mind is filled with craving and we can't think clearly. To be able to develop the skill needed to counteract our craving, we need to keep some distance from the person who brings up our strong attachment. We are not rejecting this person, but giving ourselves some time and space to reflect on impermanence and the faults of cyclic existence in order to make our mind calmer and more balanced.

At the beginning, and for a long while, our minds are totally out of control, so we need a secluded environment. Seclusion doesn't mean we go live in a cave. It means living in an environment where we aren't exposed to all the things that push our buttons, so we can have the time and space to cultivate the antidotes to our disturbing emotions. Here, seclusion refers to the environment.

However, real seclusion is mental seclusion. When our mind is secluded, it is not reactive to external objects or our internal thoughts about them. A person who has a stable Dharma practice and has trained his or her mind in the antidotes to the afflictions can maintain a balanced mind in situations in which previously she would have become very angry or attached. This is a real benefit that comes from integrating the teachings with our mind. Because the mind is now secluded from afflictions, there is more space for positive emotions and deeds.

## Simplify Your Life to Stop Distraction

When we stop living such a busy life—running around here and there, doing this and that—we aren't so distracted. Naturally, it becomes easier to focus on the Dharma. This is the value of attending retreats, whether they are for one day, a few months, or even several years. Going to Dharma class every week is beneficial, and when you attend a daylong Dharma class or retreat, your mind becomes more concentrated. You are less distracted because your cell phone is off, your computer isn't next to you, and there is no television. You are in silence. You are not busy telling everybody what you like, what you dislike, or what all your problems are. You have time to think and reflect. You are not looking at art books, advertisements, and all the other things that distract you. Retreats help you to simplify your life and your environment. Thus, there is less distraction and virtuous activities naturally increase.

When you are at home, simplify your environment. Get rid of the television. I can almost hear you gasp at the thought: "What? No television?" Stop reading all the pop-up ads on the computer. Don't browse through the catalogs that come in the mail. Put them in the recycling bin right away. Don't turn on the radio every time you get in the car. Listen to a Dharma talk instead or chant mantra. Simplify your social life too. Do you really need to go here and there and do this and that? Simplify your hobbies. Instead of trying to do everything and be everything—because that is what you think you have to be and do so that people will like you—choose a few things that you enjoy doing. Do what is most important to you. Question the thought that says, "Everybody has to love me. I have to run around and do all these things so that they'll love me." Is that true? Make your life simple.

Many people ask if Buddhism is applicable to social issues. Yes, it is. For example, the Buddhist idea of simplicity is an antidote to frantic consumerism and the environmental destruction that accompanies it. Ask yourself why you drive so much. Simplify by carpooling with people. If possible, don't go to so many places. Structure your life so you run all your errands at one go, wasting less gas and time in the process. Don't buy so many things. The more you have, the more things break, and the more time you spend having to take care of them or fix them. If we make our lifestyle very simple, we won't have so much distraction. The more we own, the more complicated our life becomes because we have to take care of it all. When we simplify our lifestyle then virtuous activities naturally increase because we have more time to practice.

### With Clarity of Mind, Conviction in the Teachings Arises

When you avoid bad objects, then there is less distraction so our afflictions are not incited as much. When your virtuous activities increase, then there's more clarity in your mind. When there is clarity of mind, then you're able to really think about the teachings and investigate with reasoning to see if they make sense. Look and see if the teachings fit what you've seen in life, how society works, and how other people's minds work. Try the teachings out and see if they actually work with your own mind. Due to your own investigation and experience, conviction in the teachings will arise.

Although having admiring faith in the Buddha makes our mind more open and receptive to the teachings, it doesn't bring stable confidence and faith in the Three Jewels. Simply thinking, "The Buddha said it so I believe it" may have some benefit, but as soon as someone tells us of another spiritual leader or teaching, our faith wavers. For that reason, gaining stable, genuine conviction in the teachings is so important, and there is no other way to do that aside from reflecting on them and putting them into practice.

Doing this takes some time. We can't rush it. Think about the teachings, put them into practice, and try them out. In this way, you will develop firm conviction that comes from your own examination and experience. It is important to give yourself the time to contemplate the Dharma. But you can only do this if you're not spending so much time watching TV, surfing the Internet, and going shopping. Undistracted time and mental space are necessary to think about the teachings.

I read about a scientific study that found that multitasking decreased people's attention span and efficacy in doing tasks. This is no surprise. With too many things to do, our attention becomes tired and fuzzy. When too many sense stimuli come at us at once, our mind gets fatigued.

The people who do the three-month winter retreat at Sravasti Abbey experience that. For three months they are immersed in a different environment, doing six sessions of meditation a day. At the conclusion, they say, "This was fantastic! I had time to think about the Dharma. I've heard so many teachings, but I'd never sat down and thought about them in such a consistent or deep way before." One man said, "I had heard the analogy of the Buddha being like the doctor, the Dharma the medicine, and the Sangha the nurse many times. But now I've understood that I'm the patient who needs to take the medicine. I'd kept the Dharma separate from myself and didn't understand that before."

The daily schedule repeats each day of the retreat, so you have a clear mind because you are not running around. You meditate, and then have breakfast. You meditate again, do yoga, more meditation, and then eat lunch. After a walk outdoors, you meditate again, read a book, meditate some more, and have medicine meal (dinner). There's another meditation session, followed by taking down the offerings, then showering, brushing your teeth, and sleep. There are chores to do in which you offer service in the community. It's a simple lifestyle. This gives us time to observe our mind, to reflect on the Dharma, and to apply it to our mind. When we do this, conviction and faith in the teachings arise because we see that the Buddha knew what he was talking about. We see through our own experience that the Dharma describes our life and our potential.

When the verse says, *Cultivate seclusion,* it means to live in a secluded and simplified environment when possible. Abstaining from contact with distracting objects—things that will spark the arising of disturbing emotions—gives us the opportunity to look deeper into the workings of our mind. But the real seclusion is when our mind is separated from ignorance, anger, and attachment. We usually think of retreat as the physical setting, but real retreat is the mind, body, and speech retreating from nonvirtue.

### Randy: A Drug-Free Clear Mind

It wasn't that I had a hard life compared to most people, but I nevertheless witnessed a lot of suffering when I was young. People's dissatisfaction with life, and their anger towards things that did not happen the way they wanted them to, was apparent to me. I saw that a great deal of suffering could have been averted but wasn't. So much misery is caused by the choices we make in our lives. With confused minds that don't realize how confused they are, we choose to take a certain direction in our lives, and then suffering comes from having to bear the weight of those decisions. In addition, we experience suffering due to the regret of having turned away from other paths or lives we could have lived.

I saw a lot of lifestyles that I didn't want to live. I didn't want to have a career, a family, or a lot of possessions. These things didn't seem very important or meaningful to me. In my confusion, I turned to drugs and alcohol, seeing them not so much as a coping mechanism, but as a method to float and not have to get involved with anything, thereby not getting hooked and wasting my life like I'd seen other people do.

Actually, drugs and alcohol did serve that purpose in that they prevented me from getting tied down by buying a house and supporting a family. However, the reality is that drugs and alcohol are like salt water, just like anything else people turn to—climbing the corporate ladder, being popular, having a marvelous social life, and so forth. My mind had the expectation of gaining some pleasure from drugs and alcohol. Thinking they would bring me happiness, I imbibed. Yet they didn't bring me as much happiness as I wanted, so I took more in an attempt to get that happiness.

The mind forms its own "logic" and creates "excellent" reasons why it's good to take drugs and alcohol. I used these substances as a method to glide and find some pleasure since I didn't have any other method. Over time, I experienced more and more clinging attachment, expectations, and letdowns. However, I kept taking these substances thinking next time it would be different. I didn't know anything outside the small box of my mind.

Although I was longing for another way of life, I didn't know one. My mind dwelt in a place of pain and sorrow. Not knowing how to find lasting and meaningful happiness, I continued to do things that were damaging to myself and others. Eventually, I went to prison for a year where I had the fortune of meeting the Buddha's teachings. After I was released, I went to live at a Buddhist monastery. In the Dharma I discovered the tools to transform my mind. At the monastery I found meaning, and now I am a monk.

As I continue to listen to Dharma teachings, I see that I'm being taught how to live my life daily in a good way and how to make my life meaningful. It all started with avoiding bad objects and distractions. As I start letting go of things that disturb my mind, kind thoughts and peace arise in my mind. Nothing external makes this happen. Rather, it seems quite natural. As I learn to set down the thoughts and emotions that are disturbing, automatically it seems that the virtuous mind comes. This is very encouraging; it's a wonderful feeling to know that I don't have to compel myself to go towards enlightenment. If I just let go of all the things that weigh me down, I'll naturally move forward and the qualities I cherish will grow.

# 3. Transitioning

## VERSE 4: LOOKING AT DEATH AND DEALING WITH LOSS

*Loved ones who have long kept company will part.*
*Wealth created with difficulty will be left behind.*
*Consciousness, the guest, will leave the guesthouse of the body.*
*Let go of this life—*
  *This is the practice of bodhisattvas.*

THE BUDDHA'S first teaching was about impermanence and his last teaching was about death, illustrating that awareness of impermanence and death are important in spiritual practice. While most people consider thinking about death to be morbid, Buddhists see it as a way to invigorate their Dharma practice. Thus we consider that death is definite, its time is indefinite, and when we die, all that goes with us are the latencies and seeds of our actions and our mental habits.

One of my friends, a German nun who is fluent in Tibetan, took her teacher, a Tibetan geshe (learned spiritual master) to the doctor one day because he wasn't feeling well. After examining him and getting the test results, the doctor informed her teacher that he had a very serious condition and that a slight circumstance would cause him to die. In short, he could die at any time.

Her teacher burst out laughing while the doctor stood there dumbfounded, thinking that perhaps my friend had made an error in translating their report. When her teacher finally stopped laughing, he explained to the astonished doctor, "As a monk, I should be instructing you that death is definite and the time is indefinite, but instead you're saying that to me!"

For me, this verse about impermanence and death is one of the more powerful verses in the text. These two topics—impermanence and death—are what get us going. They challenge us to think about the meaning of our life and what the outcome of our life will be. When we're alive we work and we're engaged and busy all the time. But what's the purpose of it all if, at the end of the day, we're going to die? When we die, **Consciousness, the guest, will leave the guesthouse of the body** and will take another body according to the karma that ripens at the time of death. Contemplating our own mortality puts our life in a new perspective. We question, "What is the long-term meaning of what I do every day? What have I done and what am I doing that are of lasting benefit to myself and others?" These are very important questions to ask ourselves and they help us set our priorities in life wisely so that when the end of our life arrives, we will have no regrets or fear.

### Loved Ones Eventually Separate

We might think, "One thing that's really meaningful to me in this life is being loved, being appreciated, being approved of, being close to people, having all these very tight relationships where I'm never separated from the people I love." Some people believe that the main purpose of life is to have a lot of family members and loved ones around them. For them, building a family network becomes a kind of refuge. All of us want to be loved, but because we're not clear on what love is, we confuse it with attachment. Often we believe that if people love us, then we must be good, we must be worthwhile. Based on this belief, we do a lot of things in an attempt to get the love we need. But here, Togmay Zangpo says, **Loved ones who have long kept company will part.** True, isn't it? No matter how much we love someone and how long we have been together, when death comes there is no choice; we must separate. It's impossible to be together forever. Either our loved ones die first or we do, or we will part in another way while we're both still alive. In addition, in future lives, the people we're close to in this life will be born in one place, and we're going to be born in another.

Realizing that we can't stay with our loved ones forever helps us have a better relationship with them now. By lessening our attachment, we will have fewer unrealistic expectations that lead to conflict and disappointment. We don't take our loved ones for granted as much, and thus stop dumping our frustration and anger on them. We stop seeing them as a projection of ourselves and accept them for the lovely human beings they are. With less attachment, not only do our relationships improve now, but also our Dharma practice is stronger.

Separation and death are part of nature. That's the way it is. As soon as we are born in a body in cyclic existence, we have no choice but to die. Seeing this situation with wisdom will spark us to seek the causes of birth and death so that we can eliminate them and be free from this cycle of existence. When we deeply search for these causes, we will find them to be what the Buddha described: ignorance, afflictions, and polluted actions. Can these be eliminated, and if so, how? The karma that causes rebirth is created due to afflictions, and afflictions have their origins in ignorance. Because ignorance grasps at phenomena existing in a way that they do not, it can be removed by cultivating the wisdom that perceives phenomena as they actually are. More explicitly, ignorance grasps persons and phenomena to exist inherently, while wisdom sees that they are empty of inherent existence. Wisdom and ignorance cannot be manifest in our mind at the same time, so when wisdom sees the lack of inherent existence, ignorance is overcome and the afflictions based on it crumble. With the eradication of afflictions, no more karma that causes rebirth in cyclic existence is created, and liberation—nirvana, the state of lasting peace—is attained. Wisdom combined with bodhicitta—the intention to become a Buddha in order to benefit sentient beings most effectively—leads to the full enlightenment of a Buddha. Thus, fulfilling our highest spiritual potential begins with acknowledging that separation and death are part of life.

## Wealth Created with Difficulty Will Be Left Behind

The wealth we gather with great effort goes quickly, doesn't it? We work very hard to get money and possessions and to build a financial portfolio.

But no matter how hard we try, we never have enough money to feel totally secure. We could always have more. But at the time we die, all the money we have received is left behind. Not one cent can come with us. We put forth so much effort while we are alive, but at the end of our lives there is nothing lasting that we can take with us.

Have you noticed how wealth and possessions solidify our ego identity? To get these things, we need a certain type of job. Once we have the job, we need to drive a certain type of car, wear particular clothes, and live in a certain neighborhood to hold the image of someone working in that profession. So we need the job to get the possessions that are necessary to be someone who has that job. It's a cycle that leaves many people feeling trapped in their lives.

Of course, using our wealth to help others is definitely virtuous. But clinging on to it to create a certain ego image or to flaunt it in front of others so that we feel successful does not fill the feeling of emptiness in our heart; nor does it benefit others. Everything we have comes to us due to the kindness of others; nothing is inherently ours. So sharing wealth with others makes much more sense on a practical level and makes us feel good about ourselves for we know the wealth is helping others.

Recognizing that we never have enough to feel totally secure and that at the time of death we separate from our wealth lessens our attachment to it. We stop being obsessed with wealth and driven to procure more. We cease being interested in presenting the image of ourselves as someone who is well-to-do and successful in a worldly way and instead become content with what we have. Contentment is real wealth. If we don't have contentment, we can have a million dollars and be very unhappy, but if we're content, our mind is at peace even if we have very little.

### Consciousness, the Guest, Will Leave the Guesthouse of the Body

Death will happen but we don't know when. Considering that our loved ones, body, wealth, and reputation cannot come with us, what is worthwhile? What goes on with the continuity of mind into the next life?

Our mind—that part of us that experiences, perceives, knows, cognizes, feels, and so forth—is formless. It is clear and aware. Life is when the mind resides together with a body, but a physical body is just a guest-house. The mind cannot stay there infinitely. Someday the body and mind will separate. That is what we call death. At that time, the mind moves on to the next life. The ego identity we constructed for ourselves based on this body, the society and social influences we find ourselves living in, everything familiar to our five senses will cease when the consciousness moves out of the body. We've spent a lot of time and energy building up an identity: "I am this nationality. I am this religion. I am this socioeconomic class. I am this educational status. I have these interests. I am this racial group. I am this ethnic group. I am this gender. I am this sexual orientation. I like these hobbies. I don't like these kinds of people. These are my political views." We mistakenly believe that all these identities are who we are—that they are permanent and exist with their own essence. Nevertheless, at the time of death consciousness moves out of this body and the whole thing crumbles.

What goes on with the continuity of mind into the next life? Karmic latencies and karmic seeds and the mental habits we have built up. Karma simply means "action"—actions of body, speech, and mind. These actions leave latencies—also called tendencies, imprints, and predispositions—on the consciousness. These latencies accompany the consciousness into the next life, influencing where we're born, who we're born as, what the environment is like, what our habitual tendencies are, what we experience in life. It's not that things are predetermined, but they're very conditioned due to the actions that we ourselves created in the past. We're creating the causes right now for what we're going to experience in the future.

Considering these facts—considering that loved ones, wealth, and body don't come with us, but the karmic latencies do—what is of long-term value in our life? It's to use our energy, as much as possible, to practice the Dharma; to use our wealth and our relationships and our body to create virtue; to put good karmic latencies in the mind; to practice generosity and ethical conduct, fortitude, joyous effort, concentration, and wisdom; and to free the mind from being totally attached to the sense pleasures of this life.

Since our *loved ones who have long kept company will part,* is being attached to them worthwhile? Is it important to go through all the things we do to try to make people love us? Or is it more important to have relationships with people without clinging and attachment and to further our spiritual practice? Relinquishing attachment does not mean we are cold and unloving. It simply means that we do not cling. When there is no clinging, there is more space for genuine affection and good communication. Instead of our loved ones being objects of attachment, and instead of generating a lot of hatred towards the people we don't like, which also creates karma, we use the ones we don't like as objects of fortitude and the ones that we do like as objects with which to create equanimity. Because we still have all these things in our lives, we should use them, employing them in a different way. We can train our mind to react in a wholesome, constructive manner towards all these things instead of just getting overwhelmed with the usual clinging and pushing away as we struggle to have happiness in this life.

Seeing that *wealth created with difficulty will be left behind,* is it important to work overtime in order to have a lot of money? Is fretting, worrying, and being obsessed about money worthwhile considering that we will separate from it when we die, if not before? Or is it more important to spend our time doing meaningful things in life? We can earn enough to keep ourselves alive and be content with simplicity because we know we don't need a lot.

Since *consciousness, the guest, will leave the guesthouse of the body,* should we keep running around all the time trying to make our mind happy with this or that small pleasure? Or is there something more important we can do with our mind? Pondering these questions, we will realize our Dharma practice is very important because at the time we die, our wealth stays behind, our body stays behind, and our friends and relatives stay behind. What follows us are the karmic seeds we created to procure and protect all these things. What comes with us are the mental and emotional habits we've developed throughout our life. These could be habits of ignorance, hostility, and attachment. They could also be habits of kindness, consideration, generosity, ethical conduct, and wisdom. What kind of habits do we want to cultivate? What kind of karma do we want to create? Thinking about this is important because that is what's going to come with us.

As our mind develops this view that considers preparing for future lives important, we relate to things and people in this life differently. In the process, we actually have more satisfaction and more happiness in this life. The more we look at our experience, the more we see that clinging brings suffering. The more we cling, the more dissatisfaction we have because we can't hold on to what we cling to. It's never as good as we want it to be. Thus we experience constant dissatisfaction, wanting more and better.

To counteract this situation we want to learn to relate to material possessions and people in a different way. Instead of allowing our mind to become overwhelmed by clinging and craving, we think about possessions differently: "I'm going to use them to create wholesomeness and virtue and so on to put good karmic seeds in my mind for the benefit of all sentient beings so that in a future life I can have a good rebirth and I can continue to practice the Dharma and I can continue to develop these good qualities for the benefit of all beings."

It is essential to maintain a balanced attitude towards our body and possessions so that we care for them wisely and without clinging, using them to further our Dharma practice. We use our wealth wisely and give some of it to others in an expression of generosity. In this way we use our wealth in ways that correspond to our spiritual values while retaining enough to live on ourselves. We live in a world with other people. We make friends with people who support our practice; we cherish those people and they cherish us. However, we do so without clinging or becoming attached to each other.

## Let Go of This Life

The solution to attachment and the problems that come with it is to *let go of this life.* This means to let go of attachment to this life. That is, we focus on what is important to do, considering that our life is not going to go on forever. In fact, we don't know when it is going to end. Although we may feel we'll live a long life, we have no idea when we're going to die. Thus, we need to be prepared to die at any moment. In this context, what does being prepared to die mean? Does it mean you have your burial plot ready? No. It means knowing how to think, how to keep our mind in virtue, how to steer our mind towards a good rebirth, liberation, and enlightenment. If we let go of obsessing about this life, and focus on what is important, we will have much more peace of mind in this life. We will be able to die without regrets or fear, and transitioning to our next rebirth will be smooth. We will be able to continue practicing the path so that we can progress towards liberation and enlightenment in our future lives.

For highly realized practitioners, death is said to be like going on a picnic. Let alone not having any fear, they are joyful and relaxed. Since we all have to die at some time, wouldn't it be nice to die like that? To do so, we need to create the causes now through practicing the path of wisdom and compassion.

## Milt: A Child's Innocence about Death

My first exposure to death was at age twelve, when my ninety-year-old great grandmother, who was the rock of my family, died. When my parents told me she was dying, I didn't know what that meant. We went to her house and everyone was crying. When I went into her room, it looked like she was taking a nap. I didn't know what was going on; I didn't understand what death meant. Whatever death was, the adults around me were acting differently than I'd ever seen them act before.

Having some time by myself to be with her in her room, I realized that she was gone. When I asked the adults, "Does this happen to all of us?" and they replied, "Yes," I was horrified to learn that we have to let go of "the guesthouse of this body." Letting go of attachment to this life is quite a task. The fact that we have to is a powerful reminder to reflect on an important question: "What does life mean?"

## Ruth: A Dress Rehearsal of Letting Go

Last year, I gave up a wonderful husband of eleven years, a house I had owned and lived in for twenty years, and a community of friends in the city I had lived in for thirty-seven years in order to come to Sravasti

Abbey to support Venerable Thubten Chodron's vision and to support the Dharma friends who want to become monastics.

At that time I had followed Venerable Chodron's retreats and teachings for fourteen years. A few years before moving to the Abbey, I noticed my interest was waning in vacations, nice restaurants, the latest movies or novels, and conversations over the constant political ups and downs. At one time my husband enthusiastically suggested, "Let's go on a trip to Costa Rica!" When I felt absolutely no wish to go, I knew I had to change. Shortly thereafter, I told him that I'd rather go to the Abbey. Although my life in the city was comfortable and fairly happy and I had good, longtime friends and an interesting part-time consulting job, I had hit some kind of ceiling and simply could no longer spend time and money pursuing all the small comforts that we had shared.

Over the next year, although I did not become a monastic, it was amazing to step away from the householder's life. As I shed the house, car, bicycle, skis, books, furniture, clothes, and pets, I felt calmer and happier. It was strange as there were two separate voices inside: one saying, "Yes! I am finally pursuing a true path to deeper wisdom and compassion," and the other saying, "How in the world can I leave everyone I love and all those who love me?" Now, I have been living at the Abbey for almost four years, and I see that most "pleasures of cyclic existence" really hold no lasting happiness. My understanding of impermanence and my upcoming death have deepened. I am glad that I had this rehearsal of letting go, of being able to give things away in order to practice for the moment when death comes.

## VERSE 5: BAD FRIENDS
## AND WHY WE DON'T NEED THEM

> *When you keep their company, your three poisons increase,*
> *Your activities of hearing, thinking, and meditating decline,*
> *And they make you lose your love and compassion.*
> *Give up bad friends—*
> > *This is the practice of bodhisattvas.*

## Give Up Bad Friends

The term "bad friends" in this verse refers to people who influence us in a way that is opposite to our ethical values and spiritual aspirations. This doesn't mean these people are bad. Rather, it means our mind gets uncontrolled around them. Bad friends are people who think only about the happiness of this life. They don't know about future lives. Or, even if they know, it's not something important to them, and their perspective focuses on enjoying the pleasure and happiness to be found in this life and avoiding or destroying anything that interferes with their happiness. Because they're our friends, they want us to be happy and therefore encourage us to be attached to wealth, possessions, reputation, good looks, social status, popularity, people, and sensual pleasures. While these things in and of themselves are not negative, because our mind gets entangled with attachment and anger in relation to them, suffering comes our way. These people love us and care for us, but because they don't understand karma or past and future lives, their way of helping us is to focus on the happiness of this life.

Parents tell their children, "Don't hang around other kids who are into drugs and alcohol." Why do they tell their kids that? Because they know if their children stay around people who drink and use drugs, they will start doing it too. Now, the big question comes: why do some parents socialize with people who drink and use drugs? They say one thing to their kids and do another thing themselves.

When we hang around people who swear, we start to swear. When we socialize with people who gossip and talk about others behind their backs, we begin to do that too. We lose our mindfulness and awareness and get involved in many harmful actions. If we become friends with people who value making as much money as possible—even doing slightly shady or deceptive activities—it is easy to get drawn into their world. If our friends are people who are the busiest of the busy, then we, too, will feel that we aren't valuable unless we're overwhelmed by too many things to do, people to see, and places to go. These people look like they're looking out for our welfare because they want us to retaliate against our enemies, and get as much money as we possibly can. But because they don't have good values, they lead us to break our precepts and get involved in the ten nonvirtues.

The reason our three poisons increase is not because the people are bad, but because our minds are uncontrolled. These people may have values that are not conducive to human happiness, or they may be totally wrapped up with sense pleasures, wealth, and reputation. Coming under their influence, we waste time pursuing things that are of no ultimate value from a Dharma point of view. This happens in very subtle ways and we're not even aware of it until all of a sudden we realize, "Oh, I stopped doing my morning practice a couple of months ago. In the evening, I'm no longer reading Dharma books. I'm in front of the video screen." It happens very gradually and subtly, causing our three poisons to increase and our activities of hearing, thinking, and meditating to decline.

Making good friends is incredibly important on the path. Our spiritual heart is the most important part of ourselves. If we meet people who value spiritual goals, they will nurture that part of us. Our mindstream contains many seeds. Depending upon what environment we put ourselves in and who we are friends with, certain seeds are watered and not others. Dharma friends nurture the Dharma seeds in our mind: lazy friends water our lazy seeds; resentful friends feed our resentment. What seeds in us do we want other people to water? According to what our answer is, we should cultivate those kinds of friends.

When we tell our Dharma friends, "I'm going to a retreat," they say, "Great! Tell me about it. I want to come with you." If you tell your worldly friends, "I'm going to go to a retreat," they say, "What in the world are you doing that for? You're going to go sit on a cushion for a whole weekend? Get a life! Do something interesting." Those people discourage our Dharma practice, and then doubts enter our mind: "Hmm, they're right; I'm going there to sit on a cushion. Why should I do that? My mind just gets distracted and my knees hurt. It's better to go to the beach with my friend." Our activities of hearing, thinking, and meditating decline because those friends don't support those activities. They want us to go out to the movies, go to a disco, go shopping, or stay home and watch TV. They make us lose our love and compassion because, instead of being able to meditate on love and compassion, we continually have to justify and explain ourselves. We get upset at their dishonesty and pretension. We argue with them, trying to get them to change, or we worry they won't like us because we don't participate in their activities. The remedy that Gyelsay Togmay Zangpo proposes is *give up bad friends.* Let's develop discriminating wisdom regarding the qualities that make someone a good friend or a bad friend. What kind of people do we want to hang out with? What kind of people do we not want to hang out with? Be very conscientious about this because it makes a huge difference. With this in mind, *give up bad friends* and relieve yourself of all the stress of being with them. This is the practice of bodhisattvas.

### Paul: Out on a Limb in Idaho

Bad friends are not necessarily evil people. They may be friends who distract us from our Dharma practice. When I lived in Seattle, I went to the Dharma center regularly. Thus, I heard teachings frequently and was connected with the network of Dharma friends at the center.

After a few years, I moved to Idaho and my teacher moved to Missouri. By that time, I was confident that I had enough Dharma in me to be able to sustain my practice wherever I went. I felt clear about my connection with my teacher and the Dharma community in Seattle. I sustained my practice in Idaho, attended some retreats, and saw my teacher occasionally, but I didn't receive teachings regularly or have the constant support of the Dharma community, and this affected my practice. While we started a Dharma group in Idaho—and that helped—I was still out on a limb. Being the facilitator of the group helped my study, but I rarely received teachings and so my practice didn't continue at the level I had before moving.

Now, I see that I was deceived, and perhaps a bit arrogant, to assume that I had enough Dharma experience to maintain my practice without being close to my teacher. Even though many years have passed since that time, I still feel that I am making up for the damage my practice suffered when I was apart from my teacher and a supportive Dharma community.

Sometimes, we may be able to clearly identify the people we don't want to hang out with; people who are bad friends in the sense of getting us involved in unethical behavior or encouraging us to lie or create disharmony between others. The people in Idaho weren't bad friends in that way. They were good people. Many of them wanted to develop a Dharma practice, and we had good Dharma exchanges. However, building new relationships with people drew time away from Dharma practice, which was where I really wanted to put my energy. Thus, the meaning of this verse is much more subtle than I would have initially thought. I came to understand that a "bad friend" is anyone with whom I spend time developing a relationship that isn't taking me towards the Dharma.

Fortunately, what began as being out on a limb in Idaho had a happy ending. Later, Sravasti Abbey was established an hour's drive away and the Coeur d'Alene Dharma Friends is now going strong.

## Verse 6: Relying on a Spiritual Friend

*When you rely on them, your faults come to an end*
*And your good qualities grow like the waxing moon.*
*Cherish spiritual teachers*
*Even more than your own body—*
      *This is the practice of bodhisattvas.*

### Cherish Your Spiritual Teachers

The previous verse talked about bad friends and how we are influenced by them. This verse is talking about the opposite—how if we have good spiritual friends, then we become influenced by them. The literal translation of the Tibetan word "geshe" is "virtuous friend." We want to have virtuous friends because they help us in our practice, whether or not they have the title "geshe." We need to have virtuous spiritual friends who support and inspire our practice. The best virtuous friends are our spiritual teachers because they know Dharma well and encourage us to learn and practice it.

In the *Samyutta Nikaya* (SN 45:2) of the Pali Canon, the Buddha's attendant, Ananda, states that spiritual friends are half of the spiritual life. The Buddha replies that the entire spiritual life depends on a spiritual friend. This quote has often been taken out of context and misinterpreted, with people thinking that friendship with ordinary Dharma students is what is referred to. However, in the sutra the Buddha is clearly speaking about himself as the spiritual guide who leads one to realize the Noble Eightfold Path.

The Buddha is our ultimate spiritual friend upon whom we rely. He's the spiritual friend from whom all the teachings have come. In order to access the teachings of the Buddha, we need to depend on other people to teach us because the Buddha is no longer alive today. There are three levels of spiritual mentors: 1) our vinaya teacher, who gives us refuge and the five lay precepts, 2) our Mahayana teacher, who teaches us the bodhisattva path and gives us the bodhisattva vow, and 3) our tantric master, who gives us tantric initiation and the tantric vow. All three of these teachers are very precious to us.

The role spiritual mentors play in our life is extremely important. Think about it—our parents love us tremendously, but can they teach us the path to enlightenment? Worldly friends may care for us, but can they teach us Dharma methods to counteract anger and clinging? Those who are able to teach us how to free our mind and escape from the prison of cyclic existence are rare and very precious.

Thus, forming a relationship with a spiritual friend is quite important. While books are useful, they do not inspire us like an actual human being who is practicing the path, who is going through or has gone through what we are experiencing. A book cannot point out our faults to us in the very moment they are manifest, whereas an actual spiritual mentor will help us look at our state of mind at precisely the time a disturbing emotion has taken over. A live spiritual mentor knows when to encourage us and when to let us figure it out ourselves. He or she will know which teaching we need to focus on now in order to progress. For these and more reasons, depending on a qualified and compassionate spiritual mentor is essential.

When you rely on qualified spiritual mentors, *your faults come to an end and your good qualities grow like the waxing moon.* This happens because when we have a healthy relationship with a wise and compassionate spiritual mentor—a relationship characterized by respect, admiration, and trust—we listen to, take to heart, and practice the teachings we receive. These teachings are usually given in a group situation, although sometimes our spiritual teacher may give us individual instructions. While our spiritual teachers do not expect us to practice everything perfectly and instantaneously, we should listen to their wise advice and start to implement it. We are beginners; we do our best; we try. By practicing the Dharma advice we receive, our faults will come to an end and our good qualities will increase.

For that reason Togmay Zangpo recommends, *Cherish spiritual teachers even more than your own body.* Why does he say this? He must have some reason for giving us this advice which is so antithetical to our gut feeling, which cherishes our own life and body above all else. Zangpo's advice makes us reflect, "How much do I actually value the Dharma?" For instance, when we don't attend a Dharma talk because sitting for so long is uncomfortable, the physical comfort of our body has become more important to us than listening to the Dharma. While we may spend the evening relaxing in a comfortable chair, which gives us a few hours of immediate pleasure, we have passed up the opportunity to learn the Dharma, which is of greater long-term benefit.

However, as we begin to understand the Dharma ever more deeply, our feeling of regard and respect for our spiritual teachers increases, and we come to see their incomparable kindness in teaching us the Dharma— the teachings that can lead us to the fulfillment of enlightenment. As we come to cherish the Dharma and the teacher who instructs us in it, we will see that it is possible, and even makes sense, to cherish our spiritual mentors even more than our own body. This is because if we lose our body, the worst thing that happens is we die. If we have created some good karma, we will be reborn in conducive circumstances where we will be able to continue to practice. But if we abandon our spiritual mentors, we throw away the opportunity for liberation and enlightenment not only in this life, but also in future lives. Without the guidance of qualified and compassionate teachers, how can we cultivate the path in our own mindstream?

Without a teacher we won't know the correct path to follow to actualize our spiritual aspirations. We may then make up our own path, but we've done that many times in previous lives and look where it's gotten us! Giving up our body harms just this life, but giving up reliable guides on the path to enlightenment brings harm in many future lifetimes and

leaves us drowning in cyclic existence. The value of meeting fully qualified spiritual teachers who will guide us over many lifetimes cannot be
overestimated. It's important to cultivate wholesome relationships with
these virtuous friends and make prayers to be reborn where we can meet
them and continue to be guided by them in many future lives.

When we cultivate relationships with spiritual teachers, our good
qualities grow because we are near people who keep ethical conduct.
They do not lie, swindle people, talk badly about others behind their
backs, or speak harshly. They do not spend time gossiping, singing, danc-
ing, playing music, watching entertainment, or playing video games.
When we stay near people like that, we will come to do what they do:
hear, think, and meditate in our daily life. When we hear, think, and meditate, of course our virtuous activities keep increasing. We become happier and share that optimism and joy with others. Our spiritual mentors
are excellent examples to follow. By their lives they demonstrate joyous
effort, fortitude, and optimism. We learn from their formal teachings and
from simply observing how they interact with others in daily life and how
they make choices.

I love being near my teachers, and one of the most difficult things
for me about being in the USA is not being near them. This is another
reason why Sravasti Abbey exists—so that like-minded people can stay
together and inspire each other through hearing, thinking, and meditating
together. We invite guest teachers and senior monastics to come, visit, and
teach us. We offer service to our spiritual mentors, helping them with their
virtuous projects that benefit other sentient beings, and doing chores and
errands for them so that they can attend to important activities that help
others. In saying that it's good to be near spiritual mentors, I don't mean
sitting, chatting, or spending four hours over lunch. I mean living in close
proximity, assisting them, and learning through observing how they act.

Once when I was in India I took a friend to visit Khensur Jampa Tegchok Rinpoche, who is the former abbot of Sera Je Monastery. He invited
us to dinner. While we were eating, a beggar came. Khensur Rinpoche
quietly went into the other room, got a blanket, and gave it to the beggar.
That made a huge impression on my friend, who kept saying, "Wow, he
gave one of his blankets to a beggar . . . and it was a nice blanket too." She
started thinking, "Would I do that?" And then she began to see his quali-

ties and generosity. If she had not been there at that time, she never would have seen him do that and she would not have been inspired by his real-life teaching. Similarly, when we offer service to our spiritual mentors, we learn so much whether we are physically near them or not.

The book that I'm using to give this commentary on *The Thirty-seven Practices of Bodhisattvas* is *Transforming Adversity into Joy and Courage* by Geshe Jampa Tegchok. He gave these teachings some years ago, another disciple transcribed them, and I edited them to make the book. That was my way of offering service to Geshe-la. It was an incredible way for me to learn the Dharma, because when we translate, transcribe, or edit our spiritual mentor's teachings, the Dharma goes into our mind in a deep way.

Relying on our spiritual mentors also means attending their teachings and retreats. We shouldn't think that it just means being around them during informal times. By listening to teachings we learn the Dharma, and by putting what we learn into practice, our faults definitely come to an end. The primary way that the Buddha benefits us is by teaching the Dharma, so we should make an effort to attend teachings and pay attention during them.

### Karen: From Despair to Dharma

My faults have not yet come to an end. In fact, and due to an increasing awareness of them, it seems that my faults are growing. Still, some days I think that my good qualities are growing as well. One measure of this is that prior to meeting the Dharma and, in particular, hearing teachings from my spiritual mentor, I was engulfed in self-doubt and confusion. In addition, there was a chronic, ever-present feeling of despair about the state of the world and what my place in it might be. Listening to the teachings, attending retreats, doing a daily practice, and engaging in purification practices—in particular the three-month Vajrasattva purification retreat—have significantly impacted and diminished the self-loathing. An understanding of how I am under the influence of self-grasping ignorance—which fuels my self-centeredness and afflictions—has allowed compassion for myself and all other sentient beings to surface. As a result, I care very deeply about and am making daily efforts to avoid words and actions that harm others.

With the determination to keep practicing no matter what, I hope to continue to develop the good qualities that are so evident in His Holiness the Dalai Lama and all the other teachers from whom I have the good fortune to hear teachings. From what I can see of my teachers' minds, practicing over time creates profound changes in the mind. Their daily example elicits in me faith that enlightenment is possible.

### Susan: Following "Charlatananda"

Putting your trust and faith in a qualified spiritual teacher is one of the fundamental teachings of the Buddha. His Holiness the Dalai Lama has spoken of this many times, urging everyone to take time to investigate anyone they are considering as a spiritual mentor. He encourages us to observe and see if they teach the pure Dharma and if they behave as they teach others to behave. It's also helpful to observe their students to see if they are trying to live ethically and have kind hearts. Only then can we decide to take a certain person as our spiritual guide.

Before I met the Dharma, I had not heard this wise advice. Thus, I experienced many afflictive states of mind by following someone who was, to put it mildly, a shyster.

Back in 1988, I was part of a therapy group that met weekly with a man who was quite talented in facilitating people's inner journeys. He introduced the group to a supposed psychologist who he said was quite amazing and encouraged us all to meet him. From what he said, this psychologist apparently had supernatural powers. When he blew on people's heads, their entire body would fill with light. He also had the ability to make people—sometimes entire groups of people—disappear.

We all were quite curious about him. Over a period of six months our group and our friends—about thirty of us altogether—went to see this psychologist. He offered individuals time on the couch where he would blow on the top of our head, and indeed, our whole body filled with light. He was charismatic and handsome—almost exotic looking—with a lovely face and charming accent. Although married, he had an unusual interest in the young women in the group and would invite us to his hotel room where one of us would entertain him.

The cost of his twenty-minute head-blowing session was $100, and within three months I had spent hundreds of dollars getting my fix of light. Those who questioned his behavior or his fee were guilt-tripped and shamed in front of the group. The pressure to show up each week—and just hang around his fancy apartment until your turn—got very intense. Along with this came a lot of jealousy over who would be his favorite that day. Afterwards, we would take him out to dinner at expensive restaurants, drinking for hours and spending money many of us didn't have. We were like addicts all out for sense pleasure deluxe.

Through a series of misadventures, his deceptive lies were revealed. We finally came out of our fog and stopped attending the sessions. This charlatan made thousands of dollars off a group of gullible, naïve people who just wanted to feel special with someone who had a few magic tricks up his sleeve. When I finally came to my senses, my savings were gone. I was $1,200 in debt and barely employed.

It took me years to get over the deception of this shyster and to make peace with my own blindness. Later, when I met a Dharma teacher, I spent a lot of time examining her behavior and her life before deciding to initiate a teacher-student relationship. I checked out the quality of the teachings and observed if they helped me. Her students were kind and sincere, which gave me the confidence that if I followed her guidance I would become like them. Sometimes, I still struggle with doubt and trust issues which are leftovers from that wild, foolish, and painful experience. However, with a lot of compassion and wisdom, my teacher is guiding me through it and out to the other side, for which I am very grateful.

## VERSE 7: TURNING TO THE BUDDHIST PATH FOR SPIRITUAL GUIDANCE

*Bound himself in the jail of cyclic existence,*
*What worldly god can give you protection?*
*Therefore, when you seek refuge, take refuge in*
*The Three Jewels that will not betray you—*
    *This is the practice of bodhisattvas.*

## Take Refuge in the Three Jewels

This verse is about refuge. It's quite an important verse, especially for those of us who have been raised in other religions. The verse begins, *Bound himself in the jail of cyclic existence, what worldly god can give you protection?* For example, as Buddhism spread in India, the Hindu gods Indra, Agni, Brahma, Vishnu, and others were incorporated into the Buddhist worldview. They're viewed as worldly gods and samsaric beings. They're not liberated, but because of good karma they were born in realms where they had a lot of power. Some of them may have psychic powers and some of them may not. But they are not beyond cyclic existence; they haven't realized the emptiness of inherent existence. Thus, such worldly gods are not worthy objects of refuge to put our faith and trust in. They can't lead us to enlightenment since they aren't there themselves. Rather than take refuge in worldly beings who are trapped in cyclic existence, it's wiser to take refuge in the Buddha, Dharma, and Sangha for they are reliable and nondeceptive. By turning to them for spiritual direction, we will not be led astray because they embody full wisdom and compassion. A worldly deity, who is bound in cyclic existence just as we are, is incapable of leading us to liberation and enlightenment.

Sometimes people are not clear about their spiritual refuge. Maybe they are half-Christian and half-Buddhist. That's fine. People can come to Buddhism, hear the Dharma and practice, and take from the teachings whatever they find useful. They can integrate this into their practice of Christianity. There is no problem with that. But in that case, it's clearer to say, "I am a Christian who uses Buddhist teachings to help me."

If you call yourself a Buddhist, your refuge should be clear; you should turn to the Buddha, Dharma, and Sangha for spiritual guidance and direction. Your mind should not be trying to cover both bases, thinking "Maybe I'd better pray to God too." Similarly, we should not substitute Buddha for God, saying, "God and Buddha are the same; they just have different names." In fact, the theistic concept of God and the Buddhist concept of Buddha are very different. While God is said to be a creator of the universe and the beings in it, the Buddha is not. The Buddha did not create the universe, sentient beings, or the path to enlightenment. Rather, he described the causes of suffering in cyclic existence and the way to attain liberation from it. The Buddha did not create rules; he described which actions bring happy results and which ones bring painful results. The Buddha neither rewards nor punishes sentient beings. While the Buddha is omniscient, he is not omnipotent, because if he were he certainly would have removed all of sentient beings' pain.

At some point, we need to figure out what we actually believe in, be clear in our own mind, and then take refuge according to that. It is important to think about who and what we are taking refuge in, what their qualities are, and what our spiritual goals are. Making "spiritual soup" with a little of this teaching and a little of that is not beneficial in the long term.

It says, *Take refuge in the Three Jewels that will not betray you.* If we look at the Buddha as the guide, the Buddha won't betray us because the Buddha has great compassion. There's absolutely no tinge of self-centeredness in his motivation to be of benefit to us. The Buddha has no intention to harm or mislead or to use or manipulate us. That compassion is what propelled the Buddha to generate the wisdom realizing reality and to then use that wisdom to purify his mindstream and become a perfect guide to liberation and enlightenment. Because the Buddha has these qualities of perfect wisdom and compassion, we can trust him. There is no possibility of his misleading us. However, if we take refuge in worldly gods, there's every chance of being misled.

The Dharma is the actual refuge. The Dharma is the true path and the true cessation of suffering. When we actualize these truths in our mind, our mind becomes free; it becomes the Dharma refuge. The Sangha that we take refuge in are the arya Sangha, those who have realized emptiness directly. The Sangha that are our objects of refuge are special because they have actual, direct realizations of reality. A monastic community of four or more fully ordained monastics is the representative of the arya Sangha. Because not all monastics have direct, nonconceptual realization of emptiness, a group of them must be the representative of the arya Sangha; it is the power of the community that inspires us.

The Dharma, as the true paths and true cessations, is the actual refuge. When we have actualized the Dharma in our mind, we are freed from dukkha. The Buddha is the teacher who instructs us and the Sangha assists us as we practice. Both of them see the nature of reality directly and not conceptually, so they are nondeceptive guides who sincerely want to help us. It takes some time as we're encountering Buddhism to understand what the Dharma is and to understand some of the qualities of the Buddha, Dharma, and Sangha. It's important to learn about them because then the faith that we have in them becomes something stable. Faith becomes based on knowing what the teachings are and understanding how it's possible to obtain liberation and enlightenment. Faith comes from our having examined things and having conviction. If we take refuge in the Three Jewels, we will be able to actualize our heartfelt spiritual goals.

### Anne: Stop Gravitating to Worldly Gods

I've had a lot of worldly "gods" in my life. Mostly they came in the form of infatuations with emotionally unavailable people. Often, they would be married. Even if they were single, they were somehow emotionally unavailable. Still, I gravitated to them like a moth to a flame. At first, when I got the buzz of the attraction, I would think, "This is it, this is the one!" and would feel so free and alive. Not realizing that the freedom and the high were ways of distracting myself from my dissatisfied and often depressed mind, I would chase after these people in coy, silly ways. I would fantasize about them for hours each day, especially at the beginning of the relationship, when I hardly knew them. They seemed so perfect!

However, it didn't take long for me to shoot them out of the sky with my own unrealistic expectations. The misery I caused myself after I would stop seeing them was unbelievable. I was hoping for perfection, security, and romance, and what I got was misery and sorrow. Now, when I feel lonely, I think of the Buddha as the perfect friend, someone who actually has my best interest at heart. Knowing that I can entrust my heart and my deepest aspirations to the Buddha helps me relax and let go of my unrealistic stories about myself and others. It's like a true, long-term, healthy relationship where I can be myself and just relax and know that the Buddha will not leave or betray me. It's all still new, and at times I feel awkward when I open my heart to the Buddha. Then, I see that he already knows all about me and that his compassion and kindness won't end no matter how badly I behave. Furthermore, the Buddha isn't trying to make me emotionally dependent on him in an unhealthy way. His wish is for me to actualize my Buddha potential and benefit others. Who could ask for more?

## Elaine: In Jail, Taking Refuge

Last year, I was embroiled in a potentially dangerous and frightening situation when I tried to protect two dogs from being seized and euthanized by the authorities. The police arrested me for trying to stop this and handled me roughly. They cuffed and leg-shackled me, something that was unnecessary to do to a woman who is almost sixty years old. I have never in my life been in a situation that even resembled this.

I was thrown in a cold jail cell, where my mind was filled with distress for the lives of the dogs and rage at the bullying by the police. I felt no fear at all for myself, which actually astonished me. All I knew was that I was going to be in that cell for a long time. I thought of the Tibetans experiencing similar, but far worse, treatment by police and realized how fortunate I was even in this situation.

My grieving for the dogs was so painful that I needed to control it to stay well. While sitting on the floor and leaning against the wall, I stopped my tears and, for the first time in my life, I was tested to truly, truly go for refuge to the Three Jewels. In such a tumultuous mental state, I was not able to visualize anything but His Holiness the Dalai Lama sitting in front of me, exchanging breaths. Reciting *om mani padme hum*, the mantra of great compassion, my very being pleaded this mantra. There was no rote recitation here; I was desperate in wanting to be compassionate.

That began at about 10:45 in the morning. After a short time, I calmly wondered what time it was, as I heard talking outside. It was 12:30 at night.

In thirty years of Dharma practice I have not experienced so intensely the power of sincerely taking refuge in the Three Jewels.

# 4. The Next Step

---

## VERSE 8: WATCH WHAT YOU'RE DOING: YOUR ACTIONS HAVE RESULTS

*The Subduer said all the unbearable suffering*
*Of bad rebirths is the fruit of wrongdoing.*
*Therefore, even at the cost of your life,*
*Never do wrong—*
    *This is the practice of bodhisattvas.*

### Don't Create the Cause of Suffering

THIS VERSE emphasizes the importance of observing the law of karma and its effects. *The Subduer*—that is, the Buddha—stated that the suffering of unfortunate rebirths—such as those in the hells, as hungry ghosts, and as animals—is the result of our own destructive actions or karma. In other words, we are responsible for what happens to us in our life and lives. We are the ones who create the causes for our experiences.

While the verse particularly mentions the *suffering of bad rebirths,* any pain or misery we experience in this life—be it physical or mental—may be included. Suffering comes about due to the destructive actions we have done in this life and in previous lives. The best way to learn from our experience is to say to ourselves, "If I don't like the result I'm experiencing now, don't accumulate any more destructive karma. Don't act the same way I did in my previous lives that led to my present suffering."

Certain actions are considered destructive karma because they result in pain and suffering. These actions are not inherently bad or sinful, nor are they destructive because the Buddha said not to do them. Rather, such actions are considered destructive because they lead to suffering. Similarly, positive or constructive karma is so called because it leads to the long-term result of happiness. Again, these actions are not inherently good. They become constructive because they bring about desirable results.

The conclusion from the verse is *Therefore, even at the cost of your life, never do wrong.* We might say, "My life's the most valuable thing I have. If I have to kill somebody or steal something or lie or whatever to protect my life, I'm going to do it." However, even if we create destructive karma in order to keep this body alive, there's no certainty our actions will be successful. We're going to lose this life at some time or another; we will not live forever. When this life ends all we take to the next life is the karma we have created. While our harmful action may extend this life for a little while, we will experience misery in unfortunate rebirths for a long time in the future. This result arises due to the strong destructive actions that we did in this life in order to preserve this life.

In short, Togmay Zangpo is saying to us, "If you don't like lower rebirths, then take care not to create the causes for them. That is, abandon destructive actions." Destructive actions include physical actions such as killing, stealing, and unwise or unkind sexual behavior; verbal actions such as lying, disharmonious speech, harsh speech, and idle talk; and mental nonvirtues such as covetousness, ill will or maliciousness, and wrong views.

The verse is very potent and it wakes us up, encouraging us to question the thought, "Well it's only a small destructive action. It's okay; even if it brings a result, it's only going to be a small one." This verse is spurring us to question what is going on in our mind when we are acting destructively. Are we unaware that this action is destructive? In this case, we need to study more about the Dharma so we can distinguish between constructive and destructive actions. Is it that we're not being mindful of our actions and their ramifications? If this is so, we need to restore our mindfulness and introspective awareness so that we know what we're doing. Is it because we're being reckless? In other words, we know it's a destructive action, but we just don't care because we're getting some happiness right now even though in the long term it will bring suffering. If this is so, we need instead to cultivate conscientiousness that cherishes virtue and thinks about the effects of our actions. Is it that maybe we know what we're doing and we realize it's destructive, but our mind is just overwhelmed by the force of afflictions and at that moment we're out of control? In that case, we need to strengthen the antidotes to the afflictions so that they don't overpower our mind and make us do harmful actions.

When we get tangled up in these unwholesome actions of body, speech, and mind, they leave seeds and latencies of destructive actions on our mindstream. Complete destructive actions—that is, ones in which we recognized the object, had a motivation influenced by mental afflictions, did the action, and completed the action—leave potent karmic latencies that bring about unfortunate rebirths. Instead of creating actions that project unfortunate rebirths, let's engage in actions of generosity, ethical conduct, and fortitude motivated by love and compassion, which propel fortunate rebirths.

It's a challenging verse, especially for the mind that knows, "I am lying and it's not so good," but then makes up the excuse, "but it's for the benefit of the other people and it's not going to bring a very bad result anyway." Do you know that thought? This is the kind of thought that the phrase *even at the cost of your life* challenges. For our own benefit as well as the benefit of others, we've got to strengthen our mindfulness, introspective awareness, and conscientiousness.

In short, if we don't like unpleasant experiences, let's not create the causes for them by doing the ten nonvirtues. Here, too, Bodhisattva Togmay Zangpo emphasizes that we are the ones who are responsible for our lives. Feeling sorry for ourselves or blaming others for our problems doesn't make much sense.

### Dennis: Healing from Harm

More than twenty years ago I experienced the loss of a significant friendship, which caused me profound pain, grief, and sorrow. Over many years

I have come to develop the courage to look deeply and honestly at my part in the fracture and disintegration of the relationship. Encountering the Dharma played a major role in giving me the ability to understand the loss with more clarity and understanding and to see the causes that brought this result.

Now I can look at the mistakes I made at that time, feel deep regret, and view them with compassion for myself and the other person. Doing purification practices helped me not to cling on to my mistakes and feel guilty about them. These mistakes that we ordinary beings all commit are rooted in ignorance, which then inspires the disturbing emotions to kick in, and then another mess begins.

It is my sincere determination to never again commit those mistakes with my thoughts, actions, and words. The inspiring words in the verse for me are, "Even at the cost of my life, never do wrong." I do not want to harm others. I realize that this goal is not yet achievable, but I do set the motivation each morning to try not to harm others and to do as much as I can to benefit them. The long-term goal to attain Buddhahood for the benefit of all sentient beings keeps lighting the fire each day, each hour, to work at never doing wrong, even at the cost of my life.

## Gabriel: Accepting Responsibility Brings Transformation

In working with a counselor I was recently diagnosed with PTSD. This explains a lot about why I experience such a powerful emotional response to situations in which I feel vulnerable or abandoned. Studying PTSD has allowed me to understand how my brain works, where the memories are stored, and why my responses to certain situations are so strong and unreasonable. Such understanding has enabled me to take responsibility for the response, as opposed to holding others responsible for my misery and peppering them with my resentment and anger. I now am beginning to learn to simply rest in the feeling itself, without judgment, attachment, or aversion. My PTSD response has now become a powerful object meditation to rest my attention on, and so is a natural extension of my training in serenity.

What my Dharma friends find interesting is that understanding the neurological workings of my brain in the PTSD response has enabled me to take responsibility for my feelings and actions. When many people learn that a genetic, biological, or neurological component is involved in creating their tangled emotions or harmful behavior, they relinquish personal responsibility. For example, some alcoholics say, "Alcoholism runs in my family" as if their own choices have nothing to do with their addiction. Or some people who suffer from depression explain their inconsiderate behavior by saying, "It is due to the chemical imbalance in my brain." Personally speaking, I found that accepting responsibility has allowed me to see that I have the power to do something about my emotions and behavior. Rather than putting myself in the role of a victim, I see myself as someone who can be proactive and gradually heal from trauma.

## VERSE 9: ASPIRING FOR FREEDOM: WHY WORLDLY PLEASURES WON'T CUT IT

*Like dew on the tip of a blade of grass, pleasures of the three worlds*
*Last only a while and then vanish.*
*Aspire to the never-changing*
*Supreme state of liberation—*
   *This is the practice of bodhisattvas.*

### Worldly Pleasures Last Only a While and Then Vanish

This verse relates to the practice of an intermediate-level practitioner— a person who aspires for liberation from cyclic existence. Why should we aspire for liberation or nirvana? The pleasures of the three worlds are transitory. They're nice while we have them, but they don't last long. Afterwards, we are left, once again, struggling for pleasure.

   The three worlds are the desire realm, form realm, and formless realm. The desire realm is so called because the beings in it are hooked on sensual objects—sights, sounds, odors, tastes, and tactile objects, as well as on proliferating conceptions resulting from these. We human beings are part of the desire realm and we can see from our own experience how geared we are to external objects—procuring the ones we find desirable and protecting ourselves from the ones we deem undesirable. Beings in the form realms have deep levels of concentration, which are very blissful. Beings of the formless realm abide in subtle states of meditative absorption in a state of equanimity, which is more refined than the joy of the concentrations of the form realm.

Cyclic existence comprises those three realms. No matter where we are born in these three realms, the joys of existence are *like dew on the tip of a blade of grass.* They are there for a short time, and then they evaporate, gone forever. We may consider our human life to be very long. However, in comparison to beings in the celestial desire realms or form and formless realms, our human life is short. At the end of our lives the most we have are good memories and a lot of photo albums and scrapbooks. But what good are they? It's pretty sad if the only happiness we have comes from remembering past experiences. It's like being happy watching other people's lives on TV. No one makes movies showing people watching TV or looking at photo albums for hours. Why not? Because that's boring. Would you watch a movie that only showed someone watching TV? Instead of having a vibrant and alive mind ourselves, our pleasure comes only from sitting there observing others' lives.

Happiness that doesn't last is not true happiness. It is not something we want to devote our life to trying to attain because there is never any end to our efforts in attaining happiness. Whatever happiness we manage to have is always in the process of fading and going out of existence. It's here and it's gone and in the meantime we experience much unhappiness trying to get it. We create a ton of destructive karma, which is what comes with us to future lives. If we really want a top-grade happiness, a triple-A type of happiness, we should aspire for the peace of liberation, which never disappears. For that reason, nirvana is also called the unconditioned and the deathless.

Some people may think, "Yes, chasing after sense objects is a futile means to bring lasting happiness, but if I don't do that, I won't be happy at all." I don't agree. The more we subdue our mind, the happier we are no matter how much we have or who we are with. A mind free from ignorance, attachment, and anger does not rely on external people and things for excitement or joy. It has a well of joy inside.

Rather than seek out the pleasures found in cyclic existence, only to have them end when a good rebirth ceases, let's aspire for the never-changing supreme state of liberation. Nirvana is never-changing in that once liberation is attained, it never ceases. Once ignorance has been completely eradicated from our mindstream, there is no cause for it to ever return. In this way, a state of lasting happiness and peace that is freedom from afflictions and karma is attained.

Americans often say they stand up for freedom, but in a consumer society we are bound by attachment and are not free. Our minds are tied up, not just by craving, but also by resentment, hostility, and a host of other disturbing emotions. Are we free when our mind is tormented by craving something—a house, a relationship, delicious food, or whatever? Are we free when our mind is overwhelmed by jealousy because others have more than we do or by competition wanting to prove ourselves and be better than someone else? These mental states aren't indicative of true freedom even if on the physical level we have the "freedom" to buy what we want or go where we like.

The Buddhas are trying to get us to open and transform our mind so that we can experience the fulfillment and bliss that doesn't disappear or let us down. They want us to have more than a photo album of good memories at the end of our life; they are guiding us to a state of bliss that comes from freeing our mind from afflictions and karma, a state of bliss that comes through generating bodhicitta and realizing the nature of reality. They want us to experience the joy of making our life meaningful for all sentient beings.

In a Buddhist sense, real freedom is not about having the ability to act on any impulse that comes into our mind. True freedom means not being enslaved by anger, clinging, craving, resentment, spite, and so on. True freedom is being able to direct our mind to any virtuous object without any interference whatsoever from disturbing thoughts and emotions. It is knowing the nature of reality, seeing things as they actually are, which frees us from the misconceptions that torment us. True freedom entails not having a body and mind under the influence of ignorance, afflictions, and karma, but being able to manifest in a form that is of benefit to others.

To attain true freedom we need to broaden our perspective of what we think is possible. Instead of having a limited view that seeks only momentary pleasure, let's expand our perspective and follow Togmay Zangpo's advice to *aspire to the never-changing supreme state of liberation.* This liberation is completely within our reach. It's something we can accomplish. But we have to have the motivation to attain it and then put in the energy to create the causes for it. Because the law of cause and effect functions, we can create the causes for a lasting state of freedom, and the result, liberation, will naturally arise.

### Barbara: The Dew of the Dharma

Just before doing the three-month Vajrasattva purification retreat, I received teachings on this verse in which my spiritual mentor explained it in the context of the Four Noble Truths. It made me question why I chased after transient people and things (true dukkha) in the belief that they would give me lasting happiness, especially because my entire life's experience has proven the opposite. Certainly ignorance, anger, and attachment were the culprits (the true origin), and since they are based on incorrectly grasping inherent existence, they can be eliminated by the wisdom realizing the emptiness of inherent existence (true path). This brings about lasting peace (true cessation of dukkha and its origins).

The image of the dew on the tip of a blade of grass in the context of the Four Noble Truths stayed with me the entire retreat and afterwards as well. All these years that little drop of dew has been continuously dripping on the hard rock of my mind. Over the years, water seeps into the cracks of that rock and, sooner or later, the rock splits and opens up.

### Katerina: But It Was Supposed to Make Me Happy

This verse describes my experience of living in China as an expat. We had a nice "mini-society," with so many ways to relax, enjoy, and make ourselves comfortable. Almost every day I went out to eat at a restaurant and enjoyed nice clubs, relaxing massages, a magnificent spa, fascinating travel opportunities. After two years of living this life, I saw how empty this lifestyle was. Those pleasures that I really enjoyed left me feeling empty. They had no essence and provided nothing more than fleeting pleasure and sometimes not even that. So I quit my job and sought to do something else, even though at that time I still hadn't encountered the Buddha's teachings. A few years later, when I met the Dharma, I knew it was better than all the pleasures of my expat life.

## Mitchell: Here and Then It Vanishes

In 2001 I worked in New York about nine blocks from the World Trade Center. I had just emerged from the subway when the buildings began to burn. My first reaction was not to believe what was happening in front of me. It felt like it was unfolding on a large TV screen, not before my eyes.

I worked in real estate and many of my clients had offices in the World Trade Center. I had an idea about their lifestyle. They worked so hard and made money, which was supposed to bring them happiness and security. Earlier that day they had gone to work just like every other morning, being part of the powerhouse of New York City, feeling successful, and thinking life is wonderful. Later that day, their lives fell apart. Many of them lost everything, including their lives. Some were jumping out of a window a hundred floors up.

A month before, I had been on the 107th floor of the World Trade Center. It's an observation roof from which you can see New York like a map on your palm. Today it was crumbling and the people who worked so hard to earn the wealth that the WTC symbolized were losing it all. Witnessing this was a good reminder of how fragile life is. This understanding energizes me to practice the Dharma while I still have time. One day I too will wake up expecting the day to be just like any other, but instead I will die and lose everything I've gathered during my life.

# 5. Cultivating Love, Compassion, and Altruism

## VERSE 10: THE KINDNESS OF OTHERS AND WANTING TO REPAY IT

*When your mothers, who've loved you since time without beginning,*
*Are suffering, what use is your own happiness?*
*Therefore, to free limitless living beings,*
*Develop the altruistic intention—*
*    This is the practice of bodhisattvas.*

### Repaying the Kindness of All Mother Sentient Beings

THIS VERSE begins the practices of advanced-level practitioners—those beings who cultivate the bodhicitta motivation and engage in bodhisattva activities. There are two methods for developing the bodhicitta motivation: (1) the seven-point instruction of cause and effect and (2) equalizing and exchanging self with others. In particular, this verse talks about the first method.

Both methods are used to develop equanimity towards all sentient beings—friends, enemies, and strangers. Usually we have very strong emotions towards these three groups of people. We are attached to our friends and dear ones, hostile towards enemies and those we dislike or fear, and apathetic towards strangers. To develop equanimity, we contemplate that these three categories are made up by our own mind. It's our mind that discriminates someone as a friend, another person as an enemy, and a third person as a stranger. In addition, one individual can move from one category to another very quickly, depending on a small change of circumstance or a small action. Given the arbitrary nature of these three categories, generating strong attachment, hostility, and apathy towards anyone does not make sense. Instead, we cultivate an equal feeling of care and concern for everyone. When we do this, we find that it's very pleasant to have a more stable mind that is free from these three deluded emotions.

After cultivating equanimity towards all sentient beings, we practice the seven-point instruction of cause and effect:

1. Seeing all sentient beings as having been our mother.
2. Understanding their kindness.
3. Wishing to repay their kindness.
4. Love, wishing them to have happiness and its causes.
5. Compassion, wishing them to be free of suffering and its causes.
6. The great resolve to undertake the task of bringing them happiness and freeing them from suffering.
7. Bodhicitta—the altruistic intention in which we seek complete enlightenment in order to best benefit all living beings—arises as a result of the previous six causes.

Some people may not be familiar with the concept of rebirth and wonder, "Have all sentient beings really been my mother?" There is a chapter in my book *Open Heart, Clear Mind* about rebirth. It may help you to read and contemplate this section of the text to get a sense of how rebirth works.

Since our mind has existed beginninglessly, we have had infinite previous lives. Thus, there was plenty of time for every being to have been our mother. As our mother, each was kind to us, just like our present mother. Each gave birth to us, fed us, taught us, nurtured us, gave us an education, etc. Thinking about this, we see that we have received much kindness from others when they were our mothers and fathers. The wish to repay their kindness automatically arises when we see sentient beings in this way. Wanting to repay their kindness, we wish them to have happiness and its causes—this is love—and to be free from suffering and its causes—which is compassion. Finally, the great resolve to bring about their temporary and ultimate happiness arises.

The way to free limitless beings is to develop the altruistic intention, bodhicitta. Bodhicitta is the mind that seeks to attain full enlightenment in order to benefit all sentient beings most effectively. When we develop this altruistic intention, our whole practice takes on a different flavor because we have this long-term view. When we take the bodhisattva vow, we're committing ourselves to all sentient beings. Thus, we find a way to work with frustration and obstacles along the path because we're doing it for a wonderful purpose. With this altruistic intention, we seek to realize emptiness in order to remove our own afflictions, to remove our own inabilities to benefit others, and to gain the abilities that will enable us to benefit others most effectively.

Seeing that a Buddha has the greatest ability and capacity to work for the welfare of all beings, we develop the aspiration to become a fully enlightened Buddha for their benefit. Having generated bodhicitta, we then learn the bodhicitta deeds—the six far-reaching practices of generosity, ethical conduct, fortitude, joyous effort, meditative stabilization, and wisdom.

## Ed: You Only Get One (In This Life, Anyway)

Many people in the West have difficulty with the meditation on the kindness of their mother. Seeing their parents' bad habits and harmful actions, they attribute their own unhappiness to their parents' behavior. In this way, they remain stuck in feelings of hurt, resentment, anger, and even entitlement. However, the way inmates speak about their mothers is very different. Although most inmates behaved extremely poorly towards their mothers when they were younger—taking them for granted, stealing from them, screaming at them, and other behaviors that rebellious and uncontrolled children do—when they are locked up, things appear very differently. They see that while almost everyone else deserted them once they were incarcerated, their mother is still there. She comes to visit when no one else does even though the prison is far away and hard to get to. She sends money to their commissary account even when she has little money herself. The appreciation the men have for their mothers knows no bounds. It was in this spirit that Ed wrote this to his mother:

I will always love you, Mom. You brought me into this world. I'm talking about you, my one and favorite girl. I got mine and you got yours, and you always better love your Mom because you only get one.

I'm so ashamed for taking you for granted. You were the first one there, and the last one to leave, and that's why I'm writing this letter. You've always been there, through all my good and bad times, when I was sick and when I was well. You took care of me when you were sick, and you were not sure how you were going to make it. All you knew was that you had family to take care of, and that's why you will always be my queen. All you wanted was for me to make you proud to be my mommy as long as you live in this world. I wish upon the heavens and the stars that I could make your dream into reality.

I never meant to hurt you. I know sometimes it is hard for you to carry on, and that's why I'm asking you to be the strong queen that you are. No matter where I'm at, you will always be special to me, Mom, because you loved me while you were in this world. Oh, Lord, I can't thank you enough for giving me my Mom.

Long live the Queen,<br>from your son, Ed

### Guy: My Mothers Spinning in Cyclic Existence

Travel to and from my job takes me through downtown Seattle during rush hour, when it's jam-packed with buses and people, and everyone is going somewhere. Sometimes I stand back and observe this spectacle, reflecting that in a hundred years, all these people will be dead. They are all trying so hard to be happy and working so hard to get what they think will make them happy, but in the process they look quite miserable. No one is successful at getting everything they want, and many times what they desire also causes them problems and brings them more suffering. I then reflect that all these people have been my mothers in previous lives and have loved and protected me. It's overwhelming to witness them running around in confusion like this, not knowing what the actual cause of happiness is. Seeing this, there is no alternative but to develop the altruistic intention and attain enlightenment. This is the best way to help them.

## Martin: The Cup of Love

I spent a summer living in the forest, where I got water from a natural well, a spring flowing directly out of the ground. However, the water was not easily accessible. When I wanted to fill my water container I needed to bend over, scoop up some water in a small cup, lift it out, and pour the water into the container. To fill a two-gallon bottle, I had to repeat this movement hundreds of times. One day, each time I bent over to fill the small cup, I repeated aloud, "I fill the lives of sentient beings with love and happiness." I said this over and over again. Throughout this process, the mosquitoes kept biting me and with every bite, I repeated, "I take upon myself all the suffering of sentient beings who experience mosquitoes biting them at this moment." Also, my body was extremely uncomfortable because of kneeling in a difficult position to reach the water. However, I practiced transforming every sensation by doing the taking and giving meditation with bodhicitta.

Initially I made my mind respond to every experience with the attitude of bodhicitta, but after that my mind gained a certain momentum and it did this automatically. After a half an hour—with pain and fatigue and hearing the melodious repetition of my prayers—my mind "changed gears" and became very tranquil. When I finally straightened my body and stood up, I stood in complete silence under the trees. Everything appeared very clear and bright and the interdependence of sentient beings and our environment became very apparent. It was as if the trees grew as an expression of affection to help sentient beings. The foliage, the rays of sun, the air—everything was compassion, love, and an intense wish for others to be happy. It was as if the nature of the world was an intense wish that all sentient beings be happy and all the trees and other things in the environment were a manifestation of this wish. I knew immediately that I had discovered something important.

## VERSE 11: SHIFTING FROM THE SELF-CENTERED THOUGHT TO CHERISHING OTHERS

*All suffering comes from the wish for your own happiness.*
*Perfect Buddhas are born from the thought to help others.*
*Therefore, exchange your own happiness*
*For the suffering of others—*
  *This is the practice of bodhisattvas.*

### Equalizing and Exchanging Self for Others

As mentioned previously, there are two main methods to cultivate bodhicitta. Verse 10 was the first method, the seven-point instruction of cause and effect. Verse 11 explains the second method for generating bodhicitta, equalizing and exchanging self for others. Here we specifically dwell on the disadvantages of the self-centered thought and the benefits of cherishing others. To meditate on bodhicitta using this method, we first contemplate that just as I want happiness and to be free of suffering, so too does everyone else. There's no difference among all sentient beings in this respect. Then we contemplate that all our own suffering comes from the self-centered thought that is preoccupied with "Me, I, My, and Mine." Considering our own happiness more important than others' happiness and our own suffering more painful than others' suffering, the self-centered thought obsesses, "How can I get what I want? I'm not getting enough support. I'm suffering so much." This constant preoccupation with ME makes us easily offended and turns almost everything in our lives into a drama starring ME.

Verse 11 begins, *All suffering comes from the wish for your own happiness.* We usually think all happiness comes from the wish for our own happiness. Although we wish for happiness, we do not have a clear understanding of the causes for happiness. Thus, we accumulate as many external things as possible to build ourselves up. While we usually think the self-centered thought is our best friend and protector, this line is telling us the opposite—that our self-preoccupation actually makes us suffer. It is important to understand the meaning of this idea correctly. It does not mean that we are bad for being selfish, that we should be miserable, that we're worthless and deserve to suffer. We should not misinterpret this verse and beat ourselves up for being selfish.

The self-centered thought is not who we are. The self-centered thought is different from the mind that wants to be happy because we're sentient beings. Everybody wants to be happy. There's no problem with wanting to be happy. The problem is the way the self-centered thought goes about thinking of our happiness and the way it goes about getting happiness. It is a distorted mental state that can be eliminated by seeing its disadvantages, applying the antidotes, and cultivating the mind that cherishes others.

Although the self-centered thought appears to be our advocate, saying, "Take care of yourself first. Make sure you get what you want. Get what's good before the other guy does," this thought is really the grand deceiver. Why? The more we look out just for ourselves, the more we create disharmony around us, and the less others are willing to help us. We want happiness, nothing wrong with wanting happiness. Everybody wants happiness. We practice Dharma because we want happiness. Buddha wanted happiness. He became a Buddha. The difficulty is the mind that says, "Me, me, me. I, I, I. I'm more important than everybody else. My happiness is more worthwhile than everybody else's. My suffering hurts more than everybody else's. Everybody else is on this planet in order to serve me because I'm the center of the universe." That kind of thinking is the problem, not the wish for happiness.

In addition, we are more easily offended and create more destructive karma, which only produces more misery for ourselves. Just seeking our own benefit is a dead end for us and creates problems for others. When we look at the situation realistically, we see that other sentient beings have been very kind to us, while our self-centered mind has only harmed us. Seeing this, it doesn't make any sense to continue being self-centered. In brief, following the self-centered attitude sabotages our own happiness.

The first sentence says, *All suffering comes from the wish for your own happiness.* Here the intention is to show us that we need to correctly identify and give up the self-centered mind because it's making us miserable and we want to be happy. We correctly identify the self-centered thought that is making us miserable and then we abandon it because it is not us. Don't identify your self-centered thought as being you because it's not you. There's a conventional "I" that exists by being merely labeled. It's only a label. The self-centered thought is something totally different. It's the conventional "I" that wants to be happy and that deserves to be happy. It's the self-centered thought that's impeding that happiness.

Meanwhile, the thought to help others is the source of happiness for ourselves and others. The second line says, *Perfect Buddhas are born from the thought to help others.* When we look at the Buddha's qualities, the two major ones we talk about are compassion and wisdom. Compassion and bodhicitta motivate us to seek Buddhahood. In other words, we seek to practice the path to the very end—removing even the subtle stains from the mind—so that we have the capacity to be of the greatest benefit to sentient beings. This motivation inspires us to continue meditating and accumulating the vast store of merit that's necessary to become a Buddha. The force of compassion creates bodhicitta and leads us to follow the bodhisattva path to full enlightenment. Only benefit comes from cherishing others. When we cherish others, they are happy and so are we. We create good karma, the cause for happiness in cyclic existence and for the attainment of enlightenment. When we cherish others, feelings of being alienated, lonely, and unloved cease. We are more open and confident, less suspicious and fearful. Others don't harm us as often because we stop creating the cause to be harmed. So many benefits come from cherishing others.

Cherishing others doesn't mean we go around hugging everyone or doing everything that others want us to do. Sometimes the proper way to cherish others is to say, "No." Sometimes the way to cherish others is to say, "I'll teach you how to do it so you will be able to care for yourself." It's important to understand that cherishing others doesn't mean that everyone bosses us around and we do whatever others want. Every parent who cherishes his or her child knows that fulfilling all the child's wishes is a disservice to the child. It's much better to teach the child various ways to handle the frustration of not getting what they want. A child who is used to having all his wishes fulfilled will have difficulties as an adult, while a child who learns constructive ways to deal with frustration, who learns to give and to share, will be much happier as an adult. Thus, cherishing others necessitates combining wisdom with compassion.

Seeing the disadvantages of self-centeredness and the benefits of cherishing others, the wish to exchange self and others grows. Exchanging self and others doesn't mean I become you and you become me. It means instead of working just for my own benefit, I now exchange that view and work for the benefit of others. Benefiting others becomes our foremost priority. Just as we previously considered others' happiness to be of secondary importance, we now consider our own selfish pleasure to be less important.

We might worry, "If I don't take care of myself, then I'll be miserable because no one else will take care of me." Seeing the disadvantages of self-centeredness and the benefits of cherishing others doesn't mean we neglect ourselves. To the contrary, it enables us to care for ourselves in a healthy way. The way the self-centered mind "cares" for us results in our being miserable now and creates the destructive karma that results in future suffering. When we care for all sentient beings—ourselves and others—we take care of our body and mind in a healthy way so that they can be used to work for the welfare of others. For example, we keep our body healthy not with self-preoccupied panic and worry, but with compassion for ourselves and others in order to use our body to practice the Dharma and benefit others. While self-centeredness causes us to not eat properly, cherishing others will lead us to care of this body by eating properly. We need a healthy body to help others.

Finally, the third and fourth lines state, *Therefore, exchange your own happiness for the suffering of others.* This is the meditation on taking and giving (Tib. *tonglen*), which is quite a powerful meditation. We imagine taking on the suffering of others with great compassion and using their suffering to destroy our own self-centeredness. Then we imagine transforming our body, our possessions, wealth, and merit into whatever fulfills the needs of others. We give these to them, imbuing them with happiness and feeling joyful ourselves.

The taking and giving meditation is a practice to increase our love and compassion. It takes great courage to do this practice, let alone actually taking on others' misfortunes and giving them our happiness. We don't

want to even think about it! We don't want to think of experiencing our
own suffering, let alone think of taking on the miseries of others. Usually we want all the good things for ourselves and jealously protect whatever possessions, positions, relationships, and status we have. However,
in the taking and giving meditation we imagine taking others' suffering
and giving them our body, possessions, and merit. Because this practice
contradicts the wishes of our self-centered thought, it is a profound way
to cultivate genuine love and compassion.

When we imagine taking on the suffering of others, we don't simply
think that their pain and misery enters us and stays there. Our becoming
depressed or emotionally overwhelmed won't benefit anyone! Rather, we
imagine our own self-centered mind—which is the source of so much of
our own misery—as a solid lump in the middle of our chest. This imag-
ery parallels what we feel when we're stuck in the middle of our own
self-preoccupation. Then imagine breathing in the suffering of others in
the form of pollution or smoke. This suffering transforms into a lightning bolt that strikes the solid brick of self-centeredness in our chest and
completely demolishes it. At this point, we think that we no longer suffer
from self-centeredness and self-grasping. Similarly, other sentient beings
no longer suffer from the results of their karma or afflictions. We have
used what other sentient beings don't want—their suffering—to destroy
what we don't want—our afflictions and karma. Thinking in this way is
crucial. Do not think that by taking on others' dukkha you become so
overwhelmed and distressed that you cannot function properly. That is
not the purpose of this meditation. Rather, with compassion take on the
suffering of others and use it to destroy your own internal enemy of self-
grasping and self-centeredness.

Your heart is open now and from within that open space in the
center of your chest radiates the light of love and compassion. Imagine
multiplying and transforming your possessions and giving them to all
sentient beings so that they fulfill the needs of each being. Then imagine
multiplying and transforming your body so that it becomes everything
and everyone that others need and send that to them. You become what
others need or whomever they need and they are fulfilled. You imagine
even your own constructive karma, your roots of virtue, multiplying

and transforming into conducive circumstances—both mental and environmental—so that sentient beings can meet and practice the Dharma. Imagine that others reap the benefit of all the virtues you have accumulated. This becomes a profound meditation on love, wishing others to have happiness and its causes.

There are a lot more details to this meditation, which Geshe Jampa Tegchok eloquently explains in *Transforming Adversity into Joy and Courage*. If you wish to be guided through this meditation, listen to the audio recording of it on www.thubtenchodron.org.

In short, bodhicitta is really the source of all good and happiness in the world, and verses 10 and 11 instruct us on ways to generate this powerful, profound, and noble mind.

### Bill: Compassion Conquers Fear

Of all of the practices I've done, the taking and giving meditation has had the most profound effects in my life. In particular, one of the emotions I have the most trouble with is fear. A lot of it is conditioned fear. I've lived my whole life in one kind of dangerous situation or another. Fear is one of those emotions that can quickly move me from acting wisely to acting irrationally. The meditation of taking suffering motivated by compassion and giving happiness motivated by love has helped me more than anything else in situations where I feel intense fear.

I am imprisoned for life without parole due to a murder I committed when I was sixteen. The following story occurred in prison. Joe, another inmate who was a friend of mine, was being sexually exploited. One day we were walking on the yard, discussing how he could put a stop to this distressing situation. As we walked and talked, he finally came to the point where he was just going to tell the guy who was exploiting him that he had had enough and then walk off. Of course, if you have dealt with prisons long enough, you know that such a confrontation usually doesn't end well. As we were walking, Joe's "friend" came out to holler at him. Joe did just what he said he was going to do. His friend quickly figured out that I was at fault for Joe's sudden courage, and now his friend wanted to holler at me. I knew what that meant, and it wasn't good.

I did my best not to respond with my first reaction, which was to strike first. Instead, while I walked towards the guy, I practiced taking and giving—taking from him his desire and greed, giving him what little virtue I had created in my Dharma practice. While doing this, I recited the Tara mantra. By the time I got over to the guy, I was calm, not feeling fight or flight. Of course the exchange between us was heated. He threatened me in various ways, wanted me to pay him money for taking his "boy," all of that. Joe went in and told the officer that his friend was out of bounds. The guy went to the Hole (disciplinary segregation) and was eventually transferred.

During the incident I didn't have to resort to violence because I never even felt moved to that level of fear beyond the initial feeling that led me to practice taking and giving. In short, taking and giving helped me to react from a more spacious place—a place where I had options other than confrontation and aggression. In the end, it worked out well. Joe isn't getting exploited anymore and the guy was transferred. Now Joe is in a much safer camp working on the inner issues that led him to that situation—he was abused as a child and quickly identified himself in that victim role.

### Jonathan: Compassion from Both Sides

A while ago, I was asked to fill in for the full-time instructor to teach Vocational Sheet Metal to inmates at a prison. I was fortunate to have had dedicated teachers instill a little good sense in me so that when I arrived to start the six-week assignment, I was able to discern that the men were more proficient in sheet metal fabrication than I was. I also knew I was not very smart about prison life. To take charge, I proposed we work on something that would benefit all of them.

After some discussion, they suggested we go to the prison dump and scavenge for something. We found an old tool chest that was in bad condition, which we hauled back to class to refurbish. I pitched in working with the men. During the course of the work our conversation consisted mostly of me hearing their stories. I gradually grew to understand that a single rash act had them behind bars, while I went home each night.

After I'd been there a few weeks, a violent, gang-related multiple-stabbing murder occurred in the exercise yard. I was upset and wanted to know more about the murder, so I asked what had happened. A gang member told me in some detail about the weapon and what had occurred. Other inmates joined in and gave me more information. This information, based on common trust between the prisoners and me, was a potential bombshell and I knew that I could not betray their trust. So I kept their disclosure to myself.

When I finished the assignment, the men approached and told me I was a nice guy, but something of a fool. They showed me a knife and told me they could have killed me at any time. After saying this, they cut the knife into small pieces and discarded them. They then surprised me by saying that they had no need for the tool chest and that it was a gift for me. But the biggest gift they gave me was the knowledge that if we can remain trusting and nonjudgmental, compassion will come from both sides. The biggest bars most of us contend with are those we construct around ourselves.

# 6. Transforming Distressing Events

## VERSE 12: LIVING WITH LOSS

*Even if someone out of strong desire*
*Steals all your wealth or has it stolen,*
*Dedicate to him your body, possessions,*
*And your virtue, past, present, and future—*
  *This is the practice of bodhisattvas.*

### Transforming Problems into the Path

THIS VERSE begins a series of practices called "mind training" in which we practice transforming adverse circumstances into the path to enlightenment. Thought training practices are very practical because disappointments and obstacles abound in cyclic existence. These practices may initially seem challenging, but when we contemplate them repeatedly they begin to make sense. They show us a new way to view circumstances—a way that prevents anger and resentment and increases joy and the sense of meaning in our lives.

### Dedicate All to the Person Who Steals from You

One of the worst things anyone can imagine is robbers stealing needed and valued possessions from your home or a shady character swindling you out of your house. Normally, what would we do? We would be enraged. We would be furious. We would want revenge. Feeling violated and sorry for ourselves, we would kick up a big fuss, rant and rave, and try to retaliate. Verse 12 instructs us to do the opposite. First, we train our mind to understand that getting angry doesn't help. It only poisons our mind and keeps us mentally trapped. Transform the mind so that you're able to look upon that person with compassion—compassion for the strong desire that made them steal your things, compassion for the destructive karma that they're creating by ripping off your stuff. Thus, instead of being angry and self-righteous, we train our mind to let go and dedicate our body, possessions, and virtue to those who robbed us. Instead of thinking, "This is mine," and trying to get it back when there's no way we can ever get it back, we mentally give it to the thief. We don't just offer the thief all of our possessions, but mentally offer our body, which can transform into whatever they need, and our virtue, past, present, and future, which becomes a conduit for them to meet and practice the Dharma.

Instead of holding a grudge and having it gnaw at us year after year, we let go and happily give the clung-to possessions to the person. Perhaps something in your heart says, "Are you kidding? That's not fair." In response, ask yourself, "What will happen if I cling on to my notion of what's fair?" You may cling on to that thought, but will you be happy? No. In that case, what happens? You have lost not only your possessions but also your happiness. Being unhappy about the loss doesn't return the possessions to us. It just makes it a double loss.

If someone takes your things without permission, think, "They must need that very badly. I give it to them." If you genuinely give it to them and decide, "Now it doesn't belong to me anymore. It belongs to him," you will have mental peace. On the other hand, if you hold on to the feeling of being wronged and make yourself into a victim of another person's injustice, you'll be miserable.

This does not mean that we allow people to cheat us or that we say to a thief, "Do you want anything else? I can show you where the key to my neighbor's house is." If someone steals our things, we can try to recover them, but do this without being angry at the person, without being vengeful and seeking retaliation. Such an approach might seem impossible. However, even trying to change our mind in that way is quite beneficial because there are only two alternatives: either we feel violated, resentful, and enraged and want revenge or we do something with our mind. There are these two choices. We either remain upset or we work with our mind. To work with our mind and subdue our anger involves looking at the other person's situation and cultivating compassion for him. If we're able to do that, then this situation, which would normally just freak us out, spurs us to Dharma practice, which will make our mind happier than before. We understand our situation as a result of our own destructive karma from stealing in previous times, and now this destructive karma is finished. It's over. All those unfortunate rebirths are done. We don't have to experience them. That destructive karma is not obscuring our mind any longer. Meanwhile this other person who stole from us is now creating the karma of stealing and, as a result, will experience an unfortunate rebirth in the future and even when he is born as a human, he'll have trouble with his possessions. Definitely he is someone to have compassion for. So generate love and compassion and **Dedicate to him your body, possessions, and your virtue, past, present, and future.** Even if this initially sounds impossible, just trying to get your mind to go in that direction is incredibly beneficial.

## Jan: Swindled

Some years ago a friend—at least someone who I thought was a friend—swindled me. We had agreed to split the cost of a hotel room that we shared for some days, but in the end I was left to pay the bill. This wasn't a total surprise because the person wasn't always so reliable, so I suspected this was a possible scenario going into the situation. However, I ignored my suspicion and didn't clarify who would pay the bill with her beforehand. I chose to share the room, and when I got stuck with the bill I wasn't happy, even though I knew I had abnegated my own responsibility by not talking with her about this before we rented the room. Although I spoke with her about it, nothing was resolved—she weaseled out and denied it. I was angry about this for a long time.

Then one day I saw a card with this verse on the fence at Sravasti Abbey. It made me think that it's time I resolved this in my mind, so mentally I gave her the money over and over again. This verse worked like a cooling salve for my burning thoughts. Nevertheless, thinking about this past event now disturbs my mind, and so I am again mentally giving the money to this person and am able to feel a smile inside me.

### Lee: Losing My Job but Winning Peace

As part of my work as a nurse practitioner and therapist I joined a new group of psychologists, psychiatrists, and nurse practitioners in independent practice. The founder and leader of the group was a psychologist. It worked well; we had plenty of work, and we were doing good work that benefited others. The people involved were good and very competent—at the height there were nine of us—and it was a good practice.

After three years, the leader started to speak about financial difficulties, saying that we needed to watch how much we spent. Most of us kept on working, thinking that the situation would turn around, but the debt grew until, in my case, he owed me about $20,000. Finally, one of the psychiatrists, supported by the rest of us, got a lawyer and had the leader investigated. He discovered that the psychologist who started the business had eight liens on his house from other people to whom he also owed money. Having a long history of dishonesty and stealing, he had been embezzling money from us.

Initially, I was devastated because my perception of who he was and what he turned out to be were so different. Also, I learned that hanging on to something and not recognizing the reality of what was happening, as well as attachment to reputation, were involved in my misery.

Finally, I gave notice and said I was leaving the group. This was hard because I didn't want to abandon my clients. When I told him I was walking away even if he didn't pay what he owed me, he got very angry, revealing another side of him that I had been ignorant of. As time went on, I saw that no matter what he or anyone else did, my interpretation of the situation and my response to it created my experience. In other words, I had to be responsible for my thoughts and emotions instead of attributing my suffering to others.

When I finally got out of the group and let it all go, it was as if a two-ton elephant had been lifted off my back. I opened my own office, which worked out well. In the process, I learned a lot about not feeling like a victim and not being angry. For example, this man had two small kids. His wife had bilateral breast cancer, and a year before he had a triple bypass. His suffering was evident. In addition, I learned how to work with my mind in a way that clarified that what others do is not the issue; it's how I think about their actions.

## VERSE 13: TRANSFORMING SUFFERING

*Even if someone tries to cut off your head*
*When you haven't done the slightest thing wrong,*
*Out of compassion take all her misdeeds*
*Upon yourself—*
    *This is the practice of bodhisattvas.*

### Compassion for the Person Who Harms Us

If we haven't done anything, at least nothing that we're aware of, and somebody is taking incredible measures to deprive us of our life and happiness, what is our instant reaction? Anger, rage, fear. We may wail that their actions are unfair and uncalled for and thoughts of possible ways to retaliate may race through our mind. Is that a pleasant mental state? No. Is it a virtuous mental state that can motivate constructive actions? Not at all. In fact, it's just the opposite. Whether we've done something wrong or haven't done something wrong, the fact is that our previous karma is ripening. In that sense, in a previous life we certainly did something that was harmful to someone else. Given that, the situation is ripening back on us in this lifetime. There's no sense being angry at the other person. It was our own self-centered thought that motivated us to do the harmful actions that brought on the harm that this person is giving us now. In other words, we are experiencing the painful result of previously created destructive karma and reacting in such a way that we are creating more destructive karma that will lead to more suffering in the future.

This doesn't mean that we deserve to suffer. It doesn't mean that we're worthless people. It simply means that in a previous life whoever we were was not very careful, was overwhelmed with negativity, and did something harmful. We don't know which life it was in. It could have been three gazillion eons ago. The main point is that once an action is done, the karmic latency stays in the mindstream. If we don't purify it, it will ripen. Such recognition can be a good motivator to do purification practice even when we don't initially feel like it. For example, in the evening when we would rather watch TV, we recall, "Some strong seed of destructive karma could be right there waiting to ripen. If I don't do purification practice, it could ripen soon. If I do purification practice tonight, I will impede its ripening." Thinking in this way will motivate us to do prostrations and confession. Of course, after we do them, we feel very good and can rejoice at our virtue.

Are there other alternatives to how we could think and feel when someone blames us for something we did not do? The reaction that Gyelsay Togmay Zangpo recommends is *Out of compassion take all her misdeeds upon yourself.* Again, it's referring to the meditation on taking and giving. Why is compassion an appropriate response to this person's actions? Because she is in a confused and unhappy state. If we focus on her, not on ourselves, we see that she is suffering greatly. In her confusion, she thinks that harming us will relieve her of her suffering. Of course it won't; she'll only create more destructive karma to experience more suffering in the future. In this life as well she could experience the misery involved in being arrested and imprisoned.

Instead of getting immersed in our own trauma and how unfair it is, out of compassion see the kind of destructive karma this person is creating, take that destructive karma upon ourselves, and take the suffering that she's going to experience upon ourselves. If we have compassion for her, wishing her to be free of suffering, then we're not harming our own mind and we won't do anything to cause her further misery. Not only do we wish her to be free of suffering, we also do the taking and giving meditation, imagining taking all her destructive karma—*all her misdeeds*—upon ourselves and using them to smash our own self-centeredness, visualized as a hard lump at our heart. After all, it is our own self-centeredness that motivated us in a previous life or earlier in this life to create the destructive karma that is ripening in us in this situation. Seeing that self-centered mind as our actual enemy, it makes sense to take what she doesn't want—the destructive karma of her misdeeds and its future suffering result—and use them to destroy what we don't want—our self-centered mind that pretends to be our friend but consistently deceives us.

If we look at the situation through the perspective of karma, we see that if we had not created destructive karma in the past, we wouldn't be experiencing this result now. Thus, it's inappropriate to blame all our fear and suffering on the other person when it's our own self-centeredness that is ultimately harming us. Rather than blame the other person, let's have compassion for her, take her suffering upon ourselves through the taking and giving meditation, and use it to destroy our self-centeredness. Imagine that it makes her happy in this life and relieves her suffering so that she can meet the Dharma in future lives, practice it, and attain enlightenment. That's the best thing to wish for those who hurt us because if they had met the Dharma, then they wouldn't be doing what they're doing.

His Holiness the Fourteenth Dalai Lama told a story about one of the Tibetan monks who was imprisoned by the Chinese Communists for many years. The monk had not done anything wrong but was imprisoned because the Communists wanted to crush the Buddhadharma in Tibet. Years later, when this monk was finally released from prison, he left Tibet and went to see His Holiness in Dharamsala. His Holiness asked him, "What frightened you the most while you were imprisoned and tortured?" The monk replied, "I was afraid of losing my compassion for the guards." Can you imagine that? He was afraid of relinquishing his compassion for the people who were torturing him. I was very moved when I heard that story. It's clear that the monk's compassion was what kept him alive for the duration of his imprisonment. Why? If you don't have compassion for the person who's harming you, then either you have hatred, which can kill you, or you just give up in despair, in which case you usually die. Instead, he felt compassion and lived.

We sometimes find it difficult to feel compassion for people who don't harm us personally. I work with prisoners, and one of the inmates that

I write to took a female guard hostage. It was all over the news in Portland. It was the first time a guard had been taken hostage in twenty years. I found out about the incident because somebody wrote to my website. Some of the inmate's writings and poetry are on my website and the person who reported the incident wrote to me via the website. He was enraged. He couldn't understand why I would put the writings of a rapist and criminal on the website. In his eyes the inmate was not fit to be considered a Buddhist. He said, "I'm a Buddhist and have concern for the image of Buddhism, especially if the media finds out that this hostage-taker was a Buddhist. I have compassion for the guard he took hostage and absolutely no compassion for him."

I wrote back and said, "This inmate is a human being. He is suffering. The Dharma has been a real refuge for him. He has made progress in some ways although he has a long way to go. He still has the Buddha nature, and I will not judge or abandon him just because he made a mistake." I had been corresponding with this prisoner for some time and knew he had a rough life and a great deal of internal suffering. His suffering and his confusion about how to stop it overwhelmed him and resulted in his terrifying the guard (who was released unharmed) and sabotaging his own happiness. I'm sure he hated himself after this episode and the internal scathing words he said to himself were probably worse than what the journalists said about him and how the authorities punished him. I believe he has some mental illness that requires treatment, but the prison system focuses on punishing offenders, not on rehabilitating them or treating their mental difficulties.

Someone may think that my saying it's suitable to feel compassion for this inmate is belittling the suffering of the guard whom he took hostage and the women whom he had raped (which was the reason he was in prison). That is not my intent. The suffering of those who were harmed is immense, but our hating the perpetrator doesn't eliminate their misery. Hatred only breeds more hatred, and hatred in our heart causes us more suffering than it causes the person we hate.

What is my point in telling this story? That it is possible to have compassion for someone who has done actions that we find despicable.

Furthermore, it is possible to feel compassion for those who perpetrate extreme harm on us. Someone cutting off our head is pretty extreme. But think of how mad we get when somebody does even a minor thing we don't like. For example, not saying "Good morning" to us. We become furious at anyone who does even the slightest little thing that we don't like. If the circumstance of someone wanting to cut off our head when we haven't done anything wrong is a situation calling for compassion, then surely we should be even more forgiving and tolerant in situations where nobody has a bad intention towards us and, misinterpreting her actions, we get angry. If we hold a grudge, who does the grudge hurt? It only hurts us. It doesn't hurt anybody else. Therefore, compassion is a medicine for our own pain as well as a balm that soothes the external situation.

## Morgan: Raining Compassion

I'm incarcerated and today was feeling rather strong aversion to a certain officer. We had a horrible storm; it was raining and the wind gusts were up to fifty miles per hour. I had to go outside to turn in my college books, which left me out in the rain at 8:45 a.m. The next regular "unlock"—the time when we can move about and I could go inside—wasn't until 10:00 a.m. I asked the building control officer to let me in according to my ducat, a pass I had to turn in my books. He came to the window and asked, "What kind of ducat?" When I told him it was for turning in my books, he said, "Come back at 10:00 a.m.," which meant I would be out in the rain and wind for an hour plus.

Over the course of an hour, many inmates went in and out with the officer. Clearly, he was letting in and out only those who he wanted to. At one point, he even let out and back in my cellmate. He made sure to only let him in, although he only had to press the same buttons to let us both in.

So, I stood out there feeling the rain soak through my many layers of clothes. I tried to maintain peace of mind. I thought about all the animals who had no warm clothing, blankets, or cups of coffee. As I felt the wind against my wet face, I told myself it wasn't personal. The officer's response said more about the officer than about me. The experience was a reminder that, at times, I had refused someone else's comfort.

At 9:50 a.m. the power went out and he had to let the eight to ten people who weren't worthy back in. That's how I felt—unworthy of a little compassion.

Now, at 4:50 in the afternoon, as my clothes are hanging on makeshift hooks and are still wet, I consider missing dinner to avoid wearing those wet clothes back out into the rain. Truthfully, I'm still not feeling equanimity, but at the same time I realize a few things. One, it isn't bringing me peace to hold on to my anger. Two, I'm pretty sure that officer isn't thinking about me out in the rain. And three, it does no good for anyone to fight dependent arising and emptiness.

While this letter hasn't been helpful in terms of explaining equanimity, it is helping me to see how hooked I am by this morning's events. Why do we hold on to our labels of friend, enemy, and stranger? Does holding on to the officer as an "enemy" perpetrate behavior on his part towards me? Does it predispose me to expect negative responses in the future? This touches on the need to go beyond hope and fear and to just let each moment be as it is.

And yet, I suppose what I feel is attachment to a victim stance. Poor me. But wait. I have the Buddha nature. So maybe what I really have is a mistaken identity.

Then I realize it is all conceptual stuff that keeps me attached to the past. I breathe in, breathe out, and let it all go.

### Renee: Compassion That Goes Beyond Horror

Daniel Pearl was an American journalist who was kidnapped and then decapitated in 2002 in Pakistan. Before killing him, his captors imprisoned him, during which time he had to live with the knowledge that he would possibly be beheaded. Thinking of him when chanting this verse, I consider how much compassion one would have to have to remain open-hearted, like the verse says, in those circumstances. This gives me an image and vision of the goal of developing compassion that is large enough to encompass such a horrific situation.

## VERSE 14: FACING BLAME

*Even if someone broadcasts all kinds of unpleasant remarks*
*About you throughout the three thousand worlds,*
*In return, with a loving mind,*
*Speak of his good qualities—*
  *This is the practice of bodhisattvas.*

### Attachment to Reputation

Imagine someone savagely criticizes you, deriding you, ruining your reputation, and telling dreadful lies about you. Meanwhile, you have no recourse to tell your side of the story and to clear your name. We don't like it when somebody makes one nasty comment about us to one person, let alone broadcasts all kinds of lies that make everyone in three thousand worlds mistrust and dislike us. Imagine the suffering you would experience if someone did this to you. This points to one of our biggest attachments, our reputation. Of course, the more attached we are to our reputation, the more upset we become when other people don't agree with how wonderful we think we are. This attachment and the anger it provokes become a big problem for us.

What does Bodhisattva Togmay Zangpo recommend we do in such a situation? Take out a full-page ad in the *New York Times* and explain our side of the story? Criticize the other person in return so that his reputation is totally shattered? Curl up in a ball and feel sorry for ourselves because no one understands or support us? None of those will work. Instead, Togmay Zangpo tells us in return to **speak of his good qualities** with a loving mind. This sounds impossible and we may wonder if Togmay Zangpo is crazy. The self-centered mind thinks, "Speak of this guy's good qualities? He doesn't have any! Anybody who criticizes me is bereft of good qualities." Here we see clearly how the self-centered thought functions. The criterion it uses to evaluate people is: "Somebody who likes me is a good person and someone who doesn't like me is a bad person." Is this a good way to evaluate other people? Is it a good way to select friends? Not at all. We are just trying to protect ourselves from any criticism and unhappiness.

We are so easily manipulated. Someone with a scheming motivation comes along and flatters us, saying how talented, wonderful, and good-looking we are. We sit there and bask in his words, wanting more praise. We think anyone who says something nice about us is a wonderful person. Meanwhile, our discriminating wisdom is out to lunch. Somebody praises us, and we love that person, even if he is trying to harm us and manipulate us. We fall for praise so easily. On the other hand, when a friend sees us act in a harmful way and out of genuine concern says, "Please be careful how you are acting," we get furious. Our defenses spring up and we scream, "You're not my friend anymore. Why are you criticizing me? People who live in glass houses shouldn't throw stones." Yet this person is commenting on our behavior because he really cares about us. He doesn't want us to create destructive karma and find ourselves in difficulty. We consider that person an enemy and vow never to speak to him again. We hold a grudge against him and say bad things about him throughout the three thousand worlds, even though he was trying to help us with compassion.

The criteria we use to discern friends and enemies are totally skewed. We fall for the ploys of someone who insincerely praises us in order to get something from us, and we hate someone who, out of genuine care and concern, says something that our self-centered thought does not want to hear, even though the words are true and need to be said. Instead, we can actually assess ourselves in a more reliable way. What qualities do I have? What are my weaknesses? What do I need to focus on to improve? What good qualities do I have that I can enhance? We all have some good qualities and we all have some weaknesses.

If we are able to assess ourselves better, what other people say won't hit us so strongly. If we're able to check our own motivations, then we know when we're acting properly and when we're not. Then other people's feedback doesn't hit us so strongly because we're in touch with ourselves. If other people say all kinds of rude, obnoxious, critical, disparaging things about us to our face or behind our backs, then we're better able to assess what is true and what's not true with a calm mind. When we have that space in our mind, when we aren't so defensive about every tiny comment that people make about us, then there's space in our own mind to look at that other person and see their good qualities. Instead of seeing them and all their faults, we realize that they have some faults but they also have some good qualities. Based on this recognition, we will be able to speak well of their good qualities.

This verse counsels us to maintain a loving, compassionate heart even towards a person who turns others against us, gossips about us behind our back, and ruins our reputation. Instead of projecting "devil" onto that person, let's recognize that she has the Buddha nature. She has the quality of kindness in her, even though she isn't showing it towards us at the moment. She has been kind to us in previous lives. In addition, reputation is of no ultimate value. It is only other people's ideas, and others' ideas are fickle and changeable.

Instead of clinging to our reputation, we say to that person, "Thank you for helping me realize that reputation does not bring happiness." One part of our mind may say, "That's wrong. Reputation makes me very happy." If this is the case, ask yourself, "What happiness does reputation actually bring? What good do others' changeable opinions about me do for me? Do they prevent me from getting sick? Do they stop me from dying? Do they make me any closer to enlightenment? Do they purify destructive karma? From a Dharma perspective, what good does a good reputation do?" Looking at our situation with wisdom, we see that a good reputation does not bring us any benefit. If anything, it could harm us by making us conceited or complacent. Seeing that reputation is empty of meaning, let's relinquish attachment to it. We work with our mind and transform our mind so that we actually do see others' good qualities. Doing so allows our mind to be peaceful no matter what others say about us. Wouldn't it be wonderful to remain calm no matter what others thought or said about you?

### Kathleen: What Is a Reputation?

A number of years ago I was an executive director of an agency and made the mistake of dating one of the employees. We had known each other as friends before working there and there was no policy against dating. But after a short time I was uncomfortable and stopped seeing him outside of work.

Shortly after that, he filed a complaint against me for sexual harassment and wrote a six- page letter that revealed some very personal information that I had told him while we were dating. He gave this embarrassing letter to the Board of County Commissioners, all the other employees in my agency, and to my supervisor. He broadcast all kinds of unpleasant remarks about me throughout the three thousand worlds of the county where I lived. I was devastated. It was really difficult because the position I was in was semi-public—I went to many meetings and people knew me, and so forth. All the people I worked with on many levels had read his letter, some of which was accurate and some of it was blown way out of proportion. Still, it was very personal.

Of course, I wasn't sexually harassing him, but it seems he thought I was. I don't suppose many other women have faced the charge of sexual harassment, and his complaint began an eighteen-month process of investigation. Some in the agency believed him, some did not. Because it was a personnel issue, I was not able to discuss it with anyone but the lawyers, so no one knew my side of the story, while he was free to tell anyone anything. Eventually, I realized this was a good boundary to have, but nevertheless this was a very painful, humiliating, and frightening time.

Around this same time, I started going to Buddhist retreats, and during one retreat I met with my teacher and told her about this situation. She said a number of things that were very helpful. First, she told me that this was simply my karma ripening from times I had falsely accused and humiliated others. The situation wasn't going to last forever and it was purifying this destructive karma. Also, she said that it was only my reputation that was at stake. What is a reputation? It is just a set of other people's opinions that shift and change hour to hour, day to day. There is nothing solid or controllable about it. Over the eighteen months of investigation, I saw people's shifting opinions, "You did it; you didn't do it," "He's right, you're wrong. You're right, he's wrong," when, in fact, none of them knew what had actually happened. I had to ask myself, "Given that they don't know and that their opinions changed so often, what am I holding on to so tightly?" My mind was clinging on to a seemingly solid reputation as a director that was at stake, when in fact there was no findable, solid thing that could be identified as my reputation. It was a good lesson in realizing the emptiness of inherent existence. People think whatever they wish— correct or incorrect—and I cannot control it.

My teacher instructed me not to think of this person as an enemy and not to talk negatively about him. During the eighteen months of the investigation, I recited a new "mantra": "You are not my enemy; you are not my enemy." I tried very hard not to speak badly about him. I wasn't always successful with that, particularly with my friends, but at least in the office I was very careful because I didn't want to create more of the same karma. Experiencing this situation was difficult and I wanted to finish with creating the karma to experience anything like it again. She also recommended that I imagine Green Tara in my office, with her green light and the sound of her mantra filling the entire space, purifying and transforming it.

I followed this advice and the situation improved slowly and, once the investigation was completed, I was cleared of all charges and the man resigned from the agency. I never got so far in the practice as to "with a loving mind speak of his good qualities," but I now see that this person was a good guide on my spiritual path. He was like a spiritual teacher in that he knocked away my arrogance, so I have to thank him. I learned so much about karma, fortitude, nonretaliation, humility, and compassion from this interaction, and now I wish him freedom from all suffering, as well as peace and joy in all that he does.

## VERSE 15: WORKING WITH CRITICISM

*Though someone may deride and speak bad words*
*About you in a public gathering,*
*Looking on her as a spiritual teacher,*
*Bow to her with respect—*
    *This is the practice of bodhisattvas.*

## Compassion for the One Who Derides Us

Here someone harms us by deriding us and speaking bad words about us in a public gathering when all our family, friends, and everybody whom we want to impress are present. We seek the approval and appreciation of a group of people, but instead someone ruins our chance to receive these by disparaging us in their presence. Try to imagine this scene. How would you feel and act? We could go completely into a rage or we could cry or we could stomp out of the room and slam the door. Or we could work with our mind. There aren't a lot of alternatives.

Trying to impress people, we put on shows. We're very clever when we try to impress someone. First, we think of what kind of person they would be attracted to. Then we try to become that person, or at least to appear like him or her. In other words, we present ourselves as being someone we think they think would be good. Confusing, isn't it? We display ourselves as attractive. We pretend to be talented, rich, intelligent, or artistic. We pretend we're interested in things we're not interested in. We pretend we know things that we don't have a clue about—all because we want somebody to like us. We want him or her to approve of us and praise us; we want him or her to love us. To get that person to say the ego-pleasing words we crave to hear or to do the ego-pleasing actions we want, we go through a big routine trying to become what we think the person thinks we should be.

Even when we go to a Dharma center we may try to impress others by boasting, "I've done this retreat. I've taken this teaching. I know this and have studied that." We try to impress people with our Dharma knowledge as well. Or maybe we brag about how many lamas have visited our home or ridden in our car. We will use anything, even the Dharma, in an attempt to make ourselves look good and to get people to like or respect us. It's very sad. This is like using gold to make a toilet.

Here's the scenario: you are speaking to an audience of distinguished guests and are trying very hard to present a good image so that they will praise you and you will have a good reputation. Then someone you know but haven't gotten along with so well stands up and starts deriding you and speaking bad things about you. She tells your faults and brings up your past history, which you don't want others to know. You watch the bright, eager faces of those whose attention you're trying so hard to get, who were looking at you before and singing your praises, now going stiff as they hear this person accuse you of being an insincere charlatan.

Maybe you aren't really everything she says you are, but surely some of the traits apply. But you don't want to admit any of them, especially in front of a group of people you've been endeavoring to impress, and whose love and adoration you're trying to win. You would rather die than go through this. And in fact, some people commit suicide when such things happen.

In this terribly embarrassing situation, what does Bodhisattva Togmay Zangpo recommend doing? *Look upon her as a spiritual teacher,* and *bow to her with respect.* Imagine. She's saying all these lies in front of the people I care most about, who I want to think well of me. If those people don't think well of me, then I'm completely shattered and I'm nothing and I'm nobody. I've completely lost all my status, all my clout, all my own self-respect. How am I going to see this person as a spiritual teacher? From the viewpoint of the self-centered mind, impossible, totally impossible. From the viewpoint of Dharma mind, very possible. You put your palms together and say, "Thank you so much for trashing me." And you mean it. You really mean it. You are not doing some kind of phony trick to look like a bodhisattva. You are not doing a song and dance trying to impress people with what a bodhisattva you are by saying, "Thank you for deriding me," while you're thinking, "See what a bodhisattva I am, being so kind and considerate to this idiot here who's deriding me. I hope these people will see how humble I am and will respect me for it."

Instead, from your heart, you speak of her good qualities and look upon her as your spiritual teacher. How is she a spiritual teacher? She is teaching you the uselessness of attachment to praise and aversion to blame. She is educating you about the vanity of trying to impress people. She is showing you that you don't have to impress other people in order to be liked or loved or to win others' approval.

When doing the emptiness meditation, we go through a four-point analysis. The first point is to identify the object of negation, the inherently existent "I" that has never existed, that we believe exists. In order to negate this false "I," we must first be able to identify what it would be like if it *did* exist. Then using probing awareness, we prove to ourselves that such an "I" never has and never will exist. How do we identify the inherently existent "I"? In the scriptures they suggest thinking of a time when we were accused unjustly or when somebody blamed us or trashed our reputation. In these situations, the inherently existent "I" appears vividly because we are angry and defensive. The object of negation is right there before us—it's the feeling in our gut of: "That's ME that he's accusing." If the object of negation is not clear in the mind, the emptiness meditation doesn't have any impact. It's only when it's clear in the mind, when we really believe that such an "I" exists and then do the analysis and see that it doesn't exist at all that the meditation really wakes us up. Here is this person who's like our spiritual teacher, very kindly helping us with the meditation, so we have to *Bow to her with respect.*

No matter how much we try to impress them, people are going to think whatever they wish about us. We might as well relax, because we don't have any control over what opinion they will form of us or when they will change it. If we behave naturally without trying to manipulate the image others have of us and are content with whatever they wish to think or say about us, others may actually like us. That's what this person is teaching us. Because of this, we have to put our palms together and say, "Thank you for teaching me that I don't need to try to create an image. Nor do I need to be attached to what people think and say about me. What I need to do is to be happy within myself. If I can be mindful of my motivations and act sincerely, I'll be happy with my decisions and I won't need others to approve of me. I'll know that ultimately my karma is my responsibility and that what others say and think about me cannot make me take rebirth in a fortunate realm or an unfortunate abode."

This person who is deriding us in a public gathering is throwing us back on ourselves. Instead of seeking others' approval in order to feel good about ourselves, she is teaching us that if our motivations are good, it doesn't matter what other people think. She's teaching us to be content with who we are and to be virtuous instead of simply looking virtuous. She's teaching us to be responsible instead of seeking to look responsible.

## Steve: Grrrr, I Get So Angry

For many years I've had problems with a colleague at work. The relation-ship was extremely difficult for me. In my perception, he was very aggres-sive, critical, and negative towards me. His disparaging comments caused me to doubt myself in an unhealthy way, and my self-confidence slid away and was replaced by tension and stress. I tried as much as I possibly could to react with compassion, understanding, and love to him, but as you can imagine, I did not always succeed.

The other day, following an episode in which he was aggressively criti-cal towards me in a team meeting, he came to apologize. He was very sincere when he did so and said that he greatly appreciated my patience and saw this as one of my great qualities.

I was pleased that my "enemy" described me as a patient person, and although I know that often my "patience" takes the form of just saying nothing while boiling with anger underneath, sometimes it is like actual fortitude. I thought the fact that he recognized this was a good sign, and he linked it to me being Buddhist, which of course it is. I felt that I was for once giving a good example of how Buddhists behave.

Our relationship has been better since then, and while I don't think that I'm right and he's wrong, it was interesting to see that if we just wait and be patient (or at least quiet) with people who are so obviously disturbed by anger and critical minds, eventually they themselves will realize that they are not acting constructively. Our being as patient as pos-sible gives them the space to understand that. So after much confusion and pain between us, this was a nice moment for me—and also for him, I believe.

I still have a long way to go before I am able to consistently relate to this colleague in a proper way. I'm pleased that I manage to try as much as possible to develop patience and compassion for him, and I do see how much he suffers from being in so much conflict with the world. Nonethe-less, I still get angry with him, and sometimes am so exhausted by the negativity—his and mine—that I just want to be very far away from him! However, since that will not happen anytime soon, I am committed to keep on cultivating fortitude and compassion.

### Alex: My Coach, the Buddha

I played basketball in high school and my coach would get so angry, sometimes randomly and at strange things. One day, he was screaming at me in my face, and I thought, "What if he's the Buddha?" He was still yelling in my face, but my mind was saying, "Whoa, this changes everything." Almost instantly there was space in my mind and my mind relaxed. All the fear went away for a while. In that moment it was quite powerful because I realized I didn't really know who my coach was and maybe he was a Buddha.

### Andrea: Public Scolding, A Sign of Confidence

Many years ago I attended an international Buddhist conference in Taiwan. After the conference they kindly took us on a tour of holy sites in Taiwan, and on the concluding day there was a large presentation in one of their branch temples. At that time the Master stood up with several of the senior monastics who were instrumental in organizing the conference and tour. Smiling, the Master introduced one nun to the audience, "This Venerable worked so hard preparing the program," and she humbly bowed. Then he introduced a monk, "This Venerable did an excellent job arranging the accommodation," and the monk bowed. The Master continued on introducing a few more of the key people. Finally, he looked at one monk and said to the audience of a few hundred distinguished guests from around the world, "But this monk was lazy and didn't do his job very well. He was negligent and let us all down."

I could hear the gasp as everyone listened to the Master scold this monk in public. But I thought, "This monk is his close disciple. The Master could criticize this disciple in public because he knew he could take it." He knew that the monk could apply the Dharma and keep his mind calm in this situation. Someone like me, who does not know how to practice this mind training verse, would feel humiliated and maybe even cry or run away. In fact, the Master was pointing out the strength of this monk's practice.

# 7. Dealing with Difficulties

## VERSE 16: BETRAYAL

*Even if a person for whom you've cared*
*Like your own child regards you as an enemy,*
*Cherish him specially, like a mother*
*Does her child who is stricken by sickness—*
    *This is the practice of bodhisattvas.*

### Expectations Crashed

THIS VERSE speaks of our relationship with someone we have cared for like our child, someone we have invested so much time and energy in, someone we love and trust very much. We expect that they will feel grateful for our efforts and that we will continue to have a loving relationship. However, that is not what happens. Instead of feeling grateful and returning our affection, this person turns around and views us as an enemy. Such things happen in families and other close relationships. One person may be very kind to another but the other person can't see his kindness. Instead, he becomes an enemy and attacks him. First, they cut off our head, then they broadcast all kinds of unpleasant remarks about us throughout the three thousand worlds. Then they deride us and speak bad words about us in front of a lot of people, and then, even though we've cared for them so much, they turn their back on us and see us as their worst enemy.

This painful and unfortunate situation is a result of our own karma created in the past. We did something similar to someone else in the past. We turned on a person who was kind to us, criticized him, hurt his feelings, and betrayed his trust. Now it's happening to us. Also sentient beings' minds are under the influence of afflictions. We know from our own experience that when our mind is under the influence of afflictions, we say and do outrageous things. That's exactly what's going on with others when they do outrageous things towards us. If we regard the person who betrays our trust in the way a mother or father would regard their child who is stricken with illness, we won't take what she is saying and doing personally because we know that she is not in her right mind. What is this person sick with? She suffers from her mental afflictions. Her mind is sick with wrong conceptions, which are causing her to repay kindness with hostility.

The instant reaction of the self-centered mind is, "I love you, I cherished you. I did so much for you. And look at how you are treating me. Poor me. What did I do to deserve this?" Some of us relish indulging in self-pity. As one of the inmates I correspond with said, we throw a pity party. We are the star of the show and sing our favorite song again and again: "Poor me. What did I do to deserve this"? Everyone feels sorry for us and we don't have to do anything except enjoy being miserable. The self-centered mind loves this. But instead of going into our "poor me" routine, this verse advises us to press the pause button and, instead, to cherish that person *specially, like a mother does her child who is stricken by sickness.*

At times like this, a couple of ways of changing our perspective is helpful. One is just to reflect on when we've done the same to other people and have some regret and make some amends for how we've treated other people. Maybe you can contact them again or write them a letter or apologize in one way or another. The second is to see them as someone who's under the influence of afflictions. That's why the analogy relates to how a mother sees her child *who is stricken by sickness.* A parent knows that if you have a child with a raging fever, what your child says isn't going to make any sense. Even adults with raging fevers don't make any sense. What they're thinking doesn't make any sense. The mind's just out of control. But a mother whose child has a high fever knows that the child is delirious and will say all sorts of things he doesn't mean. But she doesn't take it personally because she knows the child is ill. Or let's say her toddler has a temper tantrum and screams his lungs out. She doesn't get upset at the child because she knows three-year-olds behave like this at times. She is tolerant and will help the child after he calms down.

Does this mean you sit there and let the other person act in an uncontrolled manner? Once a woman came to see me with her three-year-old son. He suddenly decided it was a good time to have a temper tantrum and started hitting his mom. I held him and said calmly but firmly, "It's not appropriate to hit your mom. You cannot hit your mom. That's not something you can do." Eventually he calmed down.

Thus, it doesn't mean you let the person be disruptive. Compassion is called for here. We're working for the benefit of other sentient beings. These are the things that make a bodhisattva's mind very strong, because if we're going to practice the bodhisattva path, we have to be able to endure these kinds of things without our mind getting totally bent out of shape and without falling into anger or self-pity or self-righteousness or any of the usual things we do when sentient beings are not behaving as we think they should. In your heart, you cherish him like a mother does her sick child. Externally, you show that affection by providing structure and guidance.

### Maria: Trust Shattered

I helped to start an art project with a Chinese painter and my father, who is a sculptor from Belarus. They wanted to invite international artists to collaborate on a huge sculpture and to construct an art village so there could be ongoing art projects. Initially the project went well: we started constructing the buildings to display the artwork as well as a foundry for making the sculptures. My father arranged for several sculptors to go to China, and together they began working on a sculpture that was nearly ten feet high.

Because the founders of this project were artists, they didn't think so much about the practical aspects of their work. As much as I pleaded with them to put their plan and agreement in writing, they didn't have the type of mentality to do that. Thus, a year into the project, nothing was in writing, the sculpture was half done, and they started to argue because each of them had different ideas. Essentially the whole project blew up in our faces.

Our two families had been very close and there was a lot of affection and care for each other and a deep connection between us. We trusted each other, and that was why the project was done by gentleman's agreement. But just as this verse says, we now regarded each other as enemies. I was extremely hurt on two accounts. First, because we lost the art project and barely managed to get the sculpture out of China. Second, I felt guilty involving my father in a project that turned out so poorly.

Meanwhile, I was furious with the Chinese artist. While on the outside I was numb, I would dream of searching for a way to kill him. It was that bad. I looked civil, but in my dreams I was crazy.

After a while, I got tired of feeding all this hate. Also, I met some Buddhists who helped me change my mind. After a while, I was able to forgive him, and now I feel no remnant of hatred, although I still wonder what exactly happened. Now, I see it's true that we may trust someone very much but something can happen that turns us into enemies. But even in this case, we can still have compassion for the other person "like a mother does her child who is stricken by sickness."

### Deborah: Abandoned

In Buddhism we're instructed to train our mind to see others' kindness as a way to counteract the pain from when they have abandoned or rejected us. This is difficult to do, especially when it concerns the most important relationships in our lives. Since my childhood was not so good, I would like to share my perspective on this.

My mother could not take care of her five children. All of us kids grew up in an orphanage or were adopted. The youth welfare office took me from my mother's home when I was six years old. Later I learned from a relative that at that time my brother and I were very thin and not well cared for. My mother was an alcoholic, took a lot of drugs, and was unemployed.

Later, during my stay in this orphanage, I had some traumatic experiences that were quite intense. In addition, I saw my mother for just two or three days only once a year. She was not ready to embrace me, to talk to me, or to deal with me and my siblings. With her I felt alone and sometimes lost. But still she took me to her home for some days and later she tried to get me and my brother out of the orphanage. Finally she got us back for a few years.

But still the relationship with her was difficult. I could not be really a child. I had to work a lot from the morning until evening—taking care of my younger siblings, cleaning, washing clothes for the whole family, buying the food, and so forth. But I always loved my mother, and at least the social institutions helped me to find another way of life. At the orphanage and at school I met people who gladly spoke with me, who were friendly and well disposed. I learned from them. Also peers have done much for me and I am grateful for that. I have been able to learn and grow through contact with them.

Although I had some very difficult circumstances, there were also good moments in my life that influenced me. For example, in the orphanage we had time to study, we learned handicrafts and useful skills. We had sports lessons and made a few short trips in nature where we had good experiences and developed our good qualities. There were also educators who talked to us in a friendly and caring way. All these were positive moments.

During those years I met and learned from many different people. People took care of me and later I learned to select my own friends and teachers. I learned how to make wise decisions about whom to talk to, to live with, to learn from, and to work with, and in this way I had some good experiences. Thank goodness in Germany we have a good social system, so I never landed on the street, even though I had not a penny as a teenager and student. By others helping me, I got an apartment and some money and could go to school.

Also there were people who gave me a smile and made me happy. Later, there were people who wanted to hear about my life and took me into their own life and accompanied me. I saw and experienced many different ways that we human beings used to interrelate with each other. In all these ways, I learned the most important lesson: no one acts in negligent, violent, hateful, or apathetic ways all the time. There is love, care, and kindness in our world too.

I have also learned how much we human beings depend on each other. My mother is one person, but those who played the major role in my development were teachers, educators, my schoolmates' parents, neighbors, people who simply walk along the streets and smile or help an old person enter the subway, bakers and those who sell the bread, carpenters and construction workers, authors, and so forth. So even if I had a difficult relationship with my birth mother, I am grateful that she gave birth to me, and that I had at least some short good moments with her, too. But she wasn't the only one who kept me alive and shared her life with me. Everybody has been, is, or will be my mother. My teachers, friends, schoolmates, their parents, the baker, the builder, the architect, the authors—they too are my mothers. And of course since I began to learn Buddhism, the Three Jewels have been my wise companions, guides, and supports.

Everybody has been, is, and will be our mother. This is a reason to be happy and grateful.

## Cliff: My Mother's Enemy

This verse speaks of when someone whom we have cared for like our own child regards us as an enemy. My situation was the reverse: my mother regarded me as an enemy.

This wasn't always the case. I was my parents' youngest child, and they split up when I was very small. Mom saw me as hers, and I was brought up at her hip. We were quite close for the first twelve years of my life, and I was a spoiled brat. Then I started questioning things and found my heart draw towards Buddhism.

Now, ten years later, my mom is a fundamentalist Christian and I'm Buddhist, wanting to become a monk. In her eyes I became an "enemy" in that I didn't follow her way, and she even said at one point, "You're going to hell" and then added, "and it's all my fault." No matter what I did, I couldn't do anything that pleased her. It's been hard—she is a person whom I cared so much about and now the relationship is the opposite.

There's even been discussion that maybe we should not talk to each other anymore. The meditation of seeing the mother as kind because she gave me this body and taught me so many life skills has helped me not to fall into anger. In my heart I want to repay her kindness and hope that one day her mind will change so that I can do that.

## VERSE 17: SQUASHING OUR EGO

*If an equal or inferior person*
*Disparages you out of pride,*
*Place her, as you would your spiritual teacher,*
*With respect on the crown of your head—*
    *This is the practice of bodhisattvas.*

### Squashing Our Ego

This verse speaks about someone who has equal or less skill or talent than we do in a certain area. This person disparages you out of pride because she's jealous of you. In other words, she behaves just as we do towards the people we're jealous of. We find faults with them and harp on their bad qualities because we can't stand that they are so successful, skilled, athletic, or whatever. Our pride is piqued and in a misconstrued attempt to restore it we tear down our detractor, thinking it will build us up.

We want to be the best one and what better way to be best than to make someone else look bad? We do this, don't we? So, that's what somebody else is doing with us. He is suffering from arrogance and disparaging us in an attempt to feel better about himself. Of course, this doesn't work just as it has never worked any of the times we've acted that way towards others. Instead of retaliating and disparaging him in return, we put him respectfully on the crown of our head, as we would our spiritual mentor. In other words, this person becomes like a spiritual mentor to us.

Placing our spiritual teacher on the crown of our head is a valuable practice. Imagining our spiritual teacher in the form of the Buddha, Chenrezig, Tara, or another deity, we visualize him or her on top of our head. Then we do the seven-limb prayer, the mandala offering, purification, and so on. After the meditation session, we again visualize our spiritual mentor on the crown of our head as a witness to all our actions and as an inspiration for our actions during the day. This is a wonderful practice that makes us feel close to our spiritual teacher even when we live far away.

What is she teaching us? She is showing us the foolishness of being proud and of being attached to our good qualities. Perhaps the reason this person is disparaging us is because we acted puffed up, thinking we are better than she is. She is pointing out to us that humility, not arrogance, is a quality of a bodhisattva.

The remedy here is to *Place her, as you would your spiritual teacher, with respect on the crown of your head.* This is similar to a previous verse: *Looking on her as a spiritual teacher, bow to her with respect.* It's the same idea to see that this person is showing us our own pride. She is showing us our own inability to listen. She is showing us our own anger. Whoever the person is, whether she is in fact inferior or not, in that moment she is acting as a spiritual teacher to us in pointing out our own defilements. By putting the person who disparages us on the crown of our head, we learn humility. By paying respect to her, our arrogance is reduced. If your deluded mind thinks, "Why should I respect her? She's worse than me. She's inferior to me or, at best, just my equal. Moreover, she's criticizing me," think, "No. She is a human being who is worthy of respect. She has the potential to become a fully enlightened Buddha, therefore respecting her is suitable. I don't have to make myself Number One, and be the best at every activity and the most outstanding at every gathering."

Such an attitude contradicts our upbringing in which we were taught to want recognition and to proclaim our achievements. However, in Buddhist practice, being arrogant is not conducive for accomplishing the path. In fact, talking about our strengths and putting ourselves forward reinforces the notion of an inherently existent "I," and thus can create obstacles in our meditation practice. For this reason, amongst others, humility is important.

Humility doesn't mean a lack of self-esteem. It doesn't mean we put ourselves down. It just means that we don't go around broadcasting everything we've done or are capable of doing. We're completely satisfied without anyone knowing our good qualities. We don't have to be the most prominent one, to be on display, or to make a big show of ourselves.

These verses are quite potent ways to fight the self-centered thought, aren't they? They strike our self-centered intentions and our deluded need to be noticed, to be the best, the most famous, the most highly praised, the most loved. We are quite attached to these things and become arrogant or complacent when we have them. Arrogance and complacency are antithetical to the spiritual path. There is no such thing as an arrogant Buddha, so cultivating arrogance will not bring us closer to enlightenment. Humility, respecting others, praising others—these are traits of the enlightened ones, so cultivating them makes our mind more like the mind of a Buddha.

### Mary Jo: Control Freak

At work a younger colleague and I were setting up the refreshment table before a meeting. In my culture of origin, older people are automatically respected and treated with courtesy. In the culture of this young person, respect is earned through one's behavior, no matter what your age. While working together, I told this young man to take something out of the refrigerator. Looking back, I see that I did not ask kindly; I gave an order. He ignored me and asked another person near us whether he should do what I asked. I felt really angry and told him so, and we exchanged some angry words.

Later I went to him with the intention to apologize, but the conversation again turned into conflict. At the end of it I was very upset, but bowed to him and told him he was right in telling me that I was rude and inconsiderate. For the next three weeks, I had to wrestle with my self-centered view of this situation and with the emotions of humiliation, anger, and pride swimming through my head. I kept rehearsing over and over how I had run several businesses and agencies, taught hundreds of students, and supervised many workers, while he had done none of these things. However, blaming him and praising my own qualities did nothing to alleviate my anger.

Finally, I consulted my Dharma teacher, who kindly and clearly got me to stop my continuous recitation of his faults and deficiencies and helped me to look at my own process—what I had done and what I needed to address and clean up inside my own mind. It was tough going. I did a lot of purification around my pride and my anxiety over doing things quickly and efficiently. I carefully examined my compulsion to control everyone and everything when I felt anxious and my own rudeness when I was in "controlling mode." Gradually, as I calmed down and got more honest with myself, I saw that his feedback was very accurate—that at times I am rude and inconsiderate to others. I was able to relax and do my job more effectively than ever. At the roughest moments of this dispute, he was a good teacher for me and I am grateful to him for that.

## VERSE 18: ENDING THE PITY PARTY

*Though you lack what you need and are constantly disparaged,*
*Afflicted by dangerous sickness and spirits,*
*Without discouragement take on the misdeeds*
*And the pain of all living beings—*
    *This is the practice of bodhisattvas.*

### Self-Centered Mind Is the Culprit

This is another one of the thought training verses. It addresses transforming adversity into the path by doing the taking and giving meditation. Imagine losing almost everything in your life. On the physical level, you lack what you need, and on the social level, you are constantly disparaged and lack the support of friends and family. In terms of your body, you are sick and weak. We usually react in one of two ways to misfortune. One option is to become upset and angry, wanting to strike back at society or at whomever we deem to be the cause of our ruin. Another option is to become depressed and throw a pity party for ourselves. Feeling helpless and hopeless, we throw up our hands and say, "What's the use? Why should I live? Nobody is helping me and the whole world is against me. Poor me. I don't have what I need. The world isn't fair to me. I'm entitled to more. Poor me. People are criticizing me. They don't appreciate me. They're not supporting me. Poor me. I'm sick, I'm injured, I have spirit afflictions. I don't feel well." So we usually stay stuck in our discouragement and our pity party. That's the samsaric mind and that's why we are ordinary sentient beings, immersed in suffering. Do either of these responses solve the external problem or bring us happiness here and now? No. In fact, by thinking in these ways, we usually wind up more unhappy and upset.

Before indulging in these emotions, it's helpful to ask ourselves, "Do I really need all of these things? My living standard may be lower now, but did all those things bring me happiness? Maybe I could be just as happy, or even happier, with less?" Similarly, we could investigate, "Am I really being disparaged by others, or is it that I'm interpreting their behavior in a derogatory way that possibly they didn't mean?" After all, many times people don't mean us harm when they say certain things, but we misconstrue their words and take their comments personally when they aren't meant that way.

Behind our upset is often a feeling of entitlement—the universe owes us something, the world should treat us better. We may talk about karma, but when we go through hard times, we don't think that it is the result of our own actions. Instead, we continue to blame someone or something outside. If we thought about karma, we would see, "I'm going through a hard time due to the ripening of destructive karma I created. How did I create this karma? Self-centeredness, ignorance, attachment, and hostility had occupied my mind. Lacking what I need is the result of stealing. Being disparaged is the result of speaking harshly and using my speech to create disharmony. Being afflicted with dangerous sickness and spirits is the result of physically harming others or deliberately causing them mental and emotional tumult. Now I'm experiencing the result of the causes I created under the influence of my own self-centered mind. What use is it to become angry at others or to feel sorry for myself?"

It is important here not to blame ourselves for our misery or to feel that we deserve to suffer. Whoever we were in a previous life acted harmfully and we are experiencing the results because we are in the same mental continuum as that person. This does not mean we are bad people. It simply means that self-centeredness made the person we were in the past act in harmful ways and we are currently experiencing the result.

Rather than blame other people or ourselves, let's turn to our own self-centered mind and point the finger at it. This doesn't mean criticizing or hating ourselves, because self-centeredness is *not* who we are. It is just a thought, and a false one at that. It is not part of our nature or our mind, which is pure. But since it harms us, let's cease following its dictates and practice the methods to eliminate it. Instead of succumbing to that mind, which is the cause of suffering for ourselves and which prevents us from actualizing our spiritual aspirations, instead of just giving in to that mind, then *without discouragement take on the misdeeds and the pain of all living beings.*

Doing this without discouragement is very important. If we feel very discouraged and we're in the middle of our pity party and we try doing the taking and giving meditation—taking on the pain of all living beings and giving them our happiness—and we haven't realized that the self-centered thought is our enemy, then when we do the meditation it doesn't work very well. How do we act without discouragement and take on the misdeeds and the pain of all living beings? Do the taking and giving meditation, thinking of your self-centered, egotistic mind as a lump in your heart. Then visualize all living beings in front of you and, with compassion, wish to remove their misery. Imagine all their pain and suffering leaving them in the form of smoke and pollution. Inhale the smoke and pollution, but don't think they stay inside you, making you sick. Instead, the smoke and pollution transform into a lightning bolt that hits that lump of self-centeredness in your heart and decimates it. Feel incredible spaciousness in your heart now that the self-centeredness is no longer there. Dwell in that spaciousness for a while. Then, from that pure heart, imagine light radiating and think that you have transformed and multiplied your body, possessions, and virtue so they manifest as the people and objects that others need. Give these away happily. Imagine others receiving all they need and becoming tranquil and happy.

We should not only do this with physical suffering but when our mind is unhappy as well. When our mind is stuck on such thoughts as "Other people are blaming me and they're not appreciating me and I'm trying so much. They're not supporting me even though I'm doing so much for them and they're not repaying it. The people I was counting on to be so nice to me are turning on me. My relationships are falling apart." When we're having mental suffering, this meditation is very effective as well. This is an excellent meditation to do when you're going through hard times because it completely transforms the misfortune into the Dharma practice of developing love, compassion, and bodhicitta.

## Helen: Coping with Cancer

Three years ago I was diagnosed with breast cancer. It was a shock to receive this kind of news, even though I had been practicing Dharma for about ten years at the time and hoped I would be calmer. Fortunately I have excellent Dharma teachers and went to see one of them for advice. He was busy so I could only visit for a few minutes. I told him about the diagnosis and he looked at me in a very clear way and counseled me, "Be very gentle with yourself and practice the taking and giving meditation." That was it, but it was like a wonderful waterfall that took away a lot of my fear. I did this, imagining taking on the breast cancer of all women and, through that, freeing all of them from all disease while also destroying the self-centered attitude at my heart.

Around the same time my next-door neighbor also was diagnosed with breast cancer, but hers was a more aggressive kind of cancer than I had. She and her husband had two young children at home. Now the taking and giving meditation became more potent as I imagined taking on her virulent cancer, with months of painful, exhausting chemotherapy, followed by radiation and more surgery. I imagined taking on all this as well as her worry about her children so that she would live long and be healthy for her children.

Doing this changed my whole experience of what cancer meant and helped me get through my own situation. In fact, it was an excellent situation for practice. It was impossible for me to fall into a victim mentality when my situation wasn't nearly as dire as hers. Through this practice I understood that my sickness was due to harming others physically in previous lives. In fact, I was fortunate to have this past karma ripen so easily and quickly instead of as eons of suffering in an unfortunate rebirth. Thinking this way gave me a sense of purpose as I went through cancer treatment. Today I am cancer-free and so is my neighbor. More importantly, I have learned a lot about how to meet life-threatening situations with a peaceful mind and heart.

### John: Sitting on the Sidelines

As time marches on and the Dharma deepens, I really can't express in words how much I appreciate the Buddha's teachings. My ability to accept unpleasant situations that I cannot change and to make the most of whatever circumstances I'm in has increased. For example, every autumn I suffer from allergies, and for about a month I feel pretty ill with a stuffy, runny nose, itchy eyes, and all that. I used to dread it. I now embrace it.

Also, last month I went running, and my knee buckled, causing some severe damage. I am glad it happened. It is very good for me to walk around on crutches and feel the pain of not being mobile. It is also very good for me to feel sick. Realistically, these things are small inconveniences compared to the sufferings of others. When I first injured my knee, I was, of course, angry and upset because I knew that I would not be able to play hockey for a couple of months and I hate sitting on the sidelines. Getting around was going to be difficult, and I couldn't sit on a meditation cushion for about a month and had to sit in a chair instead. I'm a lawyer, and what really hit home was when I showed up in court on crutches, a friend of mine with horrible skin cancer and lesions all over his face and head asked me how I was doing. We all suffer. It's part of life in cyclic existence. Each and every being has to go through it until we attain liberation. Most of the time, our own suffering is really quite trivial. Why make a big deal out of it? We all get better eventually until, one day, we will die. If we practice the Dharma well while we're alive, dying will not be terrible, and we'll be able to continue practicing the path to enlightenment in our future life.

Everyone around me is chasing pleasure, worrying about things that we perceive as real, expending energy on negativity and not even realizing it. My world is chock full of opportunities to practice the Dharma from one moment to the next. I don't know that a human rebirth can get any better. I am healthy, have employment that takes care of shelter, food, and my loved ones, and have leisure to practice.

Yet, much of my life I have spent wishing I was somewhere else more pleasurable. I see others do the same thing. The attorneys around me work hard but their minds are longing for the golf course. For me, that's suffering. When we take each moment and dedicate ourselves to practice, to cherishing others and realizing their pain, a real sense of purpose and meaning for Dharma practice arises. To me, that's the Dharma. It takes time for the teachings to sink in, but daily meditation, weekly teachings, and a weekly group discussion with fellow practitioners go a long way towards helping. In other words, just living each day and practicing the best we can is the key. Why wish we were somewhere else with different conditions? We have everything we need to practice in front of our face. Just do it.

## Howard: Making Friends with Pain

Having been on narcotic pain medications for over five years, I have reached the point where they are causing major obstacles in my meditation practice and have decided to stop them. It is quite likely that my pain has actually been made worse by the narcotics as they create new pain pathways, according to recent research.

As I've made friends and peace with my pain I suspect I can manage better without pain medication. My pain clinic doctor supports my decision, but going through detox is incredibly painful. The side effects of the meds to help control withdrawal are bad too. This is the hardest thing I've ever done. My body is very sensitive to withdrawal and this has been a continual problem over the years as my tolerance increased. When the detox is over, I look forward to resuming my retreat, bright-eyed and bushy-tailed.

While my body is currently a wreck and is experiencing a lot of agony, my overall spirits remain quite positive and I feel hopeful. I remain grateful for the relief the pain meds offered while I learned the radical acceptance of chronic pain. My spiritual mentor has taught me how to relax into adversity. Only through relaxing into adversity and pain do we overcome excitation and suffering.

This last month of detox has been very hard but also tremendously rich. I am being forced to go deeper into practicing patience and fortitude. Only hardship gives one this opportunity. So many blessings! I am fortunate indeed. It is amazing to witness the power of Dharma in my life actually turning adversity into opportunity in a way I never thought possible. Adversity seems to be the golden bricks paving the way to freedom. It's as if the Buddhas and bodhisattvas are drop-kicking and punting me all the way towards enlightenment. Each hardship sends me flying down along the path, like it or not. Did I just say that? In the beginning each hardship was all bad news, but as the years go by and I work with them, they turn into more and more profound blessings and really good news.

## VERSE 19: DON'T LET SUCCESS GO TO YOUR HEAD

> *Though you become famous and many bow to you,*
> *And you gain riches to equal Vaishravana's,*
> *See that worldly fortune is without essence,*
> *And be unconceited—*
> *This is the practice of bodhisattvas.*

### See That Worldly Fortune Is without Essence

Due to having been generous and respectful of others in the past, your karma may be such that in this life you become famous and wealthy. Many people shower you with gifts, honor you, and proclaim your greatness and glory. The meaning of gaining **riches equal to Vaishravana's** is that your wealth equals that of Vaishravana, one of the deities of wealth. In other words, you're richer than Bill Gates. You have three times everything that you want. In addition to that, everyone thinks that you're wonderful. You're famous, powerful, and popular.

We may wonder, "What's wrong with that? I've got what I've always longed for. Does Buddhism say that I have to give it up?" There's nothing wrong with wealth and you don't have to renounce it. What you do have to do is safeguard your mind from miserliness and arrogance, both of which easily arise when we have worldly fortune. For that reason, we practice seeing that worldly fortune is without essence. In other words, wealth comes and goes. Fame comes and goes. Praise, honor, and respect come and go. They are impermanent, transient, arising only when the causes and conditions for them have assembled. Having them does not mean we are successful and worthwhile because they are simply a passing ripening of karma. Therefore, they are without essence and lack any ultimate meaning.

How we relate to wealth and honor influences the karma we create, and thus what we will experience in the future. If we care about others in society, want to share our wealth, and use it for ways that benefit humanity, then we create the constructive karma of generosity. If we keep our wealth for ourselves without caring about all the other sentient beings on the planet upon whom our happiness depends, then that wealth becomes the source for our future misery, because it has corrupted our mind and made us lose our good heart.

Having worldly fortune is unrelated to being a good practitioner. Someone may be famous, well-respected, and have a big name. He may receive many offerings and gifts but that does not necessarily mean he is a good practitioner. At the time of death, our worldly fortune of this life evaporates. None of it accompanies the mind into the next life. Whether we are rich or poor, famous or unknown, our karma continues to future lives, not our renown and our wealth. For this reason it's important not to be preoccupied with worldly fortune, but to focus on actual Dharma practice, which is counteracting our afflictions.

Sometimes worldly fortune can be detrimental to our Dharma practice. We get rich and then become complacent. We forget that money, possessions, respect, and popularity are impermanent. Some people become famous and wealthy and think, "Now, I'm powerful. I can make people follow my wishes. I don't need to practice the Dharma because I've got it made." This is similar to people who were lonely and then fall in love. They think, "I feel fantastic. Finally, somebody loves me," and they stop their daily meditation practice.

In reality, all things and situations are temporary. They come and they go quickly. Even if they last most of this life, at the time of death, we have to separate from them and go on to our future lives. Even while wealth, respect, and power last, if we investigate them deeply in our mind, we see that we still aren't completely satisfied and peaceful. We may have worldly success, but we're still subject to sickness, aging, and death. No amount of money, love, or fame can protect us from them. In addition, we have a new set of difficulties. We have to protect our wealth, status, and power. Thus, rich and famous people have a house that resembles a prison because they have to protect themselves from thieves and from people who resent their wealth or dislike how they use their power. They are restless and fearful of losing what they have. In other words, worldly fortune may be present, but peace of mind is absent.

A friend of mind went back to school to do graduate work. After the first semester I asked her how it was going, and she said, "I did very well and got A's on all my exams. But now I'm very anxious because I don't know how I'll ever be able to do that again." She was successful, but her mind was restless and worried because she felt pressure to maintain her excellent status. I think many sports heroes and movie stars must feel likewise. In other words, there is no security in worldly gain.

It's clear that even when we have worldly success, the fear of losing it haunts us. We have to fend off competition and enemies who are trying to take it from us. Or you fall in love, and then become insecure, fearing that the person may abandon you or may suddenly die.

It's extremely difficult, if not impossible, for a mind that is bound by ignorance, afflictions, and karma to ever be content. Even if we have good circumstances, they are unstable and lack the ability to give us everlasting peace and happiness. We have experienced such disappointment time and time again, but ignoring the disappointment, we think next time it will be different. In order to prevent that, it's important to *see that worldly fortune is without essence.* In other words, it comes and it goes very quickly in this life and when we die, it's gone.

It seems we haven't yet developed enough confidence that Dharma practice can bring a completely different kind of happiness than worldly happiness. We are locked into the narrow view that happiness comes from outside, and so we need external things, people, and situations in order to be happy. However, when we understand the type of happiness that comes through Dharma practice—mental peace that lasts longer, is more stable, and can be experienced no matter what our external situation—then our interest in worldly happiness will naturally decline.

In addition, thinking of the benefit that having a Dharma mind can bring to us and others energizes us to practice. Think of having genuine, deep compassion for others and making your life meaningful by being of service and benefit to others. Know that you have the ability to do this and generate the confidence to do it. The inspiration and joy this brings in the mind far excels that giddy feeling that worldly pleasure brings.

Think, "What would it be like to be a Buddha? I could be of great benefit to others. I'll know the right thing to say to someone at any particular moment and will have the ability to evaluate situations and do what is of greatest benefit. A Buddha can manifest many bodies and be able to serve sentient beings." When we think of having such capability, our mind becomes more confident, joyful, and energized to create the causes for it. That joy is much more worthwhile and meaningful. There is some purpose and reason to cultivate the abilities of the bodhisattvas and Buddhas, whereas worldly success comes and goes in a twinkle of an eye.

This verse recommends that you remain unconceited and humble, even when worldly success comes your way. Instead of getting puffed up and strutting around saying, "Look at me. I'm so rich. I'm so famous. I'm this. I'm that. I'm talented and successful," be completely humble. A person who has deep self-confidence is able to be humble because he has no internal need to prove himself to anyone. Those of us who lack self-confidence easily become conceited because we don't really believe in ourselves. We put on a big production about "Me," thinking that if we can get others to think we are wonderful, then we must be wonderful. When we have genuine self-confidence, we don't need conceit. There is no craving to receive others' approval because we are able to evaluate our own motivations and actions and confidence in our Buddha potential. We have become friends with ourselves.

Great practitioners are unconceited. I tend to react with doubt towards meditators and Dharma teachers who make big productions about themselves. His Holiness the Dalai Lama says that in India some people are nobody, but when they come to the West, they have five titles before and after their name, they wear big hats, and sit on high thrones. Personally speaking, I am much more attracted to the humble practitioners and teachers. I have had the good fortune to meet a number of them and they are excellent examples of what a practitioner should be—kind, generous, unassuming. They encourage others and teach them the Dharma without seeking anything for themselves. These are the people that I admire and want to be like. Look at His Holiness the Dalai Lama. No matter what his status and wealth and fame, he always sees himself as a student and behaves like a student in the sense of being quite humble and really seeing himself as the servant of others. This is exactly the same kind of behavior and attitude that we should cultivate.

## Melinda: We're Successful, So What?

A number of years ago I joined a Japanese drum group. Not having a drumming teacher, we were all self-taught, but since some of the drummers were Japanese, we thought that made us authentic. We wore these strange, exotic-looking outfits, and our drums weren't real drums; they were made out of sewer pipes covered with rawhide.

After nine months of rehearsal, we made our debut performance at the Heritage Festival, an international gathering of ethnic communities in Edmonton, Canada. Over the three-day weekend, we performed nine times, drumming and making wild and vigorous movements. Astoundingly, the crowd loved us and we were treated like rock stars from day one. Actually, we were really bad and were hopeless as drummers, but since no one knew anything about Japanese drumming, we looked impressive. Right away we had a cult following. We would wear our "Kita No Taiko" shirts—that means "Northern-most Drumming Group" in Japanese—and in the streets people would stop us and say, "You are so fantastic. I love your drumming." Needless to say, we lapped it up.

This went on for a year and our fame and admiration kept on increasing. For a New Year's program called the First Night Festival they gave us the best venue in the city because we were famous in Edmonton. The place was packed two hours before the show even began. You'd think it was the Rolling Stones the way we were greeted when we came on stage. People rose to their feet, cheering and clapping. Everyone in the group, including me, thought, "Yeah, we're the top of the heap here."

But through all that insanity and while this huge uproar was going on I began to think, "What's wrong here? I'm not happy. All this fame and adulation are not making me happy. What we're doing is fraudulent." I was conflicted inside because although we were making people happy, I still felt an ache inside. I thought something was wrong with me, until I heard Dharma teachings and then understanding dawned.

# 8. The Hated and the Desired

## Verse 20: Working with Anger

*While the enemy of your own anger is unsubdued,*
*Though you conquer external foes, they will only increase.*
*Therefore, with the militia of love and compassion*
*Subdue your own mind—*
 *This is the practice of bodhisattvas.*

### Subdue the Anger in Your Mind

COMPASSION IS a very important element on the bodhisattva path. Without it there's no way to benefit sentient beings or attain enlightenment. The chief enemy of compassion is anger because when we're angry at someone, be it ourselves or others, there is no way to have compassion in the mind for them at the same time. As we know from our own experience, anger is disastrous. Each of us can think of times when, overwhelmed by our anger, we said or did things to the people that we cared about the most. Looking back on those words and deeds, we regret them now and know that we never would have said or done those things if anger had not overwhelmed our mind.

As long as the seed of anger exists within us, we will have enemies. Why? We will find someone to project our discontent onto. It doesn't matter if this person makes a mistake or not, we will still find a reason to hate them simply because there is anger energy inside us. For instance, sometimes I wake up in a bad mood, and I'm just waiting for somebody to say, "Good morning" so I can get mad at him. That person doesn't need to do anything, but I'll make up a story about how he is harming me: "I can tell by his tone of voice when he said, 'Good morning' that he's trying to manipulate me."

We project our anger on the most convenient person around, over the tiniest event. For example, your spouse forgot to buy peanut butter and suddenly you're questioning the entire relationship: "We're out of peanut butter. You knew we were out and that I like it, yet you didn't buy any more. Now, you have the gall to tell me you forgot. Actually you're being passive-aggressive again. Our marriage has always been like this. You never do what I want, you never consider me. And when I confront you on this, you're full of excuses. I'm fed up. I want a divorce!"

Our anger has nothing to do with the other person's actions or motives. Why? One person will become enraged at a situation while another person is calm. If there were an objective fault—let's say an external situation or another person—then everyone would react the same way. But that is not the case at all. We create a description or story about the situation and the other person's intentions and actions and then make ourselves mad. This occurs because the enemy, our anger, is unsubdued. As long as this is the case, we will find somebody to resent, hold a grudge against, be spiteful towards, and be enraged at.

Although we may conquer external foes and put them in their place, they will increase. When we intentionally inflict harm on others, why would we expect them to be kind to us in return? To the contrary, they become more upset and rally others to side with them against us.

Anger not only affects us on a personal level, it also operates on an international level. A nation may conquer one external foe or destroy one enemy, but two more appear in response to that action. When a country thinks only of its own welfare and does not see that it is interdependent with all others, then it acts in a way that lacks consideration for others' welfare. Others respond with hostility. This scenario is common in human history. For that reason the Buddha said that hatred is not conquered by hatred but only by love.

Such dynamics occur in our personal life as well. No matter how many people we harm in return for what we consider their harm to us, they will respond with further harm. When we think about it, our way of thinking is silly: "I'm going to harm you until you decide to love me." Will that work? Not at all. In fact, just the opposite occurs. In our deep confusion and ignorance, our mind believes that anger and aggression will bring the peace and happiness we want. This doesn't work on a personal level or on the international scene.

On a personal level, we harp on people we love, we nag them and criticize them, thinking that will make them change and then we'll be happy. Does it work? No. But we keep doing it, and it keeps not working. In fact, it creates quite the opposite effect, distancing us from the very people we care the most about and want to be close to.

Furthermore, when we act with anger, other people lose respect for us and do not trust us. When I hear someone speak badly about another person, an alarm goes off in my mind. I know that one day that person will speak to me or about me in the same way. If that person has the habit of speaking negatively of others, denigrating and lambasting them, someday he will find a reason to do that to me too, whether I do anything wrong or not. To prevent that from happening, I keep a polite distance from that person and do not confide in him.

When people talk badly about others behind their back, they're saying more about themselves than they are about the people they're disparaging. They are sending the message to other people that they're not to be trusted because others see how they treat people. It's clear that their anger and the backbiting that it motivates bring an opposite effect from what they want. All of us seek friendship, but conquering foes and backbiting do not bring it.

Sometimes it happens that someone misunderstands what we say, and many people are upset about what they believe we have said. At those times, in order to dispel the commotion and misunderstanding, we should explain what we meant and tell our side of the story. We can do this without being angry and without saying nasty things about the person who spoke badly about us.

This happened to me a couple of years back. Someone whom I considered a friend complained to one of my teachers that I had incited discord amongst his circle of students. In fact, I had tried to pacify the gossip and bad feelings between the different factions. But, for this person, if you weren't on his side, then you were against him. Thich Nhat Hanh faced something similar, but far worse, during the Vietnam War. He tried to pacify the discord between the two warring factions without taking sides, but both sides distrusted him because he wasn't on anyone's side and wanted to help both sides get along. In my case, another one of my teachers heard about this and said to me, "You should go to your other teacher and explain what the situation was because he was told misinformation." I'm very grateful to my teacher for giving me that advice. I went to my other teacher and, without blaming the person who spoke ill of me, explained to him my view of the discord and what I had said and done.

This taught me an important lesson. I learned that when there is a misunderstanding and someone is talking badly about you and other people are getting worked up about it, it is necessary to explain your side of the story without being defensive or blaming. It is helpful to clear things up as much as you can, especially if you do not want a bad relationship with your teachers. Normally, I would have just kept quiet and let it go. However, my teacher taught me that it is important to clear up misunderstandings and not just ignore them.

When people gossip behind our back or try to harm us, we should clarify the situation with others when it is appropriate to do so without making the person who harmed us into an enemy. Ruining his reputation or taking revenge is of no benefit. One of the auxiliary bodhisattva precepts says that when people are upset with us, we should try to explain and ease their upset and reduce their anger.

Discriminating wisdom is necessary. Sometimes it's better to let the situation go because it is not a big deal. If we try to explain, it may unnecessarily stir up the conflict again. Sensitivity is needed to know how to act in various situations. But no matter what the circumstances, subduing our anger is necessary.

We subdue our anger and belligerence *with the militia of love and compassion.* If you want to stop having external enemies, then attack the hatred and resentment in your own mind with the militia of love and compassion. Just as a militia trains and works together consistently and doesn't give up until the enemy is conquered, so do we develop very strong love, wanting others to be happy, and strong compassion, wanting them to be free of suffering. With that, we combat the enemy of our own anger. By pacifying our anger, external enemies and foes are subdued because we cease to conceptualize others in that framework. Instead, we view them as suffering sentient beings who want to be happy and free from suffering but are confused about how to bring that about. That's how bodhisattvas look at the people who harm them. As Verse 17 said, put these people on the crown of your head, regard them as your spiritual teacher, and bow to them with respect. See those people as kind for giving us the opportunity to cultivate fortitude. After all, we can't practice fortitude with people who are nice to us; we need people who harm us to do that.

## Dianne: Learning to Love Myself

Before meeting the Dharma I reacted to all those around me with frustration, harsh words, and anger if my needs were not met. I would project my dissatisfaction onto those around me, often the ones I held most dear. I changed friends, jobs, and relationships but kept meeting "external foes." Miserable and confused, I only wanted to be happy and not have this suffering. Continuing to seek happiness outside of myself, I felt hopeless, especially as anger and disappointment were my "associates." Only after I met the Buddha's teachings did I start subduing my anger and begin to understand that the only way to find peace and happiness was to change my habitual pattern of thinking that happiness was dependent on how those around me behaved.

In an attempt to subdue my anger, I tried to force it out of my mind with disgust. This did not work. Transforming my mind by using the same type of mind state that I wanted to be free from didn't work. Getting angry at ourselves doesn't work to free ourselves from anger. I began the arduous task of applying gentleness when my mind was frustrated. The self-centered attitude would mock me, saying that this was a very stupid method. I practiced ignoring that mind that discounted my efforts and repeatedly brought gentleness into my mind. At first I was often unable to generate gentleness for myself—I couldn't even find that feeling inside myself—so I would think of another person's gentleness or my cats' gentleness towards me. Once I had the feeling of gentleness in my mind I would practice offering it to myself. I did this practice repeatedly, and gradually it became easier. This allowed me to be kinder to myself, which opened the way to cultivating love and compassion for others. In this way, my anger is more subdued. I aspire one day to be able to find peace and happiness no matter what the external circumstance.

## Alan: A Lesson in Compassion

Given a life-without-parole sentence at age sixteen, I've been imprisoned for the last fourteen years. During this time, my mother has been a great lesson in compassion for me. Just two weeks ago, she lost $19,000 in a casino in about six hours. When I heard about this, I was angry, mainly because my case started over her gambling debts. I felt betrayed, as if nothing in the past fourteen years mattered. More than that, I felt doubly wronged because my mother had recently explained to me that she feels responsible for my being incarcerated (even though I have tried to explain to her that I am responsible for the bad choices I made). She said that she needed to take the money she had received from a settlement to pay for an attorney. This was the same money she spent in the casino.

I struggled with writing her a letter, telling her all the things I haven't told her over the years—things such as how she stayed with my step-father even though she knew he was molesting my sister, how she had run off my fiancée because she was more interested in my money than my happiness. I particularly wanted to remind her that my case started over $2,400 in checks she had written to the casino—trying to get the money to pay off my mother's gambling debt was the situation in which my crime occurred.

What I did instead was have a conversation with my sister, who told me that the previous night my mother fell asleep in her lap, just like her children used to, just like a baby. I thought about how my mother's afflic-tions led her to hurt those who love her. I didn't make excuses for her actions, but I focused on her suffering and that made me realize how selfish I was being. Compassion arose. My mom is suffering just like any other sentient being. If she hurts me, she does so acting out of her suffering. How can I be angry at her for that?

Of course, it's a daily fight with myself. I don't always remember to be compassionate. But I always remember that I have to try to be compassionate, even when I sometimes have moments of anger.

### Marshall: From Enemy to Brother

In 1968 and 1969 I was in Vietnam attached to the 5th Special Forces Division as a member of the 199th Light Infantry Brigade. We pulled operations in the rice paddies in the south and in the jungles. Our job was to search and destroy the "enemy." I was very good at what I did.

One particular day, as we were walking silently down a path in heavy jungle, a North Vietnamese Army soldier suddenly appeared in front of us waving a white flag. As we approached him, we could see he was an officer in the NVA and obviously he wanted to give himself up. We called such soldiers "Chu Hoi" and they often would come over to our side and aid us in finding the enemy and weapons stashes. We also learned much about the enemy movements through Chu Hois. I remember thinking at the time how young he was to be a colonel in the NVA. We were told, especially me since I was a squad leader, not to talk to him or have any communication with him. After all, he was the "enemy."

One day, perhaps a week later, we were at a base camp and I was sitting on a bunker just keeping an eye out. I looked out in the middle of the camp and there, sitting on a log, all by himself, was this NVA officer. I watched him just sitting with his hands together in prayer and his eyes closed. After a while, he dropped his hands and hung his head down. I remember all this because at the time I felt this overwhelming sadness for him. It is hard to explain, but the longer I watched him the sorrier for him I got until, literally, I had tears in my eyes.

I then broke the rule; I walked over to him and nodded a greeting. I was answered with the most perfect English you can imagine, which really surprised me. He invited me to sit next to him, which I did, and we began to talk. I learned that he was a college professor from Hanoi, had been educated in England, and he was missing his lovely wife and children back in Hanoi. He showed me a book of poetry that he had written and in which he had drawn beautiful pictures of dragons and lotus flowers. He read me some of his poetry, and it was truly wonderful. He got out pictures of his wife and children and I did the same with my family. I spent perhaps a half hour with him and before I knew it, we were no longer enemies, but were friends instead. Brothers actually. He was a great guy and we both shared the same reality that neither one of us wanted to be where we were. He needed to be home with his family teaching at the university, and I needed to be out of that war.

But the wonderful lesson for me was that if we just sit down and open our hearts to each other, then we are no longer strangers. We are brothers. I do not know what happened to him later. He was picked up by helicopter and taken away. I missed him a lot. I imagine that when the North Vietnamese invaded the South he was not looked upon too kindly. I prayed that he made it home okay. But at least for that one brief moment, we shared a wonderful time together and because of that, we were able to put the war out of our minds and to discover compassion. It is easy to love when we clear our minds and hearts and allow love to enter.

## VERSE 21: THE MISERY OF ATTACHMENT

*Sensual pleasures are like salt water:*
*The more you indulge, the more thirst increases.*
*Abandon at once those things which breed*
*Clinging attachment—*
    *This is the practice of bodhisattvas.*

### Running after Sense Pleasure

This verse concerns our love affair with sense objects—all the external possessions, people, status, fame, praise, and experiences that we crave. These things in themselves are not bad, but the mind of clinging attachment that sticks to them creates so many problems for us. We obsess about what we want, are dissatisfied with what we have, crave more, and fear losing what we have. The more we are attached to people and things, the more upset and angry we become when we can't get them or when they are destroyed. This emotional roller coaster of attachment and anger—clinging and despair—is summed up in the eight worldly concerns. The first four of these are taking delight in receiving 1) material possessions and money, 2) approval, praise, and love, 3) good reputation and image, and 4) sense pleasures—attractive sights, sounds, fragrances, tastes, tactile sensations. The other four worldly concerns are not getting the previous four and experiencing their opposites—1) dejection due to lacking material possessions and money, 2) receiving blame or disapproval, 3) having a bad reputation or image, and 4) experiencing unpleasant sights, sounds, odors, tastes, or tactile sensations. When we think about it, a great deal of our time each day is occupied with these eight.

*Sensual pleasures are like saltwater.* When you're thirsty and you drink salt water you get thirstier. You think it's going to quench your thirst but it does the opposite. A good example is our consumerist culture where we are taught that having "more and better" is the cause of happiness. With this view, we are constantly craving something. Our society is hooked on sense pleasure. The media teaches this, and the government tells us that to be good citizens we should consume more because it's good for the economy. Sense pleasure is supposed to be the path to bliss, and so we chase after it and struggle to get it at all costs. We don't realize how much our mind is affected by the consumerist ethic because it is so pervasive. Indulging in this kind of consumerism makes us have more clinging and more dissatisfaction. That's why so many people in this country, no matter what they have, suffer from such incredible dissatisfaction and discontent.

Beautiful sights, melodious sounds and music, pleasant odors, delicious food, luxurious tactile objects, a good sex life, a new air conditioner or heater, the latest electronic device—the list goes on and on. We are addicted to sense pleasure, constantly running after it. But like drug addicts, the more we have, the more we need. Although we live in rich countries, we suffer from dissatisfaction and all its ramifications.

Remember when you were fresh out of school with no money and you thought having $10 made you feel rich? But as time went on, $10 was insufficient and we wanted $100. Then we needed $1000, and after that, $10,000. In this escalation, there is a pervasive feeling of poverty, of not having enough. Yet our houses, cars, garages, and basements are stuffed with things that we don't even use. Still, we have a hard time giving things away. Fear haunts us: "If I give it away, I may need it later." So we hang on to things we do not use.

The more we have, the more the thirst increases. The more we indulge in sense pleasures, the more we want. One year, we go on vacation in Acapulco, then the next, we have to go to the Bahamas. One partner isn't enough, you want another and another. The same goes with cars and material possessions. One isn't enough; then you need two, then three. There is no end to the story.

The book *Hooked!*, edited by Stephanie Kaza, discusses our tendency to get hooked by the consumerist ideal. The author of an essay in the book talked about his meditation center and said, "Many people come to do retreats. In their meditation, they realize how addicted they are to sensual objects. Some of them have enough space during retreat to see that and to take a breather from it, but they don't necessarily change their lifestyle. And, that's okay." I don't completely agree, because I believe that when the Dharma really touches your heart, you change your lifestyle. It's not that you have to change your consumption patterns completely, but there should be a shift. In other words, a mental change in our view should manifest in different behavior.

The antidote that Gyelsay Togmay Zangpo proposes is to *abandon at once those things which breed clinging attachment.* You may wonder, "I'm attached to having good food. Does this mean I should stop eating? That would be crazy!" Clearly, we need food and clothes and medicine and shelter. As social creatures, we have friends and relatives. A healthy relationship—one free from attachment—with all these things is important. Attachment is what is to be abandoned, because that emotion is a troublemaker. However, sometimes it's very difficult to abandon clinging when we're near the things to which we're extremely attached because our mind is not yet trained in other ways of relating to these things. *Abandon at once those things which breed clinging attachment* means take some space and some distance from these things so that attachment doesn't flare up and overwhelm us. As we do so, we realize that the things that we were so attached to, that we thought we couldn't live without, we can live very well without. In fact, our mind is more peaceful when it's free of attach-. ment, clinging, and craving, as well as the worrying and fear that come from being attached to external things.

Genuine Dharma understanding impacts how we live. When we realize that we use such an unfair portion of the world's resources, when we feel interconnected with other living beings, these understandings will affect what we think about when we get into our car to drive somewhere. If we care about the environment, we will try to carpool or use public transportation. Or, when the urge comes to buy something that we don't really need, we stop and ask ourselves, "Do I really need it? Maybe the one I have is okay."

When we understand that the more we indulge, the more the thirst increases, when we understand that the more we use an unfair share of the world's resources, the more we create suffering for others and enemies for ourselves, it is bound to impact our life. We will feel compelled to change our lifestyle. This doesn't mean we have to effect a huge change immediately. It may be easier to start with small changes and gradually increase. By doing so, we will know, through our own experience, that simplicity brings more peace of mind.

To me, caring for the environment is directly involved with reducing attachment because attachment is the motivation behind consuming more than we need. Attachment also makes us lazy when it comes to recycling and reusing things. I have a reputation in my family. Everyone knows that when I visit, I will look for the recycling bin to use. If there isn't one in the house, I comment on it. My family members all know that when I go to the supermarket, I bring my own bag instead of asking for a plastic bag.

There are many small ways to care for our planet and reduce consumption. For instance, I wear the same kind of clothes every day. Some of you may have noticed that, and wish I would change them! (I wear monastic robes.) But this makes things very easy. We have only one body, but look how much stuff there is in our closet. Do we really need that many pieces of clothing? Do we really need that many pairs of shoes for our two feet? If we were a centipede, having many shoes would be understandable. But we're just bipeds. Think of some examples in your life illustrating that the more you indulge, the more dissatisfied you become. Then, with compassion for yourself and for all beings with whom you share this planet, simplify your life.

Freeing our mind from attachment is an essential practice of bodhisattvas for many reasons. Attachment prevents having the determination to be free of cyclic existence. When attachment is there, cyclic existence looks pretty wonderful and we make no effort to free ourselves from it. When we are attached to sentient beings, having genuine love and compassion for them is difficult. Generating the bodhicitta motivation is also difficult when there's attachment because bodhicitta is based upon having equanimity for friends, enemies, and strangers, and equanimity isn't possible when attachment is present. Similarly, when clinging attachment has taken over our mind, meditating is difficult. The mind is not concentrated because it's always straying to the objects of our attachment. Therefore, it's difficult to generate the wisdom that sees the actual nature of these objects because the mind is too distracted. Letting go of the clinging attachment is important, and we do this in gradual steps. We can't do it all at once; instead we start with the things we're most attached to and slowly chip away at the amount of attachment in the mind. As we do so, we feel much more peaceful.

Some people may think, "If we only look at the disadvantages of cyclic existence, we'll feel depressed." That pessimistic view occurs if we look around and think, "The whole world is messed up" and decide that there's nothing we can do about it. But to stare into the face of suffering and adversity and say, "I can make a difference. I can stop even a little bit of it" transforms our attitude completely. That's the ultimate optimism. Even if we can't solve all the ills of the world by ourselves—and even the Buddha can't do that—we can make a difference. A friend told me of walking on the beach one day and seeing so many clams on the sand during low tide. He thought to put some of them in back in the water and hesitated because there were thousands of them and he couldn't rescue all of them. But thinking again, he realized that helping the ones he could help was still worthwhile—to those individuals his actions made the difference between life and death. So he began to pick some up and return them to the ocean.

## Rosie: Look at All the Unique Things We Have!

Years ago a friend was in the business of selling authentic artifacts that he had painstakingly found in India. He would go to faraway places such Rajasthan and spend months combing through collections of objects and furniture that had been taken from villages that were being transformed into concrete housing projects. He had a great sense for what was beautiful and authentic as opposed to knockoffs meant to look like old things. He handpicked unique pieces and shipped them back to Canada. These beautiful items were then offered for purchase, and my partner and I would spend several hundred dollars at each of his sales, filling our house with more and more stunning and fascinating artifacts.

I was in love with anything to do with India and so at one time I purchased three *gaus*, not knowing they were Buddhist prayer containers. I was magnetized by the *gaus*; they stirred my mind and heart. But the more we acquired, the more we wanted to acquire. Our desire was endless and what our friend made available was endless as well. We purchased things even when our house was full. Visitors to our home noticed how full it was getting, and they were always astounded at the quality and beauty of our unique possessions. It didn't stop with artifacts; then it was dinosaur bones, petrified wood, pretty rocks. It was a seemingly endless cycle, and our house became like a museum.

At some point I realized this acquisition was out of control, although my partner remained in the cycle. When I began listening to Dharma teachings, it became clear very quickly that happiness would not be found in possessions, and so my purchasing days began to slow down and eventually ceased. As my understanding of the teachings grew, I began to see how my approach to accumulating possessions—even unusual artifacts that were unlike anything my friends had—was changing. Meanwhile, my partner, who was not interested in the Dharma, continued to want more and more beautiful relics, expanding so that he began to purchase North American Indian artifacts that were worth many thousands of dollars.

It was painful and disturbing to watch how his attachment propelled him to spend large amounts of money and invest considerable amounts of time trying to find and purchase artifacts and antiquities. The most painful blow came when our house was robbed, and a huge number of these precious objects were stolen. The crowning glory was when it was all taken from him. He experienced deep grief and despair due to this loss. In contrast, even though I lost a number of things in the theft as well, I was so grateful that neither of us was home during the robbery and that we were not harmed.

I have come to understand that I created the causes in a previous life for my things to be stolen and that the karma for that activity ripened. The Dharma also showed me that seeking more and more possessions was like an addict seeking more drugs—there was no satisfaction and a lot of disappointment.

# 9. The True Nature

> *Whatever appears is your own mind.*
> *Your mind from the start was free from fabricated extremes.*
> *Understanding this, do not take to mind*
> *(Inherent) signs of subject and object—*
> > *This is the practice of bodhisattvas.*

### Whatever Appears Is Your Own Mind

THIS VERSE discusses the ultimate nature of reality. By saying that our mind and all phenomena are free from *fabricated extremes* means that they are free from inherent existence. Inherent existence is what appears to our mind and what we grasp as existing when we believe that things have their own independent nature inside them, something that intrinsically distinguishes them from other phenomena, something that is their unique essence and makes them what they are. The first line states, **Whatever appears is your own mind.** This means that our mind projects inherent existence onto phenomena and then the object appears back to us as if it had an inherent essence. For example, we look at a certain configuration of colors and shapes that seems to have consciousness because it moves and talks. On this basis, we conceive and label, "This is Joe." Thereafter, we forget that we conceived and labeled Joe. Instead, we think Joe exists out there, independent of all other factors, including the mind that conceives and labels him. In fact, Joe, and everything else that exists, exists by being merely labeled by mind.

All objects are not literally our mind, but they exist in relationship to the mind that perceives them. Phenomena are not objective entities, out there, unrelated to mind, even though they appear that way and we grasp them as such. Rather, their parts, which form the basis of designation, appear. In dependence upon the basis of designation, the mind conceives and labels objects. Then, having forgotten that our mind designated an object in dependence on a basis of designation, we believe the object has its own independent essence, existing from its own side, under its own power.

An analogy is helpful. M. C. Escher was a great artist who created pictures that could appear as many different objects, depending upon how our mind conceptualized the various shapes. In the same way, we select certain sensory data and conceptualize an object. There is no problem in doing this. Concepts can help us function in the world. The difficulty arises when we think that something is an object in its own right, independent of other factors such as its causes and conditions, its parts, or the mind that conceives and labels the object.

Our mind creates an object, such as a table, in the sense that on the basis of seeing four legs and a flat top it labels "table." However, this object is not a table from its own side, radiating out the essence of "table-ness" to us. Rather, in dependence on it having certain characteristics, all of us have agreed to refer to this object as a table. Of course, non-English speakers give it a different name. Additionally, people using this object for another purpose will think of it differently, perhaps as a platform or an altar.

Although everything exists by being merely labeled, we perceive phenomena as having their own independent essence. For example, when we say "I" as in "I am mad," it seems that there is a real person who is mad, someone who exists independent of all other factors. In fact, only a body and mind are there. In dependence on the body and mind, we label "I" or in my case, "Chodron." Aside from the person who is labeled, there is no "essence of person" or "soul" there.

However, our ignorance grasps an inherent person. If we examine our feeling of self, we'll see that we don't feel that we exist by being merely labeled. Instead, we feel that there is a solid, real, independent "me" somewhere in our body-mind complex. On this basis, we become attached to everything that concerns this seemingly solid, real person. There seems to be an "I" that wants to be happy and that needs to be protected from danger. Everything that concerns this "I" is incredibly important. Thus, attachment arises towards whatever makes the self happy and anger arises towards whatever interferes with our happiness or causes us misery. Yet, who exactly is it that we are protecting and defending? If we look for the "I," we can't find an independent, identifiable person. The only "I" that exists is the one that exists by being labeled in dependence upon the body and mind. This "I" can't be found either in its basis of designation—the body and mind—or totally separate from it. The self or person lacks any inherent or independent essence. It is empty of inherent existence.

While there is no independent self, ignorance apprehends one. For example, think of someone you don't like, let's call him "Harry." Somebody says the name "Harry," and how do you respond? Your mind conceives of a real, solid, inherently existent Harry. Anger then arises in your mind and adrenaline floods your body. But the only thing that happened is that you heard the sound "Harry." The rest is a creation of an ignorant mind that believes there is an inherently existent Harry who has inherently existent negative qualities. You become afraid and therefore speak or act aggressively towards him. Your actions leave a karmic latency on your mindstream. If this latency is fertilized by craving and grasping at the time of death, it propels a new rebirth. In this way, cyclic existence continues under the force of ignorance, afflictions, and karma.

The line **Your mind from the start was free from fabricated extremes** indicates that the mind, too, does not exist inherently. What we call "mind" exists by being merely labeled. The mind isn't a concrete, truly existent thing that exists with its own essence, independent of everything else. The mind depends on various moments of consciousness. In dependence on a stream of different moments of clarity and awareness, the label "mind" is given. Not realizing that the mind exists by being conceived and labeled, we think that it has some essence existing from its own side. In reality, however, the mind is free from the fabricated extreme of inherent existence. Still, it does exist conventionally. Thus, it is free from the fabricated extreme of nihilism.

It is important to understand that although phenomena do not exist ultimately, independently, or inherently, they are not totally nonexistent. They exist conventionally, nominally, dependently, and relatively. At first glance, it may seem contradictory for an object to be empty of inherent existence and yet exist conventionally. However, these two viewpoints are not contradictory. In fact, emptiness of inherent existence and dependent existence come to the same point and are complementary. For example, a table exists depending on its parts—the legs and top. Something that is dependent cannot be independent because dependent and independent are mutually exclusive. Independent existence is the same as inherent existence, so something that is dependent cannot exist inherently. However, while it is empty of inherent existence, it still exists dependently.

Then it says, *Understanding this, do not take to mind*—in other words do not grasp—*(inherent) signs of subject and object.* Whether it's the perceiving mind (which is the subject), or the object (the phenomena that's being perceived), see that neither of them has any inherent existence, that each exists dependent upon the other, dependent on causes and conditions, dependent on parts, and dependent on being conceived and labeled.

By understanding that the perceiving mind and the perceived object are empty of inherent existence, we do not take to mind inherent signs of subject and object. In other words, we do not mistake our mind as an inherently existent subject or perceiver, and we do not mistakenly believe that objects exist inherently. Instead, we realize that subject and object exist in dependence upon each other.

This verse refers to meditating on emptiness in a state of meditative equipoise. When someone is able to realize emptiness directly and nonconceptually, there is no appearance of perceiving subject or perceived object. Rather, only the emptiness of inherent existence appears. When great yogis meditate on emptiness, there is no thought, "I am perceiving emptiness." There's no self-conscious awareness of an independent "I" who perceives an independent object, emptiness. This is what is meant by *do not take to mind (inherent) signs of subject and object.*

*Joyce: Not Buying into the Wrong View*

Recently I had the opportunity to distinctly notice my self-grasping ignorance. A coworker did not support a decision I had made and told me so. Immediately, my anger flared up. In that moment, the "I" appeared very solid, permanent, and independent. Along with anger, the innate I-grasping had arisen in my mind. I had taken to mind inherent signs of subject and object! The person I was conversing with appeared very solid and permanent—an objectively existent enemy out there. This was definitely a wrong view.

Thankfully, although my mind was quite disturbed, I was able to watch what was happening. I told the other person that I needed to stop the conversation and calm myself down before continuing. So, I went outside and took a walk. I reviewed the process for the decision I made: I was clear that I had a good intention when I made the decision and I tried my best to carry it through. Consequently, there was no cause for remorse from my side. I was able to calm down, not be reactive, and go back and have a calm discussion with my coworker.

By mistaking myself to be an inherently existent subject, I separated myself from the other person. This mistaken view provoked anger. Although I was able to stop the afflicted reaction of my mind, I did not think at the time that the subject (me) and the object (the other person) existed in dependence upon one another. Now, my goal is to train my mind to see all phenomena as a combination of appearance and emptiness of inherent existence.

## VERSE 23: CHASING RAINBOWS

> *When you encounter attractive objects,*
> *Though they seem beautiful*
> *Like a rainbow in summer, don't regard them as real*
> *And give up attachment—*
> > *This is the practice of bodhisattvas.*

## The Emptiness of Attractive Objects

Verse 22 talks about how to realize emptiness nonconceptually in meditative equipoise. Verse 23 speaks of how you apply your understanding of emptiness towards attractive objects in break times, subsequent to your formal meditation on emptiness. When we see something that's attractive, it looks like a real object, out there, objective, having its own essence. The inherent existence comes on many levels. First of all, the beauty appears to be inherently existent in the object. Not only that, but the object itself appears inherently existent. It appears to have its own nature, to set itself up, to exist unrelated to the mind. But in actual fact the object is empty of existing in that way. It exists dependent on its parts, dependent on causes and conditions and, more subtly, dependent on our mind conceiving and labeling it.

When you see things that appear attractive, recognize that they are only appearances. There are no inherently beautiful real objects out there. They're like a rainbow in summer. When a rainbow appears, it appears so real. But is there something findable that you can touch where the rainbow seems to be? No. There is only light appearing to our mind. The rainbow is an example of something whose mode of appearance and mode of existence do not match. It appears real and touchable, but is not. Similarly, objects appear truly existent, but they are not.

We are especially deceived by the appearance of attractive objects. We think the beauty and desirability of a car, for example, lie in the car itself. In fact, there is no inherent attractiveness in the car. Our mind projects beauty onto the car and then we get attached to the beautiful car our mind has created. We think, "What a gorgeous car that is! It has this feature and that feature. I really want to buy it!" However, someone who is not at all interested in cars sees the same car, is not at all attracted to it, and has no desire to possess it. When our mind gets stuck in longing for someone or something, it is helpful to remember that the attractiveness we see in that person or thing is not inherent in it. It is projected by our mind. Besides there not being any inherently existent beauty in the car or person, there is no inherently existent car or person there to start with!

When you watch TV, there is the appearance of people. But are there real people in the TV? No. When you look at your face in the mirror, there's the appearance of a face in the mirror. But is there a face in the mirror? No. There is only the appearance of the face. When you see a mirage, water appears on the asphalt. Is there water there? No. However it's not that nothing exists. While there are no people inside the TV, no face in the mirror, and no water on the asphalt, there are the appearances of people, the appearance of a face, and the appearance of water. But how those objects appear and how they exist are different. They appear real but are not. Similarly, things appear truly existent but are not. Nevertheless, they exist on the level of false appearances.

Similarly, the things that appear attractive and real to us have no essence to them. They are just appearances, like a rainbow that appears beautiful. But if we go closer, and try to find something tangible that is the rainbow, there's nothing there to touch. Likewise, if we analyze and search for what is so attractive, we can't find it. If we analyze, trying to find something that really is the object out there, we can't find it. It's empty of inherent existence

When we see things as just appearances, and we don't regard them as real with their own essence, giving up attachment is easy. For example, you see this beautiful person on the television. Does it make any sense to fall in love with the person on the TV? No, because there is no person there. There are just light-emitting interactions between charged particles that give rise to the appearance of a person on the screen. If we think there is a real person in the TV and fall in love with him or her, we'll be very miserable. Similarly, if we think people are inherently existent—there is a real person or personality, an essence to the person, something that really is him or her—we'll be frustrated because the nominally existent person that exists and the inherently existent person that we've invented are not the same. Contemplating that attractiveness is only an appearance helps us subdue attachment. Contemplating that there is no person who has a real, findable essence helps us prevent clinging and craving.

Similarly with us, there's no inherently existent person to defend, to please, who is all embroiled in suffering. There's only a conventionally existent person. The more we grasp at ourselves as inherently existent, the more everything becomes a big deal in relationship to this very exaggerated way of apprehending the self. This is what we want to penetrate in order to really see the ultimate nature of how things exist. That is, that they are empty of all inherent existence or nature that we project onto them.

### Bob: Where Is the Happiness?

I have a precept not to eat after noon, and sometimes it is a real challenge to keep it. For example, one day someone offered homemade bread—a beautiful, black loaf of Russian rye bread—that was set out at dinnertime in the community where I live. I love this kind of bread and my mind went crazy: "Why did they put out the rye bread now? It should be put out at breakfast time when I can eat. There won't be any left over for me to eat tomorrow."

This kind of whining and complaining has been a pattern of mine since I was little, and I'm sick of it. It makes me miserable and when the complaints start pouring out of my mouth, it makes others miserable as well.

So after seeing this delicious bread I sat down and asked myself, "Where is the happiness in this bread? If you can find it, you can have it. You can break your precept and eat it. But if you cannot find it, shut up." I know this sounds harsh, but for me it's an effective way to deal with the whining mind. It took me almost no time at all to realize there is no happiness in that bread and that it doesn't matter if there is any left for me to eat the next day. Instead, I rejoiced that the others were eating and enjoying it. It was so easy to make a cup of tea and sit with the group. I didn't even watch people eat the bread. It was gone like a rainbow in summer.

### VERSE 24: SUFFERING IS LIKE A DREAM

> All forms of suffering are like a child's death in a dream.
> Holding illusory appearances to be true makes you weary.
> Therefore, when you meet with disagreeable circumstances,
> See them as illusory—
>> This is the practice of bodhisattvas.

## The Emptiness of Unpleasant Objects or Suffering

How do we give up aversion and hostility when we come into contact with ugly and unpleasant objects or with suffering? See them as being like illusions. Like an illusion or a mirage, phenomena appear to exist one way but exist in another. When driving through the desert, it looks like there is water on the road in the distance. However, there is no water there. Still, there is the appearance of water that exists due to causes and conditions—the road, the sun, our position in relation to the road, and so forth. Similarly, inherently existent phenomena appear when, in fact, there are no inherently existent phenomena there. However, things are not totally nonexistent because the appearance of things exists and arises due to causes and conditions. In other words, the way things exist and the way they appear don't match. They appear to exist independently, although they do not. Their appearance is false. However, they still exist; they exist dependently, not independently as they appear to.

The word "like" in "like an illusion," "like a mirage," or "like a dream" is very important. Without it, someone could think that things are totally nonexistent when that is not the case. They exist; they just do not exist independently or inherently as they appear to.

Similarly, the way things appear to us now is false. People exist, the environment exists, these things exist, but they don't exist in the way they appear to us. They appear to exist as having their own inherent nature from their own side with some essence making them what they are. In fact, they exist as dependent phenomena—dependent on causes and conditions, dependent on parts, dependent on being merely labeled by conception.

It is extremely important to identify the object of negation properly and then to actually negate it and prove to ourselves that it's totally impossible for any such inherently existent "I" or inherently existent aggregates to exist at all. Unless we correctly identify the inherently existent "I" and then negate it, we won't eradicate the ignorance that is the source of our dukkha or attain liberation.

The only way to remove that ignorance is by seeing that the object grasped by ignorance, inherent existence, does not exist at all, has never existed, will never exist. Let's say you want to have a child. One night you dream that you had a baby and are elated. But as the dream went on, the child died and you are overwhelmed with grief. When you wake up the next morning, you look back on your dream. Was there a real child who was born? Was there a real child who died? Does grieving for the death of the dream child make sense? No. There was no real child in the dream to start with, so there could be no child who died. It was just a dream of a child and a dream of the death. There is no child to be attached to and no child whose loss you grieve. It was just a dream.

Similarly, when we are awake, parents seem to have inherently existent children. You see your children as independent phenomena, not as something that exists by being merely labeled in dependence upon its basis of designation. Although thinking people exist inherently is incorrect, we don't realize this and instead grasp on to conventionally existent people as having ultimate, findable existence. Then we become attached to them, and the more attached we are, the more worry and fear we have for their safety. This produces anxiety and clinging and strains the parent-child relationship.

However, if you see your children as nominally existent, then you still care for them but the clinging, obsessing, worry, fear, anxiety, and frustration are gone. You realize that there is no real personality there and there is no real "you" to say, "That is MY child." Parent, child, and the relationship between them all exist conventionally, but have no findable essence. Although this may seem hard to fathom initially, by familiarizing your mind with this view, your mind will relax, and there will be space to actually love not only your child but all children.

*Holding illusory appearances to be true makes you weary.* Being continually angry, upset, frustrated, disappointed, and depressed is exhausting, isn't it? What would happen if we gave all of that up? Seeing that all these situations and the people in them are like illusions—they appear to exist in one way but do not—enables our mind to let go of the emotional upset. Still, people and situations exist, they are not totally nonexistent. They exist dependently, so we respond with compassion while knowing that we cannot control everything.

For example, let's say you won the lottery and are elated. What do you actually possess? The money is just pieces of paper with ink to which we as a society have imputed a particular meaning. Other than the meaning we have given them, those pieces of paper have no value. The lottery transfers the money to your account and now the shape of the scribbles on your bank statement makes you think you are rich. But then the stock market collapses and new scribbles on your bank statement indicate your wealth vanished and you feel depressed. Actually, what did you ever have? Why did the mind become elated at the shape of the ink on one bank statement and dejected at the shape of the ink on a later bank statement? Isn't all of that emotional drama coming from our mind? Was it at all necessary? Chasing after illusory appearance is truly exhausting.

So, when you don't get what you want, when you lose what you have, or when you meet with disagreeable circumstances, see them as like an illusion, as like a dream. If it seems that there is a real "me" that all this is happening to, or real people or things out there that are involved in the events, search to see if you can find their essence. Try to find something that makes them really them. When you can't, reflect that there's no real "me" that all this is happening to. There are no objectively existent things out there. They are just an appearance. When you watch a movie, you get emotional about what happens to the characters. But when you remember that there are no real people on the screen, your mind calms down. Life occurrences are the same. They are just illusory appearances. There are no real things out there that have their own essence for us to hold on to, crave, or grasp. In this way, the mind relaxes and then, because we are no longer overwhelmed by personal distress, there is space to act with compassion in these illusionlike circumstances.

Therefore, Gyelsay Togmay Zangpo advises us, **When you meet with disagreeable circumstances, see them as illusory.** When we see them as like illusions, then we don't get so reactive to them. We know how to handle each circumstance in a skillful and suitable way. By doing so, we save ourselves all the anxiety and weariness that result from grasping life's circumstances as truly existent.

### Sherry: What Is Mine about My Child?

If other mothers are like me, when it comes to our children we have a lot of attachment, even when they are grown up. We never want to stop protecting them, but when they are older, we realize that this is not always possible, that there is a time and place for everything, and that sometimes we just have to stand back and let them discover things for themselves.

Looking at my mind, I see that when things are not perfect with my children, my afflicted mind does two things. First, I think things used to be perfect and that I went wrong somewhere. Second, I focus on one part of the child's life—usually the part when they were the most adorable, sweet, cute, cuddly, and helpless. I then identify them with that image in my mind and compare that image with the distressed (adult) child I see now. The result is a huge emotional reaction, complete with guilt, an aching heart, and feelings of powerlessness.

Turning my mind to the teachings on emptiness is such a relief! When I search for what is "mine" or "my" in the child, I can't find anything. We may share some genes, but that doesn't make the child inherently mine. When I try to find a solid child—someone that is more than what is merely labeled on the collection of body and mind—I can't find one. The attachment melts right away and I can then work with the situation in a more balanced way.

### Maxine: Losing a Child

After having read a piece by Joan Didion in which she described having dinner with her husband who died right there at the table, I was sitting down for breakfast when the phone rang. It was Margaret, with a tight-voiced question, "Are you sitting down?" I knew this wouldn't be good news. "Jasper was shot and killed in Ecuador." A bolt of energy ran through me, and I felt like the ground had just dropped away. I sat down. Margaret is Jasper's mom; I am his godmother. For eighteen years we shared raising him and his two siblings. Jasper was almost twenty-three years old, and from the age of sixteen he traveled at least once a year to Ecuador to spend time with a family he had met during a cultural enrichment program. Jasper loved Ecuador and its people and planned to live there for several months each year.

Shortly after Jasper's death, I participated in a meditation retreat. Often my attention turned to his violent death, which seemed unreal to me, like a dream. Jasper was not a violent kid and rarely caused problems. He was intense, nervous, helpful, bright, and funny. His death was so unexpected, and I tried to understand how something like this could happen.

Meanwhile, I was going through many emotions—sadness, fear, denial, anger, despair at the state of the world—and began to look for ways to deal with the waves of tangled feelings and thoughts that made me exhausted and spun me in circles. The first helpful thought was that many parents in this world lose their children to violence—gang shootings, wars, and harsh accidents. I began to connect with all those parents, to share our sadness and to send them the light and healing energy of the Buddha in my meditation. This sense of connection, of joining in their pain and loss, began to loosen some of the knots inside me. I also thought long and hard about the parents of the young man who had killed Jasper. They must be experiencing great agony, fear, and anger. How were they handling the shattered dreams they had for their son? I realized that, in a way, those parents faced a situation more painful than I did, and I sent them and their son the Buddha's healing peace many times over.

This led me to reflect more deeply on the pervasive interdependence of all things. There are countless causes and conditions leading to this sad ending of a short life. I began to look at the karma of all of us affected by this and especially thought about Jasper's karma and how his early death was an unfolding of harms he had done in previous lives. I am deeply committed to purifying all of the negative aspects surrounding this as much as I am capable.

Now, when I read this verse, it haunts me a bit—because I don't really understand that this life is empty of true existence; usually, it seems very solid and real to me. What I do understand is that this is a complex, interdependent unfolding, and there is some relief in holding it *as though* it were a death in a dream. I know that how I meet this situation becomes part of that dream and affects everyone, and thus I intend to meet this tragedy with grace, wisdom, and loving-kindness for everyone involved, and to think repeatedly of how I can help turn this suffering into something meaningful by working on my own mind and heart. I make an aspiration to be like Buddha Shakyamuni, who took Angulimala, the murderer of 999 people, as his disciple. If I ever meet a person who has murdered, may I understand that meeting to be like a dream, and in that dream may I act with great understanding and compassion.

Since that time, my Dharma teacher has reminded me that in fact Jasper's death is like an illusory appearance in that it appears truly existent although it is not. Grasping this dependently arising appearance as a truly existent, real event does make me weary. Nourishing attachment for Jasper and clinging to my expectation of how life should be are exhausting. When I am able to see these as illusionlike events that are dependently arising, my mind relaxes and has more space.

# 10. Practices to Last a Lifetime

## VERSE 25: OPENING OUR HEART

> *When those who want enlightenment must give even their body,*
> *There's no need to mention external things.*
> *Therefore, without hope for return or any fruition,*
> *Give generously—*
>     *This is the practice of bodhisattvas.*

### Practice Giving without Expectations

VERSE 25 BEGINS the explanation of the six far-reaching practices, or six paramitas. These six are the principal practices in which bodhisattvas engage: generosity, ethical conduct, fortitude, joyous effort, meditative stabilization, and wisdom. This verse discusses the practice of generosity.

A bodhisattva is someone whose intention is directed completely at enlightenment in order to benefit all sentient beings most effectively. A bodhisattva is not interested in "What will make me feel good today? How can I get what I want? How come the world doesn't treat me well enough?" Instead, a bodhisattva wakes up in the morning with joy and delight in the prospect of benefiting others and transforming his or her mind through Dharma practice.

People with spontaneous bodhicitta aren't attached to their body. They understand the body is impermanent; it comes and goes. At death we will separate from our body whether we want to or not. We took this body under the influence of ignorance, afflictions, and karma, so there is nothing in it worth being attached to. The body is an illusionlike appearance. Although our body seems to be solid and real, in fact it is a collection of physical substances, reducible to smaller parts at each level. In dependence on these parts—none of which by itself is a body—we label "body." Not realizing this, we impute value and meaning to this body that it does not have from its own side.

This doesn't mean we should not care about this body. After all, it is the basis of our precious human life and thus is needed to practice the Dharma. Keeping our body healthy and clean is important. We allow the body to rest and we feed it, but we do all this without the clinging attachment and anxiety that ordinary beings generally have towards their body.

Clinging to this body with obsessive attachment when we can use it to benefit sentient beings doesn't make much sense. Thus, bodhisattvas use their body in whatever way possible to benefit others. At very high levels of practice, they can even give their body away. They are not attached to their body, so giving it away is like giving a carrot to someone. It's no big deal. However, for those of us at initial levels of practice, who have not realized emptiness directly, sacrificing our body is not permitted. It's better to use it for practicing the Dharma, listening to teachings, meditating, serving others, and so on. We should use the body to create virtue so that we will become bodhisattvas in the future. Saying, **When those who want enlightenment must give even their body** is giving us the idea that at some point we want to be able to relinquish everything without any fear, without any attachment.

If bodhisattvas can give their body with such ease, then there's no need to mention the ease with which they can give other things. In particular, bodhisattvas practice giving wealth and possessions, love, Dharma, and protection from fear. It's said that the highest gift is that of the Dharma because the Dharma is what can liberate us from cyclic existence altogether. Still, giving possessions, money, protection, and extending our affection and support to those who need it are worthwhile. Such actions create merit that leads to enlightenment and helps others immediately as well.

Also, this verse is emphasizing to give **without hope for return or any** *fruition.* Whatever level of practice you're at, try to give without expectation of receiving anything in return—either praise, a gift, or even the karmic fruition of a fortunate rebirth. Thus, practice giving without thoughts such as "I hope they'll give me a present in return. Maybe they'll tell others how generous I am," or "May I be reborn in the celestial realm." Practice the way bodhisattvas do, with both your motivation and dedication aimed at full enlightenment for the benefit of all sentient beings. You want to make sure that your giving is really done with a bodhicitta motivation, not just to benefit someone else because wanting to benefit others is great, because that's not bodhicitta. You want to give the gift to benefit the others, to create the merit that will ripen in your being propelled along the bodhisattva path and attaining final Buddhahood. You want to make sure that you include working for the benefit of all beings and attaining Buddhahood, otherwise it's not bodhicitta.

For those of us who are beginners, it's an incentive to us if we think, "Generosity creates good karma, so I will be generous in order to create the cause to have wealth in the future." For ordinary beings, the idea of creating good karma that will ripen as happiness in future lives is a good motivator. There is nothing wrong with that motivation for that level of practitioner. But, when we progress to a higher level of the path, limiting the ripening of virtuous karma to a fortunate rebirth is very narrow. Because a series of good rebirths during which we have conducive circumstances to practice the Dharma is necessary to attain enlightenment, we dedicate for that along the way. However, the pleasures of cyclic existence, which include fortunate rebirths, are not our real aim. Instead, we aim for full enlightenment to benefit all beings. That is, in the context of the greater aspiration for full enlightenment, we may also dedicate for lesser aims, such as a series of fortunate rebirths, that afford us the opportunity to practice the Dharma and create the causes for our ultimate aim of enlightenment.

When we are generous because we care about others and are aimed at full enlightenment, then our generosity becomes very pure. In addition to this altruistic intention, if we contemplate the emptiness of the sphere of three—that is, ourselves as the giver, the thing that we are giving, and the action of giving, as well as the recipient as empty of true existence but existing dependent on each other—our generosity becomes the far-reaching practice of generosity.

Offering water bowls on the altar each morning is a practice of generosity. We can offer water very freely. Usually, we aren't attached to water. When we offer water to the Buddha, we do not expect the Buddha to give us something back. When we offer cookies, we may have to be more careful. The next day, when we remove the plate of cookies from the altar, some attachment may arise as we look forward to eating them. It's important when we make offerings to the Buddha that we give them from our heart, without any thought of consuming them later ourselves and without any expectation of achieving worldly gain.

I've seen people make offerings to the Buddha as if they were doing business. They think, "Buddha, I'm offering you so much money. Make my son marry a nice woman, my daughter get a high paying job, and my family be in good health." Other people are more clever businessmen: they say, "Buddha, if all these things occur, then I'll make an offering to you." Implicit in this is "and if they don't occur, then you don't get an offering." Clearly this is not the correct attitude to have when making offerings to the Three Jewels!

When we give to others, let's do so without thinking, "I gave this small gift. Now, when the holiday season comes, they'll give me something back." Or "I gave them this present. Now they'll like me." Or "I made this donation. Now I'll be able to sit in the front row when a high lama comes to teach." Or "I offered service by working in the Dharma center, therefore, I'm entitled to . . ." We may have all sorts of unconscious expectations about how others should act towards us because we've given them something. Such thoughts bring a lot of disappointment, not to mention that they contaminate our motivation for being generous.

Bodhisattva Togmay Zangpo encourages us to give because we take delight in giving. The delight we take in giving itself is the "reward." Giving is incredibly enjoyable when we do it without expecting anything in return.

At Sravasti Abbey, we eat only the food that is offered to us. We want our lives to be lives of generosity and hope that others will respond by providing us with the four requisites for life: food, clothing, shelter, and medicine. When people attend a retreat at the Abbey, we encourage them to cultivate a mind of generosity when they offer food. Instead of thinking, "I better bring food to the Abbey or else I won't have anything to eat this weekend," we encourage them to think, "I'm going to a monastery and will offer food to the monastics and others who are practicing the Dharma there. How wonderful it feels to support people who are practicing the Dharma." Although the actions of shopping and delivering the food are the same, our motivation determines whether or not we are being generous. It also influences whether or not we feel happy when giving.

Whether giving food is an obligation that we do reluctantly or an act of generosity we do joyfully depends on our motivation. This applies to the monastics and lay residents at the Abbey as well. We want to live a life of giving, so we don't charge for anything when people come here. They can leave offerings in a donation basket if they wish. Some people do and some don't. But from our side, we want our lives to be lives of generosity. Many Dharma centers charge for teachings and most retreat centers charge for room and board. We don't charge for either. Why not? Because if we charge and others pay, then it's a business transaction, and neither we nor our guests create any merit. In addition, Dharma becomes something only for the well-to-do who can afford the high prices many places ask. The Buddha gave the Dharma freely to everyone, whether they had money or not. We want to do likewise and we trust that others will support us in return so that we will be able to continue living like this. When everyone practices generosity, then all of us experience the delight of giving and all of us create virtuous karma.

In our consumerist culture that puts a dollar value on everything, the practice of generosity may seem like swimming upstream. But this is worthwhile because we won't attain Dharma realizations by making Dharma into a business. The Buddha didn't say to his disciples, "I'm showing you the path to enlightenment. This is the most valuable thing you could ever receive, so turn over all your gold to me." The Buddha just sat in a grove and people came and he spoke. They were inspired and practiced the teaching. Seeing the value in this and wanting to make it possible for more people to learn and practice the precious Dharma,

Anathapindika gave a park at Sravasti to the Buddha and the Sangha. Visakha gave the Buddha and the Sangha another park, also at Sravasti. Other people in other places donated what they could because they were inspired, appreciated the Three Jewels, and wanted to spread goodness in the world. They took delight in giving. That's the model we're trying to use at Sravasti Abbey.

### Laurie: Cancer Patient Care

Life suddenly became very precious to me one year ago when I was diagnosed with a very aggressive form of breast cancer which had spread to the lymphatic system. The word "cancer" throws you into an adrenaline spell of fear, panic, and overload. The word alone is almost enough to frighten you to death! The medical staff mentioned something about stages and blah, blah, blah—the terminology sounded like Swahili to me. Regardless, suddenly I was faced with having to accept the truth. "Yes, me. I have a life-threatening disease." If left untreated, this would be the end. Death was looking my way.

I was petrified and in disbelief. While still in deep denial I began to listen to what the team at the cancer center was telling me: that the treatments could work very well. Cancer is not a death sentence. However, the treatment matches the severity of the disease; fight fire with fire after all! I reluctantly started the long process of chemo, surgery, and drug therapy which would last nearly a year. As the chemo began, my concentration left and I became unable to do my highly technical work. It was difficult to remember the year I graduated let alone which algorithm I should use. My job and I soon parted.

Then, the realities of living crept back into my awareness . . . My family lives far away. Who would take care of me when I was too sick to dress myself or cook? How would I pay my bills? Can I burden my friends? The treatments progressed. I suffered from side effects and got shingles as well. Not to mention the worst winter of the century! And the usual mishaps of life still show up whether you have an illness or not: a snow plow hit my vehicle and then ran! The power went out at 5 below. I can laugh now—a little. As my well-being began to spiral, so did my career and finances. What followed was my personal financial crash of '09.

Miraculously and simultaneously, dozens, if not hundreds of professionals, volunteers, friends, and family soon rallied to my aid. Insurance came from the Breast and Cervical Health Screening program. My family was extraordinary and lovingly provided emotional support. My friends made heroic efforts, often driving for hours to provide Reiki treatments and home care. They brought homemade meals and hats. But most of all they brought love and affection. The medical professionals were and are tireless in their dedication and efforts. The list is long—I cannot thank these people enough.

Important help came from the Buddhist community, which is my true refuge. Dharma friends provided the internal tools to rebound and restore my attitude. They advised me, "Look for the kindness in others and be kind. That's all you need to do." Opening my eyes to this one simple practice was a huge revelation. This was life-saving advice. I don't mean in the sense that it saved my life, but it made my life, while I was sick, an exploration of kindness.

For example, out of deep empathy the oncologists kept showing up, even though they knew they would make the patient uncomfortable and that the patient may even hate them for it. One very angelic nurse even wrote to my elderly mother to keep her informed the entire time I was in treatment.

I began to see just how much I had taken for granted: my health, my family, my friends, and my spiritual friends. Even those countless strangers who try to show sympathy and support with a smile or a hug or some help with the door I had hardly noticed when lost in my own problems.

Prayers from friends and strangers blossomed forth—I was even included in a prayer circle in a church on the other side of the country. Prayers from India and other countries too—such kindness. Where there is someone with cancer there is also someone with a big open heart praying for all cancer patients. And I, too, could authentically pray for cancer patients—now knowing what it is like. We could support each other.

While well supported in so many ways, bills, transportation, and food continued to be very serious issues for me. I still needed more help. Fear and depression often bubbled up as well as feeling overwhelmed at all the challenges. Sometimes I had the irrational need to find someone or something to blame. Absurd doubts came too, "Was I a bad person—had I done something wrong?" Fear can surface in so many ways. I had to continuously return to the practice of looking for the kindness of others.

One particular place I looked and found much kindness and generosity is right here in Spokane. We have a very, very special champion, one who is available to the neediest: Cancer Patient Care (CPC). Their mission is to make sure cancer patients can make ends meet with groceries, gas to get to the doctor, and other resources. This was real, practical help for my crisis.

I made my way down to their office to see if I qualified. There I met Katie, who would become my social worker. Approachable and with a good sense of humor, she came immediately to my assistance. CPC does so much more than I had imagined. They not only helped keep me warm during the blizzards with money for the power bill but also provided more personal items, such as fuzzy hats and cozy blankets knit by volunteers. They warmed my heart with hours of advice, moral support, and old-fashioned listening.

And then shopping sprees to the resource room for wigs, bandannas, and yes, more hats! As I tried on the different personas—blonde, brunette, redhead—my spirits continued to lift. The support group they led also helped to dispel the feelings of loneliness and isolation. It was easy to see the kindness of the staff—all they want more than anything is to be of help and brighten a cancer patient's day.

As the treatment progressed, the tumors shrank, and the cancer was almost gone by the end of chemotherapy. This improved my prognosis quite a bit. Surgery removed the rest, and with the help of friends I actually attended that surgery (believe me I had many flimsy excuses to be elsewhere)! Drug therapy, physical therapy, and group therapy all helped restore my health. I can now see the wisdom of the different treatments and feel much confidence in the outcome.

Cancer Patient Care stayed with me beyond the most difficult times. Once I was well enough, they helped sponsor an exercise program for me.

They sponsored other services like restorative retreats and foot massages. The annual picnic at the park keeps the Cancer Patient Care community in touch. They let you know you are not alone. As the months went by I felt I always had someone to turn to who understood my experience. I feel I have joined a large, warm extended family!

As I continue this voyage, I realize I am not alone in yet another way. Many others understand the cancer experience—I am so sorry for your battles too. It's not difficult to imagine the anxiety of those in our community who are unable to make ends meet during treatment. In my neighborhood alone, I know of two single moms facing cancer who have only state income and are in a desperate struggle to keep the household fed while trying to recover. This is a tragic situation. But there is help for them and so many others through Cancer Patient Care.

On the way to recovery I am very fortunate and grateful. I have the precious opportunity now to live on and to practice generosity and kindness. As long as we are alive—sick or well, rich or poor—we can do something very rewarding and joyful. We can be kind, giving, and caring. Now I feel a deep wish to repay the kindness of others, to give to others what they gave to me when I needed it the most.

## VERSE 26: STOPPING THE HARM

> *Without ethics you can't accomplish your own well-being,*
> *So wanting to accomplish others' is laughable.*
> *Therefore, without worldly aspirations,*
> *Safeguard your ethical conduct—*
> > *This is the practice of bodhisattvas.*

### Practice Ethical Conduct without Worldly Aspirations

Before being able to benefit others, we must first restrain ourselves from harming them. Harm can be done physically, verbally, or mentally. To help us be more aware of our actions, the Buddha delineated ten nonvirtues which he recommended we avoid. Three of these are done physically, four verbally, and three mentally. Killing, stealing, and unwise or unkind

sexual behavior are the three physical nonvirtues. Lying, creating disharmony, harsh speech, and idle talk are the four verbal nonvirtues. Covet-
ing, malice, and wrong views are the three mental nonvirtues. Physical
and verbal harms begin with the mind, however, because without the
mind having an intention, our body and speech do not act. Pratimoksha
vows—which include monastic vows, lay vows, and the one-day vow—
regulate physical and verbal actions. The bodhisattva and tantric vows
regulate mental activity in addition to physical and verbal actions. Therefore they are more difficult to keep. As our mindfulness and introspective
awareness become firmer in the field of ethical conduct, there is a carry-
over effect into our meditation because those two mental factors are very
important in developing concentration. Mindfulness and introspective
awareness also play a role in cultivating wisdom.

By restraining ourselves from destructive actions, we become someone who can actually be of benefit and service to others. You can't under-
estimate the value of ethical conduct. When you look at the pain and
suffering in our world, it all boils down to people engaging in the ten
nonvirtues listed above. Why is there disease? Because in previous lives
people harmed others' bodies. Why is there discord and dissension? The
four nonvirtues of speech are involved here. We not only experience the
results of lying and so forth done in previous lives, but people engage in
these in this life too, leading to unequal distribution of wealth, oppres-
sion, and so forth.

Here we can see exactly what this verse is warning against. Without a
good foundation of ethical conduct, wanting to do all sorts of high practices and thinking that we can actually attain results from them, or even
wanting to cultivate bodhicitta, is impossible. How in the world can we
help others and develop bodhicitta if we aren't willing to restrain our
own destructive actions? So this is why *wanting to accomplish others' (well-
being) is laughable.*

Living in ethical conduct, especially taking vows, is an excellent way
to train our body, speech, and mind and to guide them to virtue. When
we stop harming others, we suffer from less guilt and regret, and our relationships with others are more harmonious. We transform into a likeable
person whom others can trust, so automatically we'll have more friends.

To live ethically, setting our motivation every morning is essential. When you first wake up, before even getting out of bed, think, "Today, as much as possible, I will avoid harming others. As much as possible, I will help them. I will live today in accord with my long-term motivation to attain full enlightenment for the benefit of all sentient beings."

Karmically, keeping ethical conduct results in fortunate rebirths in the future. As with far-reaching generosity, it's important to practice far-reaching ethical conduct without the worldly aspiration for just a good rebirth. We practice it with the bodhicitta motivation aiming for full enlightenment. Fortunate rebirths are a by-product. Bodhisattvas seek them not as an end in themselves, but in order to have conducive circumstances to practice the path so the final goal of full enlightenment can be actualized.

Far-reaching ethical conduct is of three types: 1) abandoning harm, 2) accumulating virtue, and 3) benefiting others. These are wonderful practices that bring not only long-term spiritual results but also give meaning and purpose to this life.

### Tom: The Importance of Ethical Conduct

Recently, during a Dharma discussion with friends, I had a big "aha" moment. Sharing this experience might prevent new Dharma students from experiencing the suffering arising from my own mistaken steps along the path. We often associate "Dharma practice" with sitting on the cushion more than with our day-to-day activities in between sitting sessions. For many years I was absolutely convinced that if I just steadfastly applied myself to daily meditation and supplemented that practice with Dharma study, eventually my concentration would improve to the point of attaining some kind of significant realizations. It made sense, really—practice, practice, practice, and in time I would become a great meditator and that would make my life meaningful. In fact, the better I became at meditating, the more certain I was that my life would become more peaceful and balanced as well. The key was daily sitting practice. Only now, years later, do I see the folly of that conception of Dharma practice.

While, of course, over time my meditative concentration did improve, it did so only up to a point. Then I experienced a growing sense of being stuck or, alternatively, I just viewed my sitting practice as maintaining my meditative concentration. It didn't seem like I was progressing, and at times it even felt like I was backsliding. At the same time I became very adept at making excuses for lapses in ethical behavior, often under the guise of having compassion for myself. In my mind, I operated under the implicit assumption that when my meditative stability improved and when realizations flowed from that, then I would worry about attending to my ethical conduct. I said to myself, "My ethical conduct is a lot better than it was ten years ago, or even three years ago, and it is probably not fair to expect more of myself as a lay practitioner surrounded by all the temptations, distractions, and comforts of this modern world." Although I was still determined to improve my meditative concentration in order to move further along the path, I was becoming increasingly frustrated by my apparent lack of progress in ethical conduct. So I started checking up.

Thanks to the confluence of hearing a lucid commentary on the stages of the path and the steady hand of my spiritual mentor guiding me along the path, it finally dawned on me that the reason I was stuck was because I was placing too much emphasis on meditation and not nearly enough on the practice of ethical conduct. I now fully appreciate why the Three Higher Trainings are in this order: ethical conduct, concentration, and wisdom. Without pure ethical conduct, concentration does not progress, and without increasing concentration, wisdom (realizations) does not increase. No matter how many hours I may devote to my sitting practice, the actual practice is dealing with my disturbing emotions day in and day out. This is what one of my spiritual mentors called "the real Dharma practice."

Recently I did a "Tara Retreat from Afar," doing one meditation session a day while the sangha at Sravasti Abbey did six sessions. It seemed that every day Guru Tara was testing me with new problems—foreclosure on my house, relationship problems, you name it. As difficult as it was, I was more determined than ever to meet each new problem with a simple question: "Which of the *Eight Verses of Mind Training*[1] do I apply

1. This short text is akin to *The Thirty-seven Practices of Bodhisattvas* in being a mind training text.

here to subdue my disturbing emotions and attitudes before engaging the situation?" Here we are, drowning in the ocean of afflictions, and the Buddha constantly throws us life preservers in the form of these amazing transformative verses.

I meditate in the morning and evening, but it seems the real purpose of my meditation practice is to keep me conscientious and mindful during the intervening hours. Of course, all it takes is losing mindfulness for a brief moment to suffer an ethical downfall, in the form of acting on a disturbing emotion—lashing out in anger at someone, talking behind someone's back, "adjusting" the truth. We inhabit such a treacherous landscape in our minds.

So the good news is that I am beginning to gain mastery over my afflictions and am beginning to practice ethical conduct with more interest and vigor. Now that I am emphasizing this aspect of my Dharma practice, I am definitely noticing that my concentration is improving. I can't say I've had any special realizations at this point, except for maybe a deeper understanding of renunciation, which fortifies my determination to live ethically.

Many of us come into this with a fixed idea of what renunciation means. However, it is often a Judeo-Christian idea that is not the same as the Buddhist notion of renunciation at all. The Buddha encourages us to renounce suffering and the unsatisfactory condition of being born in cyclic existence. He also advises us to renounce their causes: ignorance, clinging attachment, and anger. In Buddhism, renunciation is not about giving up happiness; it is about leaving behind misery and its causes so that we can have excellent happiness and peace. Less attachment to the pleasures of cyclic existence leads to more ethical behavior. I don't get involved in harming others in order to procure and protect the objects of my greed and attachment.

After almost eleven years now of dedicated practice, that is where I am at—trying to cultivate true renunciation! Of course, I am also happier than I ever thought possible. The happiness I have now is more stable and not as subject to the whims of circumstance. And my life has meaning. At the beginning I never would have associated renunciation with happiness, but now I see that the more I apply antidotes to my attachment and my obsession with the happiness of only this life, the better my ethical conduct becomes. Good ethical conduct, in turn, means less guilt, fewer regrets, and this makes concentration and meditation easier. Good ethical conduct also makes me more honest with myself and others so that less time is spent in rationalization, justification, and denial. Now I have more ability to feel genuine compassion for myself and others.

My conclusion is to avoid placing the cart before the horse on the path to enlightenment. Embrace ethical conduct—it is the quickest accelerant along the path. Many of us start out thinking the hardest thing is wrapping our mind around the idea of the lack of inherent existence of self and other. However, true renunciation is the hardest thing for modern lay practitioners. And true renunciation is not possible without ethical conduct. Until we get that, we are just pretending to practice the Dharma. One of my teachers said it best: "Following desire is not practicing the Dharma. Not following desire is practicing the Dharma." All I can say as a lay practitioner is thank goodness for the *Eight Verses of Mind Training*!

### Nancy: Practicing What I Preach

I've always thought that I knew what was best for others. I love to give advice. But practicing what I preach is not so easy. It's as if giving advice to others prevented me from looking at how I was living my life. As I see it, being a hypocrite is a form of laziness since I want the whole world to change while I do nothing to cultivate my own integrity.

I would be outraged by CEOs cheating their companies and clients out of billions of dollars and not getting punished while I worked for people and got paid under the table. I would complain and whine about others' faults not realizing that I was looking into a mirror and seeing myself. Since I met the Dharma and, in particular, since I became ordained, I have become very aware that I find fault in others and that those faults exist in me too.

While my self-centered attitude finds it tempting to clean up my behavior just to look good so that others will like me—which is a worldly aspiration on my part—I now focus on correcting my behavior of body, speech, and mind for my own peace of mind, and in order to be more kind and openhearted with others.

## Verse 27: Having a Steady Mind

*To bodhisattvas who want a wealth of virtue*
*Those who harm are like a precious treasure.*
*Therefore, towards all cultivate fortitude*
*Without hostility—*
  *This is the practice of bodhisattvas.*

### Practice Fortitude Towards All without Hostility

Chandrakirti, a seventh-century Indian scholar, talks about the practice of fortitude in his *Supplement to Nagarjuna's "Treatise on the Middle Way."* He focuses especially on the faults of anger. By learning the disadvantages of anger (or any other destructive state of mind), we gain the courage and inspiration to let the anger go. After all, we care about ourselves and want ourselves to be happy, and seeing that anger makes us miserable, why hang on to it? Anger prevents our good karma from ripening, and it creates a huge amount of destructive karma. For example, if a lower bodhisattva gets angry at a higher bodhisattva, it destroys a thousand eons of merit. Think of having practiced generosity, ethical conduct, and other virtues for a thousand eons and then it getting destroyed because we got angry at a high bodhisattva. If this is the case when a lower bodhisattva gets angry at a higher one, what happens to us ordinary beings who have uncontrolled minds when we get angry at a bodhisattva? It doesn't hurt the bodhisattva much, but what it does to our own mind is devastating because it destroys so much constructive karma that we created with great effort.

In addition, anger prevents the constructive karma from ripening by making a figurative wall or a barrier around the good karma so that it can't ripen. For example, if one bodhisattva gets angry at another bodhisattva, the merit she's been accumulating on the path of accumulation is prevented from ripening and she has to start that training over again and create all that merit again in order to be able to go on to the next path.

The accumulation of merit or virtue is essential for progressing on the path and attaining enlightenment. Fortitude is the ability to endure suffering or harm without getting upset and hostile, and it is an excellent way to create a wealth of virtue. How do we practice fortitude? We need someone who harms us. We can't practice fortitude with people who are nice and kind. We can only practice fortitude with the people we perceive as harming us. For that reason, people who harm us are the most essential for our Dharma practice, the most treasured for our Dharma practice because they give us the opportunity, the circumstances with which we can practice fortitude. So we see them as a precious treasure, then joyfully practice fortitude with them, letting go of all our hostility, hurt, and anger and developing love, compassion, fortitude, and tolerance for them. Through that, we progress in our practice of far-reaching fortitude that will take us across this ocean of cyclic existence.

Therefore, bodhisattvas cherish the people who harm them and are very excited when someone does so because then they have the opportunity to practice fortitude. This is the opposite of how we ordinary beings think, isn't it? But look at the result. We have many people with whom we don't get along or who harm us. Bodhisattvas, on the other hand, have a hard time finding enemies to practice fortitude with. This could be because they've cultivated love and compassion towards all sentient beings.

Spiritual masters must practice fortitude with their disciples, but a real teacher does not find this too difficult. It is said that when Lama Atisha came to Tibet, he brought a cook with him. This cook was very argumentative and disagreeable, so much so that the Tibetan disciples complained about him and requested Atisha to send him elsewhere. But Atisha explained that the cook was essential for his practice of fortitude.

I found a few of my teacher's students very difficult to be around. They were demanding, discourteous, and self-centered, always ready to blame others. Of course, I considered myself to be just the opposite—so pleasant, polite, and harmonious. One day, two Chinese nuns visited our monastery, and I was able to arrange for the three of us to have lunch with Rinpoche. This was special because my teacher is usually very busy, so I rejoiced that these nuns would have the opportunity to meet him. We had just started our lunch when one of the difficult students barged in the room unannounced, without an appointment, while Rinpoche was busy with other guests. The student had just left a meeting of the Dharma organization and was extremely angry. He complained, "Rinpoche, you know I've been serving this Dharma organization for years, and now these people are accusing me of xyz. They are criticizing me and blaming me, without any appreciation for all I have done." He went on and on and on in a loud voice. The two nuns didn't even get a chance to talk to Rinpoche because this guy monopolized the situation. Meanwhile, I was becoming furious. Of course, I couldn't show it. I was in front of my teacher and wanted to look like a good disciple. But inside I was fuming. The thought of practicing fortitude didn't even occur to me.

I was thinking, "Rinpoche, please ask him to leave. Tell him to come back later. He has no business being in here." But Rinpoche responded to his complaints kindly, saying, "It's fine. You've done well. Don't be offended by what they're saying about you." I was thinking, "He should be offended because he does all those things the others say he does. He's so disagreeable that it's no wonder that others criticize him." But Rinpoche thought a totally different way. At the end, who was Rinpoche teaching that whole time? He was teaching me. He was giving me a real-life practical lesson on the importance of quarrelsome people and the way to practice fortitude with them.

Therefore, towards all beings let's cultivate fortitude free from hostility. Remember, fortitude does not mean letting someone do whatever they like. If someone is harming others, we should try to stop him. But we do so without being angry at him. In other words, we cultivate compassion for both the perpetrator and the victim. Without hating one side and pitying the other, we wish both parties well and do what we can to prevent harm. Recognizing the disadvantages of anger and the benefits of cherishing others helps us to do this. In that way cultivating love and compassion becomes our priority, not taking revenge or putting the people who harm us in their place.

The point of this is that when we look at a situation deeply and ask ourselves, "Does anger benefit me?" we see that, "Well, no, it doesn't benefit me. It makes me unhappy now when my mind's under the influence of anger. It creates a lot of destructive karma that's going to bring horrible rebirths in the future, and it also prevents my good karma from ripening."

### Sam: An Enemy Becomes a Friend

I am not yet able to "cultivate fortitude without hostility" towards all, but I have learned that when I believe I have an enemy, I usually don't. For the most part, whenever I have perceived a harm in my life, no one has actually been trying to harm me. That is, I might get angry and antagonistic thinking that someone is deliberately trying to thwart my way or to sabotage my happiness, but in fact no one actually has it out to get me.

For example, I just don't get along with one person I've known for a few years. I could never understand her motive or her method. Worse yet, my hostility arose in the context of our working together to plan Dharma events. I would be doing my job, and she would come in and take over my job and then accuse me of taking over someone else's job. I felt anger because she misunderstood me and frustration because I couldn't understand what she was doing or thinking. In addition, I heard other people gossip about the situation. Most of them believed me and didn't side with her, so I had some arrogance thinking I had one up on her. All this was ugly, especially because we were organizing Dharma teachings together.

At some point I realized this was an opportunity to practice and thought of this verse, which synthesizes all the points of the fortitude of voluntarily bearing suffering. By reflecting that conflict is natural in cyclic existence and that this situation is my own karmic creation, I replace the question "Why?" with "Why not?" So now I say to myself, "Why not me? Why shouldn't this be happening to me?" I also practice "blaming" the suffering on my own self-centered attitude that supported the creation of the destructive karma and supports my anger. I contemplate that the object of my anger is precious and useful so that I take the opportunity to transform the experience into a sincere Dharma practice. I'll also meditate on compassion for the enemy by remembering the faults of afflictions and karma and wanting to stop both of us from experiencing them. Recognizing the helplessness of the other person in that they are under the influence of their afflictions is also helpful. Of course, generating forgiveness from the depths of my heart and extending it out to all sentient beings is healing as well.

Having applied these methods to that situation, today I recognize the things that used to drive me crazy and make me so angry do not have the same power over me. I can make space inside my mind so that I am able to trust that the other person's underlying motivation is good, even if it gets distorted in the process of acting, or even if my mind views it as distorted.

Nowadays my relationship with this person has completely changed. She is one of the most generous people I know, and my respect for that quality in her has grown. I am grateful to have had the teachings on fortitude and the brevity of this verse that reminds me that "those who harm are like a precious treasure."

### Sharon: Being Firm, without Anger, towards a Thief

Last weekend, while I was teaching class at some friends' yoga studio, which was attached to their home, an amazing drama unfolded. A young man with a drug addiction was in the class, and throughout the weekend he stole jewelry from my friends. I had an uneasy feeling on the last day and, checking his sweatshirt, which was out in the entryway, I found some of the jewelry in his pocket. We discovered more after I confronted him. When I found it, I knew I wasn't going to let him steal it. I'm not confrontational by nature—in fact, I tend to let things pass because it is uncomfortable to talk to people directly about an issue—so I started saying Tara mantra, trusting Tara would show the way. What a blessing that practice is.

Since then, I've been thinking a lot about the situation. I can be self-critical and doubt myself, but I'm also seeing how much Dharma practice changes me, even if I think it's not as good as it could be. Here I was happy to see that my immediate reaction was not wanting that young man to create destructive karma by stealing the jewelry. I had the confidence, without even thinking, that I would find a way to deal with the situation. Although I was churning inside, I wasn't afraid. This young man was in such incredible pain and so desperate. His lies were wacky, crazy, and he couldn't stop himself.

The best news is that he starts drug rehab on Tuesday, and my friends will go to the police today. He says he needed money because he owes his drug dealer. Of course, we don't know if that is true or not, but regardless, stealing is not the way to repay debts.

I've been thinking about the karma that has brought us together. And I've been contemplating the emptiness of the events and of each person involved as a way to release the residual tension in my body and to loosen the mental attachment to the story. A potent afternoon.

## VERSE 28: JOYOUS EFFORT

> *Seeing even hearers and solitary realizers, who accomplish*
> *Only their own good, strive as if to put out a fire on their head,*
> *For the sake of all beings make enthusiastic effort,*
> *The source of all good qualities—*
> > *This is the practice of bodhisattvas.*

### Practice Enthusiastic Effort for the Sake of All Beings

Hearers and solitary realizers are practitioners whose aim is liberation from cyclic existence, not the full enlightenment of a Buddha. They cultivate compassion, but they don't cultivate the great compassion and bodhicitta, as bodhisattvas do. Although their spiritual aim is more modest than that of a bodhisattva, they are very good practitioners who work very hard to practice Dharma.

We have to understand the analogy of *strive as if to put out a fire on their head* properly. Usually we think, "If there were a fire on my head, I would panic and scream with fear. Is that how I'm supposed to be in my Dharma practice? Such an approach doesn't seem indicative of a relaxed, concentrated, and wise mind." The analogy doesn't mean that we should practice with terror. Rather, if your hair were on fire, you wouldn't sit back and lounge around, would you? You would be very focused and alert, and no matter what effort you needed to exert to extinguish the fire, you would joyfully do it.

In the same way, if we are able to see cyclic existence clearly for what it is, we will know that the situation we are trapped in right now is much worse than our hair being on fire. The suffering caused by our hair being on fire doesn't last so long compared to the dukkha we have been experiencing in cyclic existence since beginningless time. Since we would definitely make an enthusiastic effort to put out a fire on our head, we should be even more enthusiastic and energetic to get ourselves out of cyclic existence.

If even those who strive for their own liberation, such as the hearers and solitary realizers, make incredible enthusiastic effort, then for the sake of all sentient beings we too should make enthusiastic effort to accomplish the path.

Enthusiastic effort is called the source of all good qualities because it is through joyous effort that we accomplish all the other excellent qualities and realizations of the holy beings. If we practice out of obligation, thinking, "I don't really want to practice Dharma, but I guess I have to," creating merit will be tedious and a real hardship. In addition, since our mind is not virtuous, the actions motivated by it will have little virtue even though externally they may seem to be Dharma actions. Enthusiastic effort is a mind that takes delight in virtue. It is a joyful mind, not a mind that pushes us and puts us down with a lot of "should's," "supposed to's" and "ought to's." We usually think effort means forcing ourselves to do something. But here it is joyous effort that takes delight in virtue. With that delight, with that happy mind, so many other good qualities follow. Joyous effort helps us on the method side of the path, practicing generosity, ethical conduct, and fortitude. It also helps us on the wisdom side of the path because it's this mind that takes delight in virtue.

Enthusiastic effort in the Dharma does not mean being frenetic, with a mind buzzing around thinking, "I've got to do Vajrasattva practice, then the Tara practice after that. I've got to do more meditation on the stages of the path too. How am I going to do all these practices in one day?" Joyous effort means having a happy, relaxed mind that delights in purification, creating merit, serving others, and hearing, thinking, and meditating on the Dharma.

The main hindrance to joyous effort is laziness. There are three types of laziness. The first is what is commonly called laziness—lounging around, sleeping, doing nothing. The second is being busy with worldly activities. While from an ordinary viewpoint a person like this is seen as energetic and successful, from a Dharma viewpoint he is lazy because he has no energy to practice the Dharma. Having an active social life, working sixty hour weeks, spending hours thinking about the stock market, playing politics in our workplace, and engaging in other such activities are considered being lazy. In other words, just being busy is not joyous effort. It depends on what you are busy doing.

The third type of laziness is discouragement. This is the mind that thinks, "I'm incapable of practicing the Dharma. The path is too hard. Enlightenment is too high a goal." This type of thinking, which underestimates our capability and puts us down, is very detrimental.

We need to apply the antidotes to the three types of laziness. In the case of sleeping and lying around, we can reflect on death and impermanence to help us set good priorities in life. When we are overly busy with worldly activities, contemplating the defects of cyclic existence is very helpful. For depression and discouragement, thinking of our precious human life, its meaning, the rarity and difficulty of finding it, and Buddha nature are recommended. Reading the biographies of past great practitioners is also helpful. We see that they, too, went through hardship and, by persevering, they became fully enlightened beings.

With joyous effort, a mental transformation occurs. We become less motivated by the thought "should," and more motivated by the thought "I want to . . ." Greeting situations with eagerness and curiosity makes whatever we do joyful. It takes a while of training our mind to go from the "should" to "I want to." However, if we keep working on it, we will find that our life can be happy doing many, many different kinds of things that we previously could never have imagined being happy doing. In this way engaging in virtuous activities becomes a pleasure.

### Connie: Sergeant Joy S. Effort

For my first few years at a new job I prided myself on the effort I put out, but didn't really understand the concept of "joyous"; mine was imposed effort. As time went on, a caricature appeared of this outstanding competent worker who could get everything done efficiently. At first, I created her unintentionally because I thought she was quite lovely and remarkable. In my mind, everyone at my workplace loved her and the company could not last without her for any period of time. At one of our office skits, I officially created her—Sergeant Joy S. Effort—and everyone laughed. Thereafter, Sergeant Joy S. Effort began to take on a life of her own, and for the following two years I felt I had to uphold, sustain, and embody her through thick or thin, darkness or light, snow, hail, and sleet.

Eventually, I crashed into a wall (figuratively) and had months of health problems that were rooted in pushing myself. I had to stop (literally) and rethink my approach. In another office skit, Sergeant Joy S. Effort went on permanent holiday to the Bahamas, bless her heart, and may she never return. If she does, the loving community I live with will remind me that she is on permanent vacation.

For my new life, as I recreate myself once again, I'm trying not to make the self too solid. Sergeant Joy S. Effort has become a symbol of all the things joyous effort is not. It is not about striving, dictating, controlling, imposing authority, or driving myself and others to the point of exhaustion. Now, I'm learning to understand what joyous effort is, mostly because I'm still recovering my health and don't have much effort these days, even though I have an increasing amount of joy.

One of my personal aspirations this year is to be able to define for myself, as well as to model for others, the far-reaching practice of joyous effort. I hope to inspire myself and others with light-heartedness, fortitude, and self-acceptance. With joyous effort, we have the capacity to do what is possible to the best of our ability. In this way we attain great results.

## VERSE 29: MEDITATION

*Understanding that disturbing emotions are destroyed*
*By insight with serenity,*
*Cultivate concentration which surpasses*
*The four formless absorptions—*
    *This is the practice of bodhisattvas.*

## Cultivate Insight with Serenity

This verse talks about the far-reaching practice of meditative stabilization and incorporates discussion of both insight and serenity. Insight (Skt. *vipashyana*, Pali *vipassana*) is a penetrative mind that is on the side of analytical meditation. Analytical meditation examines phenomena and develops understanding. Serenity (Skt. *shamatha*, Pali *samatha*) is a peaceful mind which is on the side of stabilizing meditation. Stabilizing meditation makes the mind focused and single-pointed. Insight is a penetrating mind that probes and investigates the nature of reality—how things actually exist. This ability to scrutinize and examine intensely must be complemented by a concentrated mind.

Initially insight and serenity are generally cultivated separately. Later the mind becomes so skilled that analytical meditation is able to produce the responsiveness that is indicative of serenity. When an analytical meditation leads to the responsiveness associated with a concentrated mind, the union of serenity and insight has been attained. That insight is conjoined with an extremely still and clear mind that can be directed towards any object and remain there single-pointedly. There are different kinds of insight, but the one that we want to develop specifically is the insight that realizes emptiness.

At first this union of serenity and insight sees emptiness through the veil of a conceptual appearance. However, as the meditator continues to practice, this conceptual appearance is gradually eliminated until she sees emptiness directly and nonconceptually. At this point, her meditative equipoise on emptiness is capable of gradually eradicating the layers of ignorance and afflictions that support cyclic existence. As these are eliminated, she progresses on the path until the point where ignorance and all afflictions are forever eradicated and liberation is attained.

This verse advises us to *cultivate the concentration which surpasses the four formless absorptions.* Earlier we discussed the three realms—the desire realm, which consists of hell beings, hungry ghosts, animals, humans, demi-gods, and celestial beings; the form realm, which consists of four states of meditative absorption (Skt. *dhyana*, Pali *jhana*); and the four formless realms, where the beings remain single-pointedly focused on infinite space, infinite consciousness, nothingness, or have such a subtle mind that it is difficult to tell if there is perception or not. Beings are born in the form and formless realms because they attained a comparable level of concentration when they were human beings.

As a human being, you can attain the level of concentration of the form and formless realms. If you develop those levels of meditative absorption without also cultivating wisdom, you are born in the form and formless realms. While the mind is very blissful and equanimous there, you are not liberated from cyclic existence. When your karma to enjoy those deep states of concentration runs out, you plummet down to lower realms of cyclical existence due to the ripening of other karma.

Even non-Buddhists can practice concentration and attain the four formless absorptions. It is said that all of us have been born in these realms of meditative absorption before. Believe it or not, we have had single-pointed concentration before. We have been born for eons in these blissful realms of pure concentration.

And yet, we are still in cyclic existence today because we neglected to renounce all of cyclic existence and to cultivate the wisdom realizing emptiness, which has the power to cut the root of cyclic existence. Therefore, now we want to do something different from what we did before. In this life, we want to train in *concentration which surpasses the four formless absorptions*. This means to cultivate concentration that is conjoined with insight realizing the emptiness of inherent existence. In this way, we will be able to cut off the ignorance that is the source of the afflictions and karma and to free our mind from the afflictive obscurations that keep us bound in cyclic existence. Because we are committed to benefit all sentient beings and seek full enlightenment in order to do so most effectively, we will continue to practice until all cognitive obscurations—the latencies of afflictions and other stains—have been removed from the mind and we have become fully enlightened Buddhas.

## Claire: Confidence in Concentration

I have had the experience of feeling very peaceful and happy while sitting in the meditation hall listening to teachings, walking in nature, pausing by a river, and having an honest and open conversation with someone. Sometimes the experience is fleeting and lasts just a few seconds, sometimes it lasts longer. Those tastes help me imagine what it would be like to be free of disturbing emotions. How fantastic and amazing it would be to be free of the afflictions that make us and everyone around us miserable! I would love to be able to smile at a person who normally evokes my anger and to be completely calm in a situation that usually provokes strong aversion. To rejoice when receiving harsh criticism and to feel love for the person delivering the words are such radical and challenging responses that they are appealing.

At the moment it is enough to know that there are teachers and practices that exist that can lead us to reaching a state of concentration that surpasses the four formless absorptions—a meditative state that destroys the afflictions that bring us constant suffering. I aspire to develop that level of concentration. In the meantime, I rejoice that we are living at a time when His Holiness the Dalai Lama, who exemplifies the beauty and grace of having a heart and mind that are virtuous in every moment, is present. His teachings concerning how a bodhisattva interacts in the world to benefit all sentient beings gives me a glimpse of what I can become and the inspiration to become that.

## VERSE 30: FAR-REACHING WISDOM

*Since the five perfections without wisdom*
*Cannot bring perfect enlightenment,*
*Along with skillful means cultivate the wisdom*
*Which does not conceive the three spheres (as real)—*
    *This is the practice of bodhisattvas.*

### Conjoining Wisdom and the Other Far-reaching Practices

The first five far-reaching practices of generosity, ethical conduct, fortitude, joyous effort, and meditative stabilization are essential aspects of the path. However, by themselves, they can't bring full enlightenment. Only the far-reaching wisdom can cut ignorance—the root of cyclic existence—and eliminate it, its seeds, and its latencies completely so that they are not able to reappear in the mind ever again. Thus, along with skillful means that know how to benefit sentient beings, we also want to cultivate wisdom that doesn't conceive the three spheres as real. and to contemplate these three as being empty of inherent existence and as dependently arising.

The *three spheres*, also called the "circle of three," are the agent, object, and action. These three do not exist independently, from their own side, but do exist by being merely labeled in dependence upon each other. For example, when we practice generosity—let's say we give a donation to a temple—the agent (ourselves), the object (the temple that is the recipient of our gift), and the action (the action of giving) have no inherent essence. Sometimes "action" refers to the object acted upon, in this case the gift that is given. All of these do not exist under their own power, independent of other factors. The recipient cannot exist without the person who is giving, the object given, the gift, and the action of giving. The other elements are similarly dependent on the others. They all exist by being merely labeled in relationship to each other.

Everything exists by arising dependently. Functioning things depend on 1) their causes and conditions, 2) their parts, and 3) being conceived and labeled by the mind. Dependent arising and the emptiness of inherent existence come to the same point. They are not contradictory. Dependently arisen phenomena lack independent or inherent existence. But emptiness does not mean total nonexistence. Phenomena exist. How do they exist? Dependently. Thus, emptiness and dependent arising are complementary.

When doing bodhisattvas' activities, we see all the components— agent, object, and action—as dependent on each other, on their individual causes and parts, and on the mind that conceives and labels them. Being dependent, they cannot be independent, possessing their own true essence.

For instance, Harry criticizes you, and you feel anger starting to arise. You choose to practice fortitude because you understand the disadvantages of anger. Fortitude doesn't mean stuffing your anger. It means seeing the situation from a different viewpoint so that there's nothing to get angry at. You remember that Harry is a sentient being caught in cyclic existence. He doesn't really intend to harm you, he's just under the influence of his own confusion and anger right now, and that's why he is criticizing you. Thinking this, your mind calms down and you think about his suffering. You even begin to feel some compassion towards him. That's the practice of fortitude.

Then conjoin this with wisdom by seeing that the "I" who is practicing fortitude exists in dependence upon the action of practicing fortitude and also in dependence upon Harry, the person you are practicing fortitude with. Harry isn't the object of your fortitude from his own side. Rather, he becomes the object of your fortitude because you are practicing fortitude and because there is the action of practicing fortitude. Similarly, you become the one practicing fortitude because of Harry and the action of practicing fortitude. All these elements are interdependent. Everything that exists becomes what it is in relationship to other phenomena. Nothing has its own independent existence or its own findable essence that makes it what it is.

If we practice the first five far-reaching practices (perfections) with bodhicitta and then conjoin them with far-reaching wisdom by meditating on the emptiness of the circle of three—agent, action, and object—then our actions become the cause to attain full enlightenment. Here method and wisdom are combined.

### Marilyn: Missing the Object of Negation

Many years ago, we nuns went to a monks' monastery to receive teachings five days a week. Our teacher was instructing us on a text that had to do with realizing ultimate reality. An important step in that process was identifying the object of negation—the false way the self appears to us. This, he said, was the most difficult part of the meditation. According to our teacher's instructions, a good time to check how the "I," or self, appeared to us was when we were under the influence of a strong, afflictive emotion such as anger.

One afternoon, just after our teacher left at the conclusion of the teaching, a monk who was a good friend of mine stood up and announced,

"From now on, all the nuns should leave the monastery within fifteen minutes of the end of the teaching." I couldn't believe what I was hearing—how dare the monks be so prejudiced against the nuns that they essentially kick us out each day, calling a halt to what had previously been good-natured and friendly talk at the end of teachings!

Furious, I told my friend—or the person I thought had been my friend—that I needed to speak to him, "Now!" As we walked down the road, I told him how hurt and angry I was. Reacting to my harsh speech, he got stirred up too. However, we both kept listening and sharing and after a while we calmed down and felt like friends again.

At that moment, he turned to me and said, "Looks like we just missed the opportunity to observe the object of negation," and we both started to laugh.

# 11. Joyfully Staying on the Path

## Verse 31: Facing Our Faults

*If you don't examine your own errors,*
*You may look like a practitioner but not act as one.*
*Therefore, always examining your own errors,*
*Rid yourself of them—*
 *This is the practice of bodhisattvas.*

### Look Within and Examine Your Own Errors

THE NEXT FEW verses discuss how to practice skillful means so that our own practice stays on track and so that we can continue to benefit sentient beings. This is the verse that keeps us clean, clear, and straight on the path because otherwise it's so easy for us to fade into complacency or fade into hypocrisy. Thinking, "I'm a Dharma practitioner" doesn't make us one. Taking monastic vows does not make us holy. Taking the bodhisattva vow or tantric initiations does not mean our mind has been transformed. We must actually live according to the precepts we have received, do the practice of the deity whose initiation we have received, and transform our mind by subduing disturbing emotions and relinquishing destructive actions. In addition, we need to purify our previously created negativities and put effort into creating virtue. The point of Dharma practice is to purify our own mind and enhance our own good qualities. Our purpose is not to look like a practitioner, but to be one. Only then is the label "Dharma practitioner" suitable.

It is easy to look like a practitioner by wearing robes, sporting elaborate titles, or having an entourage of people following us around. It's not too hard to impress people if we receive lots of offerings and praise, publish books, and travel around the world giving teachings. You can look like a good teacher. That's not too hard to do because it is just superficial external appearance. But inside, if our mind doesn't accord with the mind of someone practicing the Dharma, then the main one we're deceiving is ourselves, because we are the one who will experience the results of our actions. Eventually our defects will come out and others will notice. Unfortunately, this is very harmful for any students or admirers we may have.

That is why it is important, if we are in the position of being an example to others of how to practice, to always examine our own errors. Otherwise, we wind up being a hypocrite, don't we? We wind up having a Dharma appearance, but not a Dharma mind.

When people ordain as monastics, the most important thing for them to develop is a "monastic mind." Taking ordination is not too hard. Some lamas will even ordain a person who is very new to Buddhism and doesn't understand what monastic life is about. However, developing a monastic mind that is humble, respectful, and cherishes others—this takes time, requires the guidance of a spiritual mentor, and is more difficult.

It is not too hard to come to the West, gain a position, receive some titles, and have followers. But to practice deeply and cultivate a Dharma mind is very difficult. Why? Because to have a Dharma mind we have to do so many other practices like giving up attachment and pacifying anger. Are such practices easy to do? No.

If we are really going to have a Dharma mind, we have to look inside and be attentive so that we recognize our own ignorance, anger, and attachment when they arise. We must be able to notice our own self-centeredness, jealousy, and competitive mind, our own arrogance, laziness, and excuses. We must acknowledge our tendencies to justify, rationalize, and defend our destructive attitudes and actions. The Dharma path entails continually turning the mirror back on ourselves. Even when we do actions to help others, we always need to watch our own body, speech, and mind and examine our own errors.

Sometimes, when we first meet the Dharma, we become so enthused by the idea of bodhicitta and of benefiting all sentient beings that we become busy helping others but forget to look at our own mind. We think, "I'm working so hard to benefit sentient beings." We might be busy doing charity work or setting up a Dharma center, but we forget that the bottom line of benefiting sentient beings is not to harm them. And to not harm them we have to examine our own mind and motives.

Let's also remember that part of benefiting sentient beings is transforming ourselves into as worthy a practitioner as we can be. It is not enough to do some Dharma practice and then say, "Okay, now I've finished doing formal meditation practice. I'm going to go out and serve sentient beings." We have to continue to meditate. If we stop learning, reflecting, and meditating on the Dharma, our mental state will degenerate. If we don't survey our mind with introspective awareness, very soon deeply rooted disturbing emotions will rear their ugly heads. Therefore, it is crucial to always make time for Dharma study and meditation.

Lots of people are eager to become Dharma teachers. They want to be respected and appreciated and to feel that they are doing something beneficial. However, it is not that easy to be a Dharma teacher. Being a teacher is not about sitting on a high throne and smiling while a group of devoted students look at you with appreciation. Guiding people in the Dharma necessitates incredible fortitude because students will do all sorts of things that you do not like. They will come to you for advice and then ignore it. They will criticize you when you say something that doesn't accord with their opinions. They will promise things and then be too busy or distracted to carry through. Dharma students are sentient beings after all, which means that they are not perfectly consistent, reasonable, and reliable. This requires great patience, fortitude, and compassion on the part of spiritual mentors.

If we do not observe our mind, we will fall back into the same old unrealistic expectations and judgmental attitudes as before. Thoughts such as "I'm working so hard for these students and they don't appreciate me" will appear. If we don't examine our own errors, we may look on the outside like an accomplished practitioner or like a respected Dharma teacher with many students, but on the inside we are not acting as one. Eventually, the façade will be shattered. Even if it isn't, we will still experience the results of our actions.

Therefore, the antidote is to always examine our own errors and rid ourselves of them. That is the bottom line. When people come and say to me, "I want to ordain so I can teach the Dharma," I'm cautious. I want to check what their actual motivation is. How can they aspire to put out the fire in others' houses if they don't first want to extinguish the blaze in their own home? I believe our foundational motivation for requesting ordination should be that we want to tame our own mind, we want to stop harming others and start benefiting them. To do this, we see that our body, speech, and mind need restraints and that living in precepts can provide the structure that we need to tame our unruly mind. As instructed in Verse 26, *Without ethics you can't accomplish your own well-being, so wanting to accomplish others' is laughable.* Isn't it a bit idealistic to want to teach others if we lack the intention of establishing the foundation by practicing the Dharma ourselves?

Verse 31 emphasizes the importance of practicing ourselves. Only on the basis of ridding ourselves of our own faults can we then act in ways that benefit others. Therefore, learning the Dharma so we can teach others or wanting to ordain so we can teach others should not be our initial motivation. Our primary motivation should be, "First, I need to get my own mind under control. After I have done that, I can then begin to think about teaching others." Without knowing ourselves well and restraining our own ignorance, anger, and attachment, our intention to benefit others will make us what is called a "Mickey Mouse bodhisattva." A "Mickey Mouse bodhisattva" seems to have a lot of compassion but, lacking wisdom and skill, he creates havoc.

We don't need to wait to become Buddhas to benefit others. While we are on the path we can benefit others in whatever ways we are capable. But we avoid making ourselves appear like something we are not. Rather, we remain humble, more concerned with correcting our own errors than in pointing out those of others.

## Philip: Freedom from the Victim Mentality

Due to some causes and conditions that occurred when I was little, I placed myself in the role of a victim from very early on. I've carried this identity of being a victim like a banner, never considering that it was a concept in my mind. Thinking it was reality, I viewed every experience I encountered through the eyes of a victim and blamed whatever suffering I experienced in life on others.

One summer I spoke with my spiritual mentor about this, and she helped me to realize that my victim identity was a concept in my mind, created after a situation that happened early in my life. She helped me to recognize that this identity lacked any basis in reality and was, in fact, one of the major causes of my misery and my inability to engage my life in the moment.

Inside there was constant inner dialogue going on that put me in a victim space, made me oversensitive and easily offended, and very self-centered. At the same time, because I was so attached to my reputation, I put up a façade that I was capable, in control of any situation, and decisive, when in fact none of that was true. Underneath, it was great attachment to my reputation and a sense of never being treated fairly. This façade made me look like a practitioner, but many times I certainly didn't act like one. As I later discovered, this fabricated façade deceived only me; the people around me didn't like it and often didn't believe it was real.

A couple of years later I became very ill and weak. The slow process of recovery showed me how much I abandon and disengage myself from my life. I live so much in the past. This way of living fosters the feeling of being an innocent victim of life, being defensive even if someone asks me a simple question, and continuously projecting the causes of my unhappiness on others. I also do "future traveling," which causes a lot of anxiety, worry, and fear of things that haven't yet happened. Seeing these habits, I said to myself, "If I don't examine my own errors, which are the misconceptions of who I think I am, and if I don't stop repeated habitual behaviors that neither serve me nor anyone else, I will never be free."

Now, as Verse 31 instructs, I will examine my own errors in order to understand how I deceive myself. As Verse 24 recommends, I have been seeing "all forms of suffering are like a child's death in a dream." Holding these made-up and illusory appearances as real has left me exhausted. Therefore, I'm making a commitment: When I meet with difficult situations, I will practice seeing them as illusory. I will examine my own misconceptions about them and rid myself of them. To do this, I will investigate and acquaint myself with the nature of reality.

## VERSE 32: THE INTERNAL JUDGE AND JURY

*If through the influence of disturbing emotions*
*You point out the faults of another bodhisattva,*
*You yourself are diminished, so don't mention the faults*
*Of those who have entered the Great Vehicle—*
     *This is the practice of bodhisattvas.*

### Comment on the Action, Not the Person

This verse is talking specifically about pointing out the faults of bodhisattvas with a judgmental, critical, or angry mind. Some objects are potent objects for the creation of karma. For example, due to their excellent qualities and the help they give us on the path, any actions we do with respect to the Buddha, Dharma, Sangha, and our spiritual mentors become very potent. Arya bodhisattvas are included in the Sangha, and even lower bodhisattvas are very admirable because of their great qualities. They are beings who are working for the benefit of all sentient beings, who have dedicated everything in their lives—their body, their speech, their mind, and every single moment of their existence—to the practice of Dharma and to the welfare of all sentient beings. Thus, if we develop a negative attitude towards someone who is working for all sentient beings, where has our mind gone? What is going on in our mind that we now see a person who has such love and compassion as an enemy or as someone who's doing wrong?

When you talk badly to or about others, *you yourself are diminished.* This happens on many levels. On an interpersonal level, when you trash somebody else behind her back, you diminish yourself in the eyes of others in the sense that others will not trust you in the future. On another level, you create a lot of destructive karma, which diminishes your Dharma practice. Furthermore, when you're busy finding faults in others and gossiping about them behind their back, you're diminishing your love and compassion.

Therefore, *don't mention the faults of those who have entered the Great Vehicle.* The Great Vehicle is the Mahayana and someone who has entered it is a bodhisattva. Criticizing someone who has the aspiration to benefit all sentient beings and attain enlightenment only creates horrible destructive karma. We already have enough destructive karma and dukkha; why create more for ourselves? If we truly care about our own happiness, we don't damage it by creating destructive karma by pointing out the faults of others, especially a holy being such as a bodhisattva.

The masters recommend that since we lack clairvoyant powers and cannot discriminate who is a bodhisattva and who isn't, it's better not to criticize or point out the faults of anyone. What, then, do we do when we see someone doing something that doesn't seem very good? Do we just say, "That person could be a bodhisattva. I don't want to create destructive karma and diminish myself, so I just won't say anything and will let him continue with what he is doing"? No, it doesn't mean that. If someone is doing an action that appears harmful to you, you can talk about the action, and ask that person questions about his behavior. But you can do this without denigrating him.

People and their actions are different phenomena. We can discuss the appropriateness and inappropriateness of an action or the benefit and harm of an action. But we cannot attack another person, accusing him of being evil, sinful, or hopelessly corrupt, because that person still has the Buddha nature, the Buddha potential.

For example, let's say somebody's behavior appears questionable. Rather than jump to conclusions and criticize either the person or the behavior, we can go to that person, and say, "You're doing this and that. I don't understand it. Please explain to me why you're doing this." Then we should be quiet and listen to his explanation with an open mind. If the leader of a group is doing something that doesn't look too good, approach him and respectfully ask him to explain his way of thinking or give him some useful feedback. If his explanation is not satisfactory, talk to the other members in the group and say, "This is what I observe. These are my doubts. I'm not making an accusation, but I need my doubts clarified." That is very different from making an accusation when you don't know the real story. This is very different from imputing various motivations on someone when we don't know if that person has those motivations. It is very different from creating a stir by blaming a person when it is actually the behavior that you want to comment on.

There is a beautiful quote in the confession ceremony that the fully ordained monastics do twice a month. It says:

> Just as a bee feeding on flowers only extracts their nectar without spoiling their color or fragrance, so a bhikshuni entering a city or village is mindful only of her own behavior to see if it is correct and does not interfere in others' affairs or inspect what they do or do not do.

Just as a bee knows that its purpose is to extract nectar and pays attention to just that without disturbing or harming the flower, so too when we are with people, we should be heedful of our own physical, verbal, and mental activities without putting our own feelings on others or getting involved in things that we don't need to get involved in. It seems that a lot of judgment and criticism towards others arise in our mind when we get involved in situations unnecessarily. Instead of looking outward at what others have done or left undone, let's look inward at our own behavior, what we have done and what we have carelessly neglected to do.

Sometimes, we may have a difficult time differentiating pointing out someone's faults with a critical mind and speaking about someone's difficulties with a caring attitude. Sometimes these two situations are confused in our mind and we think, "I can't say anything about anybody if they're not here." But there are some situations when we should definitely talk about someone else's behavior.

One example is when someone is experiencing difficulties and stewing in his problems. His bad mood is affecting others around him, making them miserable too. First, we do our best to calm our own mind so we are not reactive to the situation. Then we reflect if there is someone else to whom we could talk who could possibly help this person or suggest ideas to us on how we can help him. Here talking about someone who is not present is an act of kindness towards the person; since he does not know how to ask for help, we ask for help on his behalf.

When we look at it this way, we see that there is no benefit to anyone if, with hostility or jealousy, we talk about other people behind their backs. Creating factions in a group by bonding with others because we have a common enemy is equally damaging. This is especially harmful when people gang up against another person in a class, on a team, or in a social group and make that person into a scapegoat. How will harming one person make the rest of us feel better?

Instead, let's try and use our speech to create harmony. When a problem with someone exists, we need to work it out. We need to practice listening and learn how to express what we're thinking and feeling without blaming anyone. Communicating with others is an important skill, but unfortunately our school system doesn't teach this, nor do most parents, because they never learned it either. However, when we see how crucial good communication skills are, we'll make an attempt to learn and practice them.

### William: Picking Faults Feels Awful

Although I have no idea which of the people around me is a bodhisattva, I find this verse helpful because it makes me look at my critical mind that picks faults in other people. This mental state is definitely self-centered, and when it is active, my inner experience is that I feel diminished. There's nothing about being critical and belittling other people that feels good. In fact, it feels rotten. Recognizing that helps me to see that my motivation is not what I want it to be. When I'm being critical of someone, there's not genuine concern for him, and when I have genuine concern for another person, I don't see his traits or actions as faults. Instead, I see them more as reflections of the other person's unhappiness and suffering. Then compassion arises in my mind.

## VERSE 33: REPUTATION AND REWARD

*Reward and respect cause us to quarrel*
*And make hearing, thinking, and meditation decline.*
*For this reason give up attachment to*
*The households of friends, relations, and benefactors—*
     *This is the practice of bodhisattvas.*

### Give Up Attachment to Households of Friends, Relations, and Benefactors

This verse is directed particularly to monastics who live due to the kindness of others' donations. When we depend on the kindness of others to receive the four requisites of food, clothing, shelter, and medicine, we may become attached to these things or to the people who give them to us. Or we become manipulative in order to get people to give us the things that we need for our lives because we can't just go out and buy them at the store. If we haven't been trying to subdue our attachment, we may think we can't do without these things. With that attitude, we then try to make friends with people who could possibly give us the things that we want. Not cultivating a sense of contentment in our practice can lead to such ugly behavior.

Someone may be known as a Dharma teacher or a great practitioner even if he or she hasn't reached high levels of the path or had direct insight into the nature of reality. Thus, he is still susceptible to attachment, jealousy, or envy arising in relation to receiving reward and respect. For instance, someone respects you and you get a little bit arrogant. Or someone gives you a lot of offerings and you think you must be pretty great. Or you are envious when someone respects another teacher more than they respect you because you want the students to come to your Dharma center and not go to the other one. Perhaps you get jealous when a benefactor gives to someone else but not to you. These things happen. Craving reward and respect leads to envy, jealousy, and attachment. When actions are motivated by these disturbing emotions, quarrels and conflict ensue.

Clearly, when we become competitive, our mind is just thinking about our own reputation, status, and wealth. Therefore, hearing, thinking, and meditating decline because we are more concerned about gaining a good reputation for ourselves and being better than the other person than with subduing our own mind. We forget about hearing teachings, thinking about them, meditating, and integrating them. Instead, we do "single-pointed meditation" on the eight worldly concerns—honor, respect, wealth, praise, sensual pleasure, and so on.

Not only does our own practice degenerate, we also harm others when we are in a leadership position. Politicians butter up prospective donors with flattery and promises; CEOs deceive others with under-the-table business deals; spiritual leaders pretend to be kind and caring when their interest is in pleasure, money, or fame. Eventually, others see these corrupt motivations and lose faith in these people. This deception and broken trust damage everyone concerned, especially when it happens in a religious or spiritual setting.

What is the antidote for craving to have a big name as a Dharma teacher, lots of followers, and a heap of offerings? *Give up attachment to the households of friends, relations, and benefactors.* These are the people who praise us, make offerings to us, respect us, and boost our reputation and renown. Rather than being attached to their households and cultivating their friendships with the motivation of trying to get something from them, we contemplate the disadvantages of attachment so that we want to relinquish it. By doing this, as well as enhancing our sense of personal integrity and consideration for others, we will not take advantage of others or manipulate them. Instead, let's cultivate genuine appreciation for the people who support us and dedicate our merit for their welfare. In addition, it is extremely important to use their offerings wisely and not waste the donations or goods that they give to us.

Giving up attachment to those who make offerings doesn't mean we become rude or ignore those people. We may still have students, relations, and benefactors. But we deal fairly and equally with all people, and give up any motivation of trying to get something out of them or use them for our own benefit. Spiritual mentors must continuously work to benefit their students with a compassionate motivation that wants to help them progress on the path to enlightenment.

Sometimes we use others for our own advantage, don't we? When we desire reward and respect, we know how to manipulate people by flattering them, dropping hints, or giving them a gift so they will give us something bigger in return. We put them in a position where they cannot say, "No," and they feel obliged to give us something or to praise us. Sometimes we'll act very holy and proper when our benefactors are around, but very sloppy and self-centered at other times. We are very good at creating the illusion of a Dharma practitioner. However, we cannot become a real spiritual practitioner if we rely on these wrong ways of earning our livelihood that seek material possessions, honor, and reputation.

In such instances, we remember that it is due to others' kindness that we have the opportunity to practice the Dharma. Therefore, having deep gratitude for them and praying for their well-being is natural and appropriate. We pray not only for their well-being, their health, and long life, but also for their ability to practice in this and all future lives. We pray that they meet the Dharma in all of their future lives, and that they have the inclination and wish to ordain in future lives so that they have a good relationship with the Dharma and can hear teachings and contemplate and then meditate on them and quickly attain enlightenment.

One of the things that initially attracted me to Buddhism was that it points out our hypocrisy and cunning no matter how much we try to hide it or pretend it's not there. Whenever we try to put on a show for ego's benefit, there is a verse in a thought training text that points our error out to us.

### Jessica: Going to the Ends of the Earth for Appreciation

Once, while I was in retreat, the thought came to me very strongly, "I will go to the ends of the earth to seek appreciation!" The thought was so clear and stark, and I saw that in many ways I have done that in my life. Having a glimpse of the depth of my attachment to appreciation was a real eye-opener and recognizing how much time and energy I have spent in my life to procure it was a shock. I now recognize this attachment as a compulsive and impulsive force that can manifest in many interactions and endeavors in life. The task now at hand is to slow down, look closely at my motivations and then "clean them up" by training my mind in nonattachment to praise. This means seeing praise for what it is: someone else's opinions. Another person's ideas about me are not the reality of who I am; their praise doesn't make me good and their criticism doesn't make me bad. I need to know my inner reality, evaluate what is virtuous and what isn't, and then steer my actions of body, speech, and mind towards virtue.

## VERSE 34: ZIPPING OUR LIPS

> Harsh words disturb the minds of others
> And cause deterioration in a bodhisattva's conduct.
> Therefore, give up harsh words
> Which are unpleasant to others—
>     This is the practice of bodhisattvas.

### Give Up Harsh Words

**Harsh words disturb the minds of others.** What are harsh words? This refers to speech that is motivated by a harmful thought to put someone down, to humiliate him, to make oneself look good, to vent one's anger or one's feeling of turbulence inside. There are so many different possible motivations for harsh words. What they share in common is an attitude that doesn't care about the effect of our speech on others and is more concerned with our getting out what we want to say.

We spoke about harsh words in previous verses. For example, Verse 8 is about karma, and "harsh words" is one of the ten destructive actions. However, while still including all cases of harsh words, this verse refers specifically to giving up harsh words when we are in the position of a leader such as a Dharma teacher, counselor, administrator, and so forth. When we are in a leadership position, it is very easy to become arrogant and feel as if we are infallible. So many scandals with CEOs, politicians, and even religious leaders are due to such arrogance. When some people are in a position of authority—having wealth, power, and respect—they forget their own ethical values. They do things that get them into so much trouble and make other people lose faith in them.

Harsh words are one example of this. Until we have direct realization of emptiness we have to watch our mind, because it is easy for such foibles to come up. You may try to be a leader and instead of leading people in virtue, you abuse your authority, thinking, "I'm the leader and these people respect me, so I can scold them, I can boss them around, I can criticize them to their face if they don't do what I want. I can embarrass them and humiliate them because I'm the person in power. They believe in me and will follow me no matter what." Arrogantly thinking like this diminishes your love and compassion, impedes your bodhisattva conduct, and leads to harming others through harsh words.

One of the reasons we speak harsh words is because we interpret others' words as harsh. Here questioning our own perceptions can be very useful. Sometimes a person may be making a simple comment, but our self-centered mind is so easily offended that we interpret the other person's words as speaking harshly to us, doubting us, or challenging us. When our mind makes up such inaccurate stories about others' motivations and the meaning of their words, we respond with our own harsh words and an argument ensues. Thus, examining our mind and cutting our proliferating projections on others is an excellent way to prevent speaking harshly to them. In short, when we stop "hearing" harsh words, our own harsh words will decline.

When common people utter harsh words they often don't see it as deteriorating their own conduct. However, uttering harsh words is a huge interference for spiritual practitioners who are trying to cultivate impartial love and compassion for all beings. The anger, resentment, rage, belligerence, and spite that motivate harsh words are contradictory to love and compassion. A mind seeing sentient beings as disgusting and a mind seeing them as worthwhile cannot exist simultaneously. Clearly the motivation for harsh words interferes with our own spiritual practice and separates us from what we really long to do, which is to fulfill our spiritual aims. Therefore, Togmay Zangpo advises us to *give up harsh words which are unpleasant to others.*

Does that mean that when you are in a leadership position you never say things that are unpleasant to other people? No. From your own side, you don't have the motivation to hurt or embarrass others. However, there are times when you have to speak in a straightforward manner to get across a point that is important for others to understand so that they can prevent suffering and attain happiness.

When you speak with a good motivation, does it mean that you will always be successful in not saying things that are unpleasant to others? No. People will find a way to be offended even if nobody is intending to offend them. We know that ourselves, don't we? Sometimes people tell us things out of kindness, but our ego doesn't like to hear those things, so we get upset and angry. We accuse them of speaking harshly to us when actually the words were said out of kindness and compassion.

If you are in a leadership position or are practicing as a bodhisattva, it doesn't necessarily mean that all you say is, "You're such a sweet dear loving person. You are so wonderful. You're talented and never do anything wrong, blah, blah, blah." People may lap that up and love you because you flatter their ego, but that isn't necessarily what is most beneficial for an individual to hear at that particular moment. Sometimes you have to be direct and assertive in order to protect them from harm, and they may find your words painful. But you know that is what they need to hear to wake them up on the path.

My teachers have spoken like that to me. Once I asked His Holiness the Dalai Lama some questions about a certain topic. He explained the point, but I didn't understand the context in which he was explaining it. I just kept on saying, "I don't understand." At one point he looked at me and said, "I've explained this many times before in teachings. Were you sleeping?" Ouch. I immediately got defensive and tried to explain myself. But then I realized I probably was sleeping when he explained it before. What he said woke me up. I realized I needed to listen better and try harder to understand. Instead of bothering him with a lot of questions, I needed to remember and reflect on what he had taught before.

Many years ago Zopa Rinpoche asked me to lead a meditation course in Kopan. I was just a baby nun who didn't know much at that time and responded, "I can't do that." Rinpoche told me to talk with Lama Yeshe about it. So I went to Lama Yeshe and said, "Lama, I can't lead this course. I don't know anything." Lama just looked me straight in the eye and said, "You are selfish." Gulp. Silence. "Okay, Lama, I'll lead the course,"

I answered. He had to speak that way to me because I was so dense that he would not have been able to get the point across to me if he spoke in a sweet, encouraging voice. He wanted me to understand that whatever I know I should share and however I can help, I should try to help. He made me see I couldn't just hide behind a façade: "I'm just little old me. I can't do anything." I was caught in the extreme of self-deprecation, putting the focus on me instead of on others and thinking about how I could benefit them, even if only in a small way.

Sometimes our Dharma teachers have to tell it to us as it is. We have to be able to take it when they do and not think, "I work so hard for my teachers. They are so privileged to have *me* as their student. But look at how they treat me!" That kind of attitude is the opposite of what we should be cultivating in our spiritual practice.

While this verse specifically addresses harsh words, it also brings up the larger topic of how we use our speech. We must be very attentive to when we engage in idle talk. Often we spend hours chatting about this and that and then wonder why we have no time to read a Dharma book, meditate, do volunteer work, or even help a friend. Avoiding idle talk does not mean that we only have serious, deep discussions with people. Rather, in situations where a little friendly talk is appropriate, we do that, but we don't let it slip into gossip and we talk for an appropriate length of time. For example, in the workplace it's important to say, "Good morning" and ask how people are. Our colleagues may like to share what they did over the weekend or what is going on in their life, and so do we. In such instances, we are careful not to say more than is appropriate and to return to our tasks after a few minutes.

### Michelle: Swearing

When I was growing up, my mother would put Tabasco sauce on our tongues whenever she caught us swearing. Of course I hated this and thought that she was very cruel for doing it. Now I wonder about my interpretation of her action, because her discipline kept me from making a habit of harsh words.

Once I was a teenager, however, it was very cool to swear, and swearing seemed to be required behavior to show how tough I was. From age fifteen on I created a habit of using many swear words, especially the "f---off" phrase. Everyone around me engaged in this so it seemed normal and harmless. One of the phrases I loved to say was "I don't give a flying f---." Whenever I said that phrase, I thought it made me feel better.

Later in life I met the Dharma and began to think deeply about the connection between thoughts, words, and actions. I could see how easily harsh thoughts led to harsh words and those led to uncaring acts. During this time I noticed that one of my closest friends used a really violent phrase when describing winning at sports: "We kicked the sh-- out of them." I started to wince whenever I heard that and gently called it to his attention. Surprised, he said he had never thought of what a violent image it conjured up. He had viewed it as just a habit of speech that he had picked up without thinking. He then asked me to call it to his attention if he used that phrase around me. I did that, and he began to change.

Years later a carpenter was working on a building for us. He was in the habit of swearing whenever something didn't go smoothly, which is often the case in carpentry work. I politely told him that I would appreciate it if he didn't swear on this one project, that it was adversely affecting me each time I heard him. He was also surprised and said he would try it out.

A few days later, we talked and he shared that his day was so much more peaceful when he worked on our project. He was still swearing on other job sites, but not on ours. This led to a good conversation about how swearing can set up an angry mind and is painful to those around us and to ourselves. He commented that he got angry too often at home, and that his wife and the pets would "clear out" when he started swearing. A week later he told me that he had spoken with his wife about our conversation and that he was trying to change his swearing habit bit by bit. His wife replied that that conversation had lifted her spirits immensely.

### Meredith: The Temptation to Scream "Hypocrite!"

Some years ago I was in a work situation in which a colleague and I developed a romantic interest. Due to the nature of our work, romantic relationships were against company policy, so we kept quiet about it. But when my boss found out, he immediately called me into his office. Normally a calm person, he was furious; I had never seen him so enraged, and without mincing words he told me I would have to leave the company. There was something about the way this happened—perhaps his derogatory tone or his fury—that stayed with me as heaviness in my heart, even though I got another job that I enjoyed.

Several years later, I came to know that my boss had been fired because he had developed a romantic relationship with a company employee. I would like to say that my first reaction to the news was one of equanimity, but it wasn't. What arose was shock, then a huge upwelling of anger bordering on rage, simultaneous with acknowledgment of the almost unbelievable karmic irony regarding my relationship with him. I wanted to stand in front of him and yell, "Hypocrite! Hypocrite! Hypocrite!" until my vocal cords were raw and I could no longer get any sound out. I felt sick. I went into my bathroom, grabbed a towel, and had one good long scream and cry.

Then I let the storm come and go. I couldn't think of anything else to do but go sit on my cushion and just let the dust settle and calm the mind down a little. When I was able to step away from my self-centered view and look at the big picture, my heart just broke for everyone at the company, especially the junior employees who respected him and whom he had looked after and tutored with much care. I could only imagine what they were going through. They are human and I was sure that their sadness, shock, and feelings of betrayal were putting them all through deep suffering. In light of that, I allowed myself to feel that suffering as well, and a sense of overwhelming compassion for all of the employees arose in my heart. And, eventually, that compassion made its way to my former boss. Whatever had led him to foster that relationship, well, I certainly knew first hand all about that. It's what got me out the gates as well. I've been there in my own fashion. I know he's suffering greatly, and I feel great empathy and deep sadness for him. I dedicate the merit of my practice to him and hope that he will find his way to some kind of peace in his heart.

### Randal: The Harsh Words Evaporated

My wife, who is now pregnant, and I have been living and working in Thailand. Yesterday I was on my motorbike, going to the post office down a small road within a government complex. I was going about 40 km per hour. As I was going straight, a truck that was parked pulled out from the side of the road and hit me. The impact sent me and the bike down; I slid a few meters due to the force of the impact. Fortunately, I was wearing a helmet, which saved my head, but my legs and shoulder are bruised and very sore.

But the part that I wanted to share with you was that I never got angry during the entire episode. I usually have a temper and let people know quite clearly what I think of them. When I asked the driver why he hit me, he said he could not see. I realized that even if he would have checked to see if anyone was coming, he could not have seen me. His eyes were clouded by cataracts.

He and his wife were older and very poor, and he was obviously scared and concerned about the police coming. I felt compassion for him and let him know that I was all right. When the police officer came, he brought a mechanic to assess the damage to the bike. I felt conflicted taking money from this couple, but there was another side of me that thought that if they paid, it would send them a clear message so that this would not happen to someone else in the future. In the end, I accepted only half of what the estimated damage was, hoping that this was enough to make him more careful when he drives in the future but not so much as to be a severe hardship on them.

Later, when I told the story of what happened to a friend, he got upset and angrily said what he would have done in that situation. I realized that most people would have been outraged having been hit by a truck due to no fault of their own, but I still felt grateful that I did not respond in that way.

I often doubt my spiritual growth and my ability to practice Dharma in my daily life. I see myself as being filled with delusion and affliction. Yet, after this accident, I am grateful that I was able to have a calm head throughout the situation, and more grateful that I was able to generate compassion for the person who hit me. Most of all I am grateful for my teacher and the Dharma. Being faced with adversity is the true test of one's practice and spiritual growth. I was proud of myself and happy that I was able to turn the situation into a Dharma experience.

## Verse 35: Banishing Bad Habits

*Habitual disturbing emotions are hard to stop through counteractions.*
*Armed with antidotes, the guards of mindfulness and introspective awareness*
*Destroy disturbing emotions like attachment*
*At once, as soon as they arise—*
  *This is the practice of bodhisattvas.*

### The Importance of Mindfulness and Introspective Awareness

This verse acknowledges the fact that habitual disturbing emotions (afflictions) are hard to stop through counteractions. Unless we have the wisdom directly realizing emptiness, we can't cut their root. Until we have that wisdom, we have to be armed with the guards of mindfulness and introspective awareness. Mindfulness has different meanings according to the context. Here it means mindfulness of the bodhisattva practices, mindfulness of our vows and precepts, and mindfulness of our spiritual aspirations. With mindfulness we try to live according to our precepts and aspirations. Since the mind has so many nonvirtuous tendencies, we employ introspective awareness to see if our mind is still focused on the constructive or if it has gotten overwhelmed by an affliction or distraction. Here introspective awareness is a part of the mind that is aware of what we are saying, thinking, feeling, and doing. It alerts us if we have gone astray from being mindful of what is wholesome. Introspective awareness allows us to see if we are actually living up to our aspirations and if we are actually applying the counterforces to the disturbing emotions. With this kind of introspection we're able to check up and see if our mindfulness is still holding on to our precepts and the bodhisattva practices. It checks up to see if we actually have a good motivation or are just rationalizing things.

The two mental factors of mindfulness and introspective awareness are important, not only for living in pure ethical conduct but also for cultivating single-pointed concentration. In the practice of concentration, mindfulness focuses on the object of meditation, and introspective awareness checks up to see if we are still focusing or if we have gotten distracted. If we discover that our mind is under the influence of agitation, laxity, dullness, or distraction, we apply the appropriate antidote.

Disturbing emotions come into our mind when we least expect them. Once they arise, we can't just sit there and say, "Oh, attachment, you are coming into my mind. Welcome. Come in. Sit down and have a good time." Or "Anger, you are coming into my mind. Fantastic! I haven't gotten angry for a while. I could use a good buzz of adrenaline. Anger, my friend, sit down and have a cup of tea." The disturbing emotions are said to be like thieves because they steal our happiness and they steal the happiness of others. If a thief comes into your house, you don't ask him to sit down and serve him tea, do you? You call the police, you sound the burglar alarm, and you chase him out.

Disturbing emotions and the negative attitudes are more harmful than external thieves because they make us create destructive karma and cause us to do things that are harmful to other living beings. Thus, when they enter our mind, we should not tolerate them for even an instant. We must identify them and then evict them, using the guards of mindfulness and introspective awareness. We chase them out right away. We don't let them hang around and create mischief.

Catching and counteracting them right away takes some practice. Our mindfulness and introspective awareness must be very strong, and that comes about through repeated and patient practice. In other words, we know the antidotes; however, when we are not well-practiced in the antidotes to the different disturbing emotions, the emotions are very hard to stop. We may know that it's good to meditate on impermanence when attachment arises, but often we don't even notice attachment has taken over our mind. Only when it has completely consumed us, we think, "Oh, maybe this is attachment." But then we forget what the antidote is and we just stay in that suffering state. Later, when we progress, then we say, "Oh, there's attachment. Oh, yes, meditating on impermanence is the antidote. I'll do that tomorrow." In this way, we stay stuck in our misery. Then we progress a little bit more on the path and we identify the attachment, we remember the antidote, we start to meditate on it, but it takes a lot of time and practice and habituation for the antidotes to be effective. If we expect that all we need to do is hear one teaching or do the meditation one time and then that affliction will be gone forever, our expectations are too great. We have to keep coming back to the fact that changing our mind requires practice, practice involves repetition, and repetition takes time. There is no shortcut. Let's practice counteracting habitual tendencies that have existed since beginningless time with joy and confidence that what we're doing is both meaningful and beneficial.

Meditation on impermanence is the antidote to free our mind from attachment. If anger, annoyance, irritation, rage, or hatred arise in our mind, meditation on fortitude is very helpful. Fortitude is the ability to remain calm when we are confronted by harm or suffering. We also want to generate fortitude when we experience physical or mental suffering in order to counteract anger that arises in response to that suffering. While sometimes it is possible to do as Togmay Zangpo suggests and drop the anger as soon as it arises, other times we have to work hard to subdue this unruly mind and get it to release the thoughts "I'm right!" and "I must win at all costs!"

When jealousy comes in the mind, meditating on rejoicing is an excellent antidote. Jealousy doesn't want others to have happiness and its causes while rejoicing wants them to have happiness and its causes.

When the mind gets overwhelmed by arrogance and conceit and pride, one of several antidotes may be applied. One is to meditate on a difficult topic, such as the twelve sources and the eighteen elements. These topics are difficult to understand, and thus meditating on them deflates our conceit. Another antidote to arrogance that I have found very helpful is thinking of the kindness of others. Here I reflect that everything I know, every talent and skill I have, came due to the kindness of others who taught and encouraged me.

Those are some of the antidotes to work with. Try to apply them as soon as you can when you notice your mind is off balance. Apply them consistently, realizing at the beginning that your defilements are very great and the antidotes are small. It's going to take some practice for the antidotes to become more familiar and for their power to increase. Thus, fortitude, patience, and consistency are needed to work with our mind and strengthen the antidotes to afflictions. If an affliction doesn't vanish instantaneously, just keep on practicing. Eventually it will.

## *Jason: Stop Fooling Myself*

Because I was raised by a scientist and a nurse, I have trained myself to be better and smarter than everyone else. If you ask me, I'm really smart and I'm charming and I'm a good athlete and people like me. I'm such a good guy and I'm really good at my job too, just ask around. Of course this is the view of my arrogance, which I'm slowly coming to realize after years of being an alcoholic and lying about it to myself and others. It took doing some exceptionally stupid things—like getting emotionally involved with a prostitute and trying to help her separate from her boyfriend/pimp, which she was not ready to do—and nearly ruining my professional career for me to just begin to stop believing everything I think. Now I'm going to focus on the second verse of the *Eight Verses of Thought Transformation*:

> Whenever I am with others
> I will practice seeing myself as the lowest of all,
> And from the very depth of my heart
> I will respectfully hold others as supreme.

I really need to start to get over myself. I don't even know why I need to be that cool guy that people like but I better get that figured out too.

During a recent meditation I had a strong momentary insight into the fact that I don't even know my own mind. I can't trust my own thoughts, and I should not believe everything I think. That's a little bit scary. One moment, one thought. The next moment, another thought that is the opposite. Dealing with the habitual disturbing emotions associated with all these thoughts is tumultuous. For example, I know I need to stop the relationship with the prostitute. It is unhealthy and is not benefiting either of us. I have my resolve, and then five minutes later I'm trying to rationalize a way to get in touch with her. Then I think of the Dharma and come to my senses.

With each day of Dharma practice, the floodwaters of attachment abate a little more, but I need to be careful and to increase my mindfulness and introspective awareness and maintain them for a long time. The support of AA, my spiritual mentor, and my Dharma friends is essential to this process.

### Gary: Guarding the Mind and the Mouth

My mind indulges in the habit of judging and criticizing other people. I'm very appreciative of living at the Abbey, where we have the space to watch our minds more carefully. One day when my critical, judgmental mind was just winding up and preparing to go to work, I stopped and listened to the sounds around me. I heard two people in the kitchen making lunch. I could hear another person on the phone speaking with the contractor who was building the new monastic residence. I could see someone fixing the fence. "They're all offering service to others and I personally will benefit from their efforts," I thought, and the judgmental complaining mind ground to a halt.

This is a reminder that with the guards of mindfulness and introspective awareness I'm getting better at turning off that yapping, critical voice and am able to actually recognize how kind the people around me are. This completely changes the inner space of my experience and makes living anywhere joyful. I appreciate this environment in which there is the space so that the guards of mindfulness and introspective awareness can function. Before I came to the Abbey, I thought I had some level of mindfulness, but now I realize it was nearly zero. Developing these helpful mental factors is like flexing muscles, it takes practice. While we may not have the most conducive environment at our fingertips, wherever we are becomes the field in which we cultivate mindfulness and introspective awareness so that we can destroy disturbing emotions and accomplish others' good.

## VERSE 36: MINDFULNESS

*In brief, whatever you are doing,*
*Ask yourself, "What's the state of my mind?"*
*With constant mindfulness and introspective awareness*
*Accomplish others' good—*
    *This is the practice of bodhisattvas.*

## Constantly Check the State of Your Mind

To sum up the previous thirty-five verses, whatever you are doing—whether you are standing, lying down, walking, or sitting, whether you are awake or asleep, whether you are happy or miserable, whether people like you or don't like you, whether you are dying or living, whether you are in pain or are healthy—no matter what is going on in your life, ask yourself, "What is the state of my mind?" Because the mind is the source of happiness and suffering, it's important to check what state it is in. Also, be aware that we have this precious human life for just a short time. Therefore, every single moment is very precious for creating the cause for happiness in the future. Thus, it is important to keep watch on our mind moment by moment because we're constantly creating the causes for happy, painful, or neutral experiences moment by moment.

Then, being aware of the state of the mind, ask yourself, "Is my mind involved in what is constructive and virtuous now? Or have the thieves of disturbing emotions taken over and are they running the show?" If our mind is involved in what is beneficial and wholesome, let it be or encourage it. If disturbing emotions have entered the mind and are destroying our happiness and the happiness of others, apply the counterforces.

These two mental factors, mindfulness and introspective awareness, come in the context of the higher training of ethical conduct and the higher training of concentration. In terms of ethical conduct, mindfulness remembers our precepts and introspective awareness checks what's going on in our body, speech, and mind to see if we're abiding by our precepts. Thus, these two mental factors are clearly important in order to subdue our body, speech, and mind.

By continually being mindful of what is wholesome and being alert to see that our mind has not gotten distracted from spiritual goals, our good qualities will increase and we will accomplish others' good. In this way, we fulfill our main motivation—accomplishing the welfare and benefit of other beings, as well as our own. That is the essence of the bodhisattva vow.

When introspective awareness discovers that the mind has strayed and is involved in greed, stinginess, arrogance, vengeance, and the like, we then apply the remedy to that disturbing mental state and remind ourselves of a virtuous emotion or activity. We do this no matter what's going on in our life. We don't have to sit in a meditation hall to do this. We don't have to be healthy. We don't have to be seated in vajra position in order to do this. Whatever we are doing, whatever is happening, we practice. We keep integrating our mind with bodhicitta no matter what situation we find ourselves in.

So this verse is saying through mindfulness and introspective awareness, both in ethical conduct and developing concentration, then *Accomplish others' good.* The whole purpose of doing all of this is accomplishing others' good. In terms of ethical conduct, we must stop harming them before we can accomplish their good. In terms of meditation and concentration, by developing those skills we then focus on the bodhicitta meditations in order to develop the method side of the path and we focus on the meditations on emptiness and impermanence in order to develop the wisdom side of the path. Then we're able to eliminate both the self-centered attitude and the self-grasping ignorance and through that attain Buddhahood. Both while we're on the path and after we've attained the goal of Buddhahood, we work to accomplish others' good as much as possible.

### Graham: What Is the State of My Mind?

One day before teachings we Dharma students were standing around waiting for our Dharma teacher to come and teach us. She was a little late. When she walked in, she looked at us and asked, "What's the state of your mind? What are you doing with the time that you're standing here waiting for me?" I was blunt and impish as usual, "Oh, just standing around." However, someone in the community adopted the phrase, and whenever he saw something he wanted to point out, he said, "What's the state of *your* mind?" I'd hear that and think, "That's not what the verse says. The verse says, 'What's the state of *my* mind?' So why are you pointing the finger at me when you are supposed to be looking at your own mind?" I thought this way every time he said it, until I realized that maybe I should read the verse myself and ask myself, "What's the state of *my* mind?" instead of getting irritated at the other person.

It happens when we live together in community that someone says something we don't like. Nevertheless, such occurrences can be useful if we just let go of whatever meaning our opinionated mind was projecting onto it and instead take the essence and apply it to our mind.

### Kevin: Coming Back to the Present and to Bodhicitta

*Transforming Adversity into Joy and Courage,* Geshe Jampa Tegchok's commentary on *The Thirty-seven Practices of Bodhisattvas,* was a pivotal book for me in my Dharma practice. I read and reread it during a one-month retreat and it really spoke to me. At the end of a three-month retreat at Sravasti Abbey, we participants read *The Thirty-seven Practices of Bodhisattvas* out loud together and then shared stories about how we applied these practices in our lives. This inspired us to print out the verses on little cards that we decorated and to put in different places around the Abbey— on the fence, in the truck, on the stairway—all over so that we would be reminded of them.

Sometimes I talk to myself, saying "Kevin, what's going on?" I may do this in the garden, while working at the computer, or wherever, checking in with myself: "What are you thinking?" I say it gently, not harshly, "Where is your mind now? What's going on? How can I come back to the present moment?" I tune in to see if my mind is disturbed by afflictions or feeling joyful by what has transpired during the day. The mental factors of mindfulness and introspective awareness are crucial when I ask myself, "How do I work with what's in front of me now?" and "How can I remember to come back to the present when I veer off into the gutter or the hedges?" For me, this involves bringing my mind and heart back to the bodhicitta motivation, going beyond the wish for my own happiness, and seeing that everywhere I go, the path is lined with sentient beings.

## VERSE 37: DEDICATING THE GOODNESS

> To remove the suffering of limitless beings,
> Understanding the purity of the three spheres,
> Dedicate the virtue from making such effort
> To enlightenment—
> > This is the practice of bodhisattvas.

### Dedicating Our Merit to Attain Enlightenment

In this last verse we dedicate all the merit from the previous practices to removing the suffering of limitless beings by attaining full enlightenment. Only when we have attained the enlightenment of a Buddha do we have the full compassion, wisdom, power, and skillful means to be able to be of utmost benefit to all. As a Buddha we won't be prevented from benefiting living beings by disturbing attitudes, negative emotions, or incapability of our body and speech.

So how do we dedicate the merit? First of all, we dedicate through the method aspect of the path, which concerns actions done with bodhicitta, in other words, with the idea *to remove the suffering of limitless beings.* We also dedicate the merit through the wisdom side of the path by *understanding the purity of the three spheres.* This means we contemplate the lack of inherent existence of all the factors involved in the dedication—the agent (ourselves as the one dedicating the merit), the objects to whom we dedicate (sentient beings), the aim we dedicate for (full enlightenment), the action of dedicating, and the merit we dedicate. In addition, we reflect that all of these exist by being merely labeled and are mutually dependent upon each other. By contemplating dependent arising and the emptiness of inherent existence in this way, we make a perfect dedication.

*Dedicate the virtue from making such effort to enlightenment.* Here we dedicate for enlightenment because that's the most noble, wonderful goal to dedicate for. By dedicating for enlightenment, all of the other positive things come about quite naturally. If we dedicate just for a future rebirth, then merit ripens as that and then it's finished. If we dedicate for enlightenment, then since enlightenment has to do with the happiness of all living beings, the merit becomes very strong. It multiplies so that it doesn't get exhausted until all sentient beings are enlightened.

### Chuck: Slowing Down to Dedicate the Merit

My teacher sometimes likes to chant prayers extremely slowly. He does this in order to contemplate their meaning and to meditate on the emptiness of the person dedicating, the merit being dedicated, and the action of dedicating. Sometimes my mind is restless and I want to dedicate quickly and move to the next activity.

And so it was one afternoon at the conclusion of teachings. My teacher was relishing drawing out each Tibetan syllable as long as possible. Plus the person sitting next to me was chanting in a very loud and off-tune voice the Chinese version of Tibetan phonetics, which it seems were done incorrectly and did not match the Tibetan pronunciation. My mind started its own cacophony inside me in reaction to all this. A precious opportunity to rejoice at the merit of myself and others was going down the tubes, and I was unhappy and angry to boot!

I told myself to focus all my attention on the meaning of the dedication verses and to ignore everything else. "Contemplate each word you are saying," I told myself, and slowly my mind began to be inspired. By the end of the prayer my mind was calm and filled with a genuine sense of rejoicing at the virtue and goodness in the world. Instead of wanting to get out of that room as fast as I could, I was marveling at my good fortune to be part of a group of people, headed by my teacher, who had made removing the suffering of living beings the purpose of their lives.

## Daniela: My Money and My Merit

When I earn money or create merit, I want to use it all for myself. I think I deserve it—because the money or merit came from MY work. But I've begun to see that this thinking ignores the reality that I am completely interconnected with others. I could not have earned or created anything without the generosity and kindness of others. To challenge that kind of self-centeredness, I imagine giving away all my merit. After all, it didn't belong to "me" in the first place and I can never, ever repay all the kindness of sentient beings that has come my way since beginningless time. Dedicating the merit challenges my usual habit of taking the good results of my efforts for myself. Also, it opens my heart to others and to the illusory nature of phenomena.

# Epilogue: Putting It into Practice

*For all who want to train on the bodhisattva path*
*I have written* The Thirty-seven Practices of Bodhisattvas,
*Following what has been said by the excellent ones*
*On the meaning of the sutras, tantras, and treatises.*

*Though not poetically pleasing to scholars,*
*Owing to my poor intelligence and lack of learning,*
*I've relied on the sutras and the words of the excellent,*
*So I think these bodhisattva practices are without error.*

*However, as the great deeds of bodhisattvas*
*Are hard to fathom for one of my poor intelligence,*
*I beg the excellent to forgive all faults,*
*Such as contradictions and non sequiturs.*

IN THESE VERSES the author, Gyelsay Togmay Zangpo, was being very humble. He credited all the words of wisdom he has just spoken to the Buddha and to the lineage of great masters who have preceded him. You can see that he truly treasures others and is not concerned with his own reputation or place in history. He doesn't say, "I wrote this text. Look at me, aren't I wonderful? These are all my ideas." He says instead, "All the words of wisdom here came from the Buddha. I have poor intelligence and lack of learning. I don't write things very well, so I may have made some mistakes. But, I tried my best to rely on my teachers and the teachings they have given me. As far as I understand, what I said here is without error."

Through the way he wrote the epilogue he shows us an example of a real bodhisattva. Perhaps we read it and say, "This guy has no self-confidence." But actually that was not the case. He is showing us, through his own actions, the activities of a bodhisattva.

> *Through the virtue from this may all living beings*
> *Gain the ultimate and conventional altruistic intention*
> *And thereby become like the Protector Chenrezig,*
> *Who dwells in neither extreme—not in the world nor in peace.*

This is Gyelsay Togmay Zangpo's dedication. The ultimate bodhicitta is the wisdom realizing emptiness. The conventional bodhicitta, the altruistic intention, is the aspiration for full enlightenment for the benefit of all beings. Here he dedicates so that, through the virtue of his writing this text and of us studying it together, all living beings may gain the ultimate and conventional bodhicittas and, thereby, become like the Protector Chenrezig, the Great Compassionate One.

Like all Buddhas, the Great Compassionate One dwells in neither extreme—his mind does not dwell in cyclic existence or in the self-complacent peace of his own personal nirvana. Concerning cyclic existence, he does not dwell in the eight worldly concerns or in attachment to the bliss of samadhi. Concerning nirvana, he does not dwell in the blissful state of self-complacent peace without benefiting sentient beings. Chenrezig has attained full enlightenment, which enables him to be of the greatest benefit to all beings. May we aspire for and dedicate for this as well, just as Chenrezig did.

> *This was written for his own and others' benefit by the monk Togmay, an exponent of scripture and reasoning, in a cave in Ngülchu Rinchen.*

This text was written for his own and others' benefit by the monk Togmay, an exponent of scripture and reasoning, in a cave. The translation was prepared by Ruth Sonam. It was published in the book *The Thirty-*

*seven Practices of Bodhisattvas,* which records the oral teaching by Geshe Sonam Rinchen, who is one of my precious teachers.

We have shared many instructions in this text. That's the step of "hearing." Now it is time for us to continue our study. I recommend that you read Geshe Sonam Rinchen's book *The Thirty-seven Practices of Bodhisattvas,* as well as Geshe Jampa Tegchok's book *Transforming Adversity into Joy and Courage.* Study and think about these teachings deeply. Contemplate them repeatedly over time so that you first get a correct conceptual understanding of the teachings. Talk about the meaning of these verses with your Dharma friends. Gather in discussion groups and discuss what they mean and how to practice them. Also, meditate on them in your daily meditation practice. Do analytical meditation by reflecting on the points in this teaching in relationship to your own life. Think about the logic in these new and different ways of viewing things. When you reach a conclusion, or have an experience of the meaning of a verse, rest your mind on it single-pointedly. By doing this you will understand these teachings correctly and will be able to apply and integrate them into your life. Then these verses will have a truly transformative effect on you.

It is not enough to listen to teachings and then do only practices in which you visualize and recite mantras. We should also think deeply about and meditate on the meaning of these teachings as well as practice them in our daily life. This text is so practical. It talks about how to deal with situations that we encounter in our daily life. For instance, we need to practice as explained in situations where somebody, out of strong desire, steals our wealth or has it stolen. In situations where somebody broadcasts all kinds of unpleasant remarks about us, let's practice as it says in that verse. When we find that desire and attachment plague us, we need to recall the verse about attachment being like salt water—the more we indulge, the more the thirst increases. We ask ourselves if we'll ever find satisfaction and peace by chasing objects of attachment. Or will we only encounter frustration in the struggle for happiness?

Recall events that have happened to you in the past, and bring what you have learned in the Dharma to apply to those past situations. In that way transform your mind. That is the true meaning of practicing the Dharma. In addition, using past experiences as examples of each verse helps you process your previous experiences and actions so you can make peace with them. Use the verses to help you forgive others. Meditate on the verses so that you forgive yourself for previous mistaken actions as well.

We have all made mistakes in the past. Instead of sitting and feeling guilty about your mistakes, use the Dharma teachings and apply them to previous situations. Ask yourself, "If I had known the teachings at that time, how could I have seen the situation and freed my mind from affliction?" Contemplate, "How would a bodhisattva have felt and acted in that situation?" When we meditate like this, we see alternatives to what used to be knee-jerk emotions, where we believed we did not have any choice about how to feel or react in a situation. Seeing that there are other ways to feel and think gives us choices. We don't have to suppress negative emotions; we can let them go and retrain our minds. As we become less self-centered, our feelings and thoughts will be more peaceful and amicable to ourselves and others. That will enable us to heal from past issues and will help purify mistakes that we have made. It also gives us some training in these techniques, so that when similar situations come up in the future, we will have some familiarity with these methods and can recall and apply them in the situation. Even if we forget to apply them in the situation, we will go home and pull out this text to read. Figure out which verse applies to what happened during the day and reflect on it to transform your mind.

In this way, you will have a taste of the Dharma. Tasting the Dharma isn't an intellectual process, it's experiential. When you experience the effects of practice in your life, your conviction in the Dharma will automatically increase. Realizing the validity of the teachings from your own experience will enhance your faith in the Buddha, Dharma, Sangha, and your spiritual mentor. That, in turn, increases your eagerness to learn and practice the Dharma even more. If you practice with a motivation of bodhicitta, your actions will be beneficial to all living beings and one day you will become a fully enlightened Buddha.

# Appendix I: Root Text:
## *The Thirty-seven Practices of Bodhisattvas*

By Gyelsay Togmay Zangpo

Homage to Lokeshvara.

I pay constant homage through my three doors
To my supreme teacher and protector Chenrezig,
Who while seeing all phenomena lack coming and going,
Makes single-minded effort for the good of living beings.

Perfect Buddhas, source of all well-being and happiness,
Arise from accomplishing the excellent teachings,
And this depends on knowing the practices.
So I will explain the practices of bodhisattvas.

1    Having gained this rare ship of freedom and fortune,
Hear, think, and meditate unwaveringly night and day
In order to free yourself and others
From the ocean of cyclic existence—
     This is the practice of bodhisattvas.

2    Attached to your loved ones, you're stirred up like water.
Hating your enemies, you burn like fire.
In the darkness of confusion you forget what to adopt and discard.
Give up your homeland—
     This is the practice of bodhisattvas.

3   By avoiding bad objects, disturbing emotions gradually decrease.
    Without distraction, virtuous activities naturally increase.
    With clarity of mind, conviction in the teaching arises.
    Cultivate seclusion—
        This is the practice of bodhisattvas.

4   Loved ones who have long kept company will part.
    Wealth created with difficulty will be left behind.
    Consciousness, the guest, will leave the guesthouse of the body.
    Let go of this life—
        This is the practice of bodhisattvas.

5   When you keep their company, your three poisons increase,
    Your activities of hearing, thinking, and meditating decline,
    And they make you lose your love and compassion.
    Give up bad friends—
        This is the practice of bodhisattvas.

6   When you rely on them, your faults come to an end
    And your good qualities grow like the waxing moon.
    Cherish spiritual teachers
    Even more than your own body—
        This is the practice of bodhisattvas.

7   Bound himself in the jail of cyclic existence,
    What worldly god can give you protection?
    Therefore, when you seek refuge, take refuge in
    The Three Jewels that will not betray you—
        This is the practice of bodhisattvas.

8   The Subduer said all the unbearable suffering
    Of bad rebirths is the fruit of wrongdoing.
    Therefore, even at the cost of your life,
    Never do wrong—
        This is the practice of bodhisattvas.

9    Like dew on the tip of a blade of grass, pleasures of the three worlds
     Last only a while and then vanish.
     Aspire to the never-changing
     Supreme state of liberation—
         This is the practice of bodhisattvas.

10   When your mothers, who've loved you since time without beginning,
     Are suffering, what use is your own happiness?
     Therefore, to free limitless living beings,
     Develop the altruistic intention—
         This is the practice of bodhisattvas.

11   All suffering comes from the wish for your own happiness.
     Perfect Buddhas are born from the thought to help others.
     Therefore, exchange your own happiness
     For the suffering of others—
         This is the practice of bodhisattvas.

12   Even if someone out of strong desire
     Steals all your wealth or has it stolen,
     Dedicate to him your body, possessions,
     And your virtue, past, present, and future—
         This is the practice of bodhisattvas.

13   Even if someone tries to cut off your head
     When you haven't done the slightest thing wrong,
     Out of compassion take all her misdeeds
     Upon yourself—
         This is the practice of bodhisattvas.

14   Even if someone broadcasts all kinds of unpleasant remarks
     About you throughout the three thousand worlds,
     In return, with a loving mind,
     Speak of his good qualities—
         This is the practice of bodhisattvas.

15  Though someone may deride and speak bad words
    About you in a public gathering,
    Looking on her as a spiritual teacher,
    Bow to her with respect—
        This is the practice of bodhisattvas.

16  Even if a person for whom you've cared
    Like your own child regards you as an enemy,
    Cherish him specially, like a mother
    Does her child who is stricken by sickness—
        This is the practice of bodhisattvas.

17  If an equal or inferior person
    Disparages you out of pride,
    Place her, as you would your spiritual teacher,
    With respect on the crown of your head—
        This is the practice of bodhisattvas.

18  Though you lack what you need and are constantly disparaged,
    Afflicted by dangerous sickness and spirits,
    Without discouragement take on the misdeeds
    And the pain of all living beings—
        This is the practice of bodhisattvas.

19  Though you become famous and many bow to you,
    And you gain riches to equal Vaishravana's,
    See that worldly fortune is without essence,
    And be unconceited—
        This is the practice of bodhisattvas.

20  While the enemy of your own anger is unsubdued,
    Though you conquer external foes, they will only increase.
    Therefore, with the militia of love and compassion
    Subdue your own mind—
        This is the practice of bodhisattvas.

21  Sensual pleasures are like salt water:
    The more you indulge, the more thirst increases.
    Abandon at once those things which breed
    Clinging attachment—
        This is the practice of bodhisattvas.

22  Whatever appears is your own mind.
    Your mind from the start was free from fabricated extremes.
    Understanding this, do not take to mind
    (Inherent) signs of subject and object—
        This is the practice of bodhisattvas.

23  When you encounter attractive objects,
    Though they seem beautiful
    Like a rainbow in summer, don't regard them as real
    And give up attachment—
        This is the practice of bodhisattvas.

24  All forms of suffering are like a child's death in a dream.
    Holding illusory appearances to be true makes you weary.
    Therefore, when you meet with disagreeable circumstances,
    See them as illusory—
        This is the practice of bodhisattvas.

25  When those who want enlightenment must give even their body,
    There's no need to mention external things.
    Therefore, without hope for return or any fruition,
    Give generously—
        This is the practice of bodhisattvas.

26  Without ethics you can't accomplish your own well-being,
    So wanting to accomplish others' is laughable.
    Therefore, without worldly aspirations,
    Safeguard your ethical conduct—
        This is the practice of bodhisattvas.

27  To bodhisattvas who want a wealth of virtue
    Those who harm are like a precious treasure.
    Therefore, towards all cultivate fortitude
    Without hostility—
        This is the practice of bodhisattvas.

28  Seeing even hearers and solitary realizers, who accomplish
    Only their own good, strive as if to put out a fire on their head,
    For the sake of all beings make enthusiastic effort,
    The source of all good qualities—
        This is the practice of bodhisattvas.

29  Understanding that disturbing emotions are destroyed
    By insight with serenity,
    Cultivate concentration which surpasses
    The four formless absorptions—
        This is the practice of bodhisattvas.

30  Since the five perfections without wisdom
    Cannot bring perfect enlightenment,
    Along with skillful means cultivate the wisdom
    Which does not conceive the three spheres (as real)—
        This is the practice of bodhisattvas.

31  If you don't examine your own errors,
    You may look like a practitioner but not act as one.
    Therefore, always examining your own errors,
    Rid yourself of them—
        This is the practice of bodhisattvas.

32  If through the influence of disturbing emotions
    You point out the faults of another bodhisattva,
    You yourself are diminished, so don't mention the faults
    Of those who have entered the Great Vehicle—
        This is the practice of bodhisattvas.

33 Reward and respect cause us to quarrel
And make hearing, thinking, and meditation decline.
For this reason give up attachment to
The households of friends, relations, and benefactors—
     This is the practice of bodhisattvas.

34 Harsh words disturb the minds of others
And cause deterioration in a bodhisattva's conduct.
Therefore, give up harsh words
Which are unpleasant to others—
     This is the practice of bodhisattvas.

35 Habitual disturbing emotions are hard to stop through counteractions.
Armed with antidotes, the guards of mindfulness and introspective
     awareness
Destroy disturbing emotions like attachment
At once, as soon as they arise—
     This is the practice of bodhisattvas.

36 In brief, whatever you are doing,
Ask yourself, "What's the state of my mind?"
With constant mindfulness and introspective awareness
Accomplish others' good—
     This is the practice of bodhisattvas.

37 To remove the suffering of limitless beings,
Understanding the purity of the three spheres,
Dedicate the virtue from making such effort
To enlightenment—
     This is the practice of bodhisattvas.

For all who want to train on the bodhisattva path
I have written *The Thirty-seven Practices of Bodhisattvas*,
Following what has been said by the excellent ones
On the meaning of the sutras, tantras, and treatises.

Though not poetically pleasing to scholars,
Owing to my poor intelligence and lack of learning,
I've relied on the sutras and the words of the excellent,
So I think these bodhisattva practices are without error.

However, as the great deeds of bodhisattvas
Are hard to fathom for one of my poor intelligence,
I beg the excellent to forgive all faults,
Such as contradictions and non sequiturs.

Through the virtue from this may all living beings
Gain the ultimate and conventional altruistic intention
And thereby become like the Protector Chenrezig,
Who dwells in neither extreme—not in the world nor in peace.

This was written for his own and others' benefit by the monk
Togmay, an exponent of scripture and reasoning, in a cave in
Ngülchu Rinchen.

This translation is excerpted from *The Thirty-seven Practices of Bodhisattvas: An Oral Teaching by Geshe Sonam Rinchen*, translated and edited by Ruth Sonam, 1997, with permission from Snow Lion, an imprint of Shambhala Publications, Boston, Massachusetts.

# Appendix II: Outline of
## *The Thirty-seven Practices of Bodhisattvas*

---

The text is divided into three parts:

1. The virtue at the beginning—the introduction
2. The virtue in the middle—the main part of the text
3. The virtue at the end—the conclusion

## 1. THE VIRTUE AT THE BEGINNING—THE INTRODUCTION

1.a. Stating the name of the text

1.b. Offering of praise

1.b.1. A brief explanation

1.b.2. An extensive explanation

1.c. Promise to compose

## 2. THE VIRTUE IN THE MIDDLE—THE MAIN PART OF THE TEXT

2.a. The preliminary practices (Verses 1-7)

2.a.1. The difficulty of obtaining a precious human life (Verse 1)

2.a.2. Giving up one's native land (Verse 2)

2.a.3. Relying on solitude (Verse 3)

2.a.4. Being mindful of impermanence (Verse 4)

2.a.5. Giving up bad company (Verse 5)

2.a.6. Relying on good friends (Verse 6)

2.a.7. Taking refuge (Verse 7)

2.b.3.b.2.b. How to overcome the beliefs that the desired and hated are real between meditation sessions (Verses 23-24)

2.b.3.b.2.b.1. Overcoming the belief that objects of attachment are truly existent (Verse 23)

2.b.3.b.2.b.2. Overcoming the belief that objects of aversion are truly existent (Verse 24)

## 3. THE VIRTUE AT THE END—THE CONCLUSION

3.a. Engaging in the trainings of bodhicitta (Verses 25-37)

3.a.1. The six far-reaching practices (Verses 25-30)

3.a.1.a. The far-reaching practice of generosity (Verse 25)

3.a.1.b. The far-reaching practice of ethical conduct (Verse 26)

3.a.1.c. The far-reaching practice of fortitude (Verse 27)

3.a.1.d. The far-reaching practice of joyous effort (Verse 28)

3.a.1.e. The far-reaching practice of meditative stabilization (Verse 29)

3.a.1.f. The far-reaching practice of wisdom (Verse 30)

3.a.2. The four points taught in the sutras (Verses 31-34)

3.a.2.a. Check our own faults and give them up (Verse 31)

3.a.2.b. Desist from criticizing bodhisattvas (Verse 32)

3.a.2.c. Sever attachment to the households of benefactors (Verse 33)

3.a.2.d. Refrain from harsh words (Verse 34)

3.a.3. The way to abandon the afflictions (Verse 35)

3.a.4. Training in mindfulness and introspective awareness (Verse 36)

3.a.5. Dedication of virtue to complete enlightenment (Verse 37)

3.b. Conclusion of the root text

# Glossary

Please note: the following are the general meanings of terms and are not necessarily the detailed definitions found in the philosophical texts.

**afflictions** Disturbing attitudes: attitudes such as ignorance, anger, attachment, pride, and jealousy, which disturb our mental peace and make us act in ways harmful to others.

**afflictive obscurations** Afflictions and polluted karma that cause cyclic existence.

**aggregates** The psychophysical factors on which the "I" is labeled. There is one physical aggregate (the form aggregate, the body) and four mental aggregates (feeling, discrimination, volitional factors, and consciousness).

**altruistic intention** (Skt. *bodhicitta*) The mind dedicated to attaining enlightenment in order to benefit all sentient beings most effectively.

**analytical meditation** (checking meditation) Meditation that involves investigating a subject. It is done to develop insight into the nature of reality. It principally leads to insight (Skt. *vipashyana*; Pali *vipassana*).

**arhat** A person who has attained liberation and is free from cyclic existence.

**arya** A person who has realized emptiness directly and is thus one of the Sangha Jewels of refuge.

**attachment** An attitude that exaggerates the good qualities of a person or thing and then clings to it.

**basis of designation** The parts or attributes upon which something is labeled. In the case of the "I," it is the aggregates.

**bodhicitta** *See* altruistic intention.

**bodhisattva** A person whose spontaneous reaction upon seeing any sentient being is "I aspire to become a Buddha in order to benefit them."

**Buddha** Any person who has purified all defilements and developed all good qualities. "The Buddha" refers to Shakyamuni Buddha, who lived 2,500 years ago in India.

**Buddha nature** (Buddha potential) The innate qualities of the mind enabling all beings to attain enlightenment.

**Buddhahood** *See* enlightenment.

**cognitive obscurations** Latencies left on the mindstream by the afflictions and the appearance of inherent existence. These prevent us from attaining Buddhahood.

**compassion** The wish for sentient beings to be free from suffering and its causes.

**concentration** (Skt. *samadhi*) A mental factor that focuses single-pointedly on an object of meditation.

**cyclic existence** (Skt. *samsara*) Taking uncontrolled rebirth under the influence of disturbing attitudes and karmic latencies.

**designate** (label, impute) To give a label or name to an object; to attribute meaning to it.

**designated object** The object designated, labeled, or imputed on its basis of designation. For example, the "I" is designated on its basis of designation, the aggregates.

**determination to be free** (renunciation) The attitude aspiring to be free from cyclic existence and to attain liberation.

**Dharma** In the most general sense, Dharma refers to the teachings of the Buddha. Most specifically, it refers to the realizations of the path and the resultant cessations of suffering and its causes.

**direct nonconceptual realization of emptiness** A mind that sees directly and without conception the lack of inherent or true existence.

**distorted views** Stubborn and close-minded views that the Three Jewels, cause and effect, and so on do not exist; believing that sentient beings are inherently selfish and cannot become enlightened.

**disturbing attitudes and negative emotions** (Skt. *klesha*): *See* afflictions

**dukkha** (Pali; Skt. *duhkha*) Any unsatisfactory condition, including physical and mental pain, fleeting worldly happiness, and having a body and mind under the influence of ignorance and karma.

**emptiness** (Skt. *shunyata*) The lack of independent or inherent existence, the ultimate nature or reality of all persons and phenomena.

**enlightenment** (Buddhahood) The state of a Buddha, i.e., the state of having forever eliminated all obscurations from the mindstream and having developed all good qualities and wisdom to their fullest extent. Buddhahood supersedes liberation.

**equalizing self and others** The attitude that feels that the importance of others' wish to have happiness and be free of suffering is equal to our own.

**equanimity** Having an equally open attitude to all sentient beings, free of attachment, anger, and apathy.

**exchanging self and others** Exchanging the object of importance from self to others, i.e., cherishing others the way we used to cherish ourselves and neglecting the self the way we used to neglect others.

**existing from its own side** Existing without depending on causes, conditions, or any other factors.

**grasping at true existence** Grasping at the objective existence of phenomena through their own entity without being posited by thought.

**great compassion** Wishing all sentient beings to be free from suffering and its causes.

**great resolve** Determining to take the responsibility upon oneself to bring about the happiness of sentient beings and to eliminate their suffering.

**hearers** Those who follow the path to liberation and become arhats. They are so called because they hear the Buddha's teachings and teach them to others.

**inherent** or **independent existence** A false and nonexistent mode of being that we project onto persons and phenomena; existence independent of causes and conditions, parts, or the mind conceiving and labeling phenomena.

**innate self-grasping** The inborn, spontaneous grasping at self-existence that all beings in cyclic existence have.

**insight** (Skt. *vipashyana*; Pali *vipassana*) Discriminating analytical wisdom. Special insight into emptiness realizes the empty nature of phenomena.

**introspective awareness** (vigilance, clear comprehension) A mental factor that is watchful so that we are aware of the contents of our mind. It enables us to bring our mind and actions back to ethical behavior or to the object of meditation if it has strayed.

**karma** Actions done by our body, speech, or mind. Our actions leave latencies on our mindstream and later bring about our experiences.

**karmic latency** (karmic seed) The residual "energy" left on the mindstream when an action has been completed. When these latencies mature, they influence what we experience.

**liberation** (Skt. *moksha*) The state of having removed all afflictions and karma, which cause us to take rebirth in cyclic existence, as well as their latencies.

**love** The wish for sentient beings to have happiness and its causes.

**Mahayana** A Buddhist tradition that emphasizes the development of the altruistic intention.

**mandala offering** Offering the universe and everything beautiful in it to the Buddhas and bodhisattvas.

**mantra** A series of Sanskrit syllables spoken by a Buddha that expresses the essence of the entire path to enlightenment. They are recited in order to concentrate and purify the mind.

**meditation** Habituating ourselves with positive attitudes and correct perspectives.

**meditative equipoise on emptiness** The time of single-pointedly meditating on emptiness.

**mental factor** A type of mind that apprehends a particular quality of an object or has a specific function in the process of cognition.

**merit** That which results in happiness in the future; latencies of constructive actions.

**mind** The experiential, cognitive part of sentient beings; clarity and awareness. Formless, the mind isn't made of atoms, nor is it perceivable through our five senses.

**mindfulness** A mental factor that enables the mind to stay on its chosen object without forgetting it and prevents distraction to other objects.

**mindstream** Continuity of mind.

**nirvana** The cessation of dukkha and its causes; the emptiness of the mind in which dukkha and its causes have been ceased.

**object of negation** What is to be negated or proven nonexistent in the meditation on emptiness, for example. It is essential to identify this properly before meditating on emptiness.

**offerings** Actual or imagined objects that we offer to the merit field in order to generate delight in giving and to create merit.

**permanent** Not changing moment by moment. Permanent phenomena are not necessarily eternal; many do not exist forever.

**person** The mere "I" which is designated in dependence upon any of the five aggregates.

**phenomena** That which holds its own entity. In general, this is synonymous with "existent." In the context of the self-grasping of persons and of phenomena, however, "phenomena" refers to all existents other than persons.

**precepts** Guidelines set out by the Buddha to help us refrain from destructive actions and to train our mind.

**realization** A clear, deep, and correct understanding of the conventional or ultimate natures. It may be either conceptual in nature or a nonconceptual direct experience.

**sadhana** The method of meditating on the Buddha or a Buddha figure that is often written in the form of a text.

**Sangha** Any person who directly and nonconceptually realizes emptiness. In a more general sense, sangha refers to any community of four or more fully-ordained monks or nuns.

**self-existent** Being able to exist without depending on anything, be it causes and conditions, parts, or the mind that conceives and labels it. This type of existence is negated on all existents, both persons and other phenomena.

**selflessness** The nonexistence of the object of negation.

**sentient being** Any being with a mind who is not a Buddha. This includes ordinary beings as well as arhats and bodhisattvas.

**serenity** (Skt. *shamatha*) The ability to remain single-pointedly on an object of meditation with a blissful and pliant mind for as long as one wishes.

**seven-limb prayer** A recitation in which we 1) bow, 2) make offerings, 3) reveal with regret our destructive actions, 4) rejoice in our own and others' virtue, 4) request the Buddhas to remain in our world, 6) request our teachers and the Buddhas to guide and teach us, and 7) dedicate our merit for the enlightenment of all sentient beings.

**six far-reaching practices or perfections** (Skt. *paramita*) States of mind and practices cultivated with the bodhicitta motivation. The six far-reaching practices are generosity, ethical conduct, fortitude, joyous effort, meditative stabilization, and wisdom.

**solitary realizers** Those who, in their last lifetime before becoming arhats, practice in solitude at a time when no Buddha has appeared in the world.

**stabilizing meditation** Meditation that stabilizes the mind by developing concentration. It leads principally to serenity.

**suffering** (Pali *dukkha*) Any unsatisfactory condition. It doesn't refer only to physical or mental pain, but includes all problematic conditions in cyclic existence.

**sutra** (Skt.; Pali *sutta*) A discourse given by the Buddha.

**taking and giving meditation** A meditation in which we imagine taking on others' suffering with compassion and giving them our body, possessions, and merit with love.

**taking refuge** Entrusting our spiritual development to the guidance of the Buddha, Dharma, and Sangha.

**tantra** A scripture taught by the Buddha describing the Vajrayana practice.

**Three Higher Trainings** Ethical conduct, concentration, and wisdom.

**Three Jewels** (Triple Gem) The Buddha, Dharma, and Sangha.

**three poisonous attitudes** Ignorance, anger (hostility), and attachment. They poison our mind and motivate actions that poison our relationships.

**true cessation** The state of some or all of the afflictions having been abandoned; the extinguishment of true sufferings and true causes.

**true existence** The objective existence of phenomena through their own entity without being posited by thought.

**unsatisfactory circumstances** *See* dukkha.

**Vajrayana** A Mahayana Buddhist tradition popular in Tibet and Japan.

**wisdom realizing emptiness** A mind that correctly understands the manner in which all persons and phenomena exist, that is, the wisdom realizing the emptiness of inherent existence.

# Further Reading

Berzin, Alexander. *Wise Teacher, Wise Student: Tibetan Approaches to a Healthy Relationship*. Ithaca, N.Y.: Snow Lion Publications, 2010.

Chodron, Thubten. *Buddhism for Beginners*. Ithaca, N.Y.: Snow Lion Publications, 2001.

———. *Cultivating a Compassionate Heart: The Yoga Method of Chenrezig*. Ithaca, N.Y.: Snow Lion Publications, 2006.

———. *Guided Meditations on the Stages of the Path*. Ithaca, N.Y.: Snow Lion Publications, 2007.

——— *How to Free Your Mind: Tara the Liberator*. Ithaca, N.Y.: Snow Lion Publications, 2005.

———. *Open Heart, Clear Mind*. Ithaca, N.Y.: Snow Lion Publications, 1990.

———. *Taming the Mind*. Ithaca, N.Y.: Snow Lion Publications, 2004.

———. *Working with Anger*. Ithaca, N.Y.: Snow Lion Publications, 2001.

Dhammananda, K. Sri. *How to Live Without Fear and Worry*. Kuala Lumpur: Buddhist Missionary Society, 1989.

Dhargyey, Geshe Ngawang. *An Anthology of Well-Spoken Advice on the Graded Path of the Mind*. Dharamsala, India: Library of Tibetan Works and Archives, 2001.

Dharmarakshita. *Wheel of Sharp Weapons*. Dharamsala, India: Library of Tibetan Works and Archives, 2007.

Dilgo Khyentse Rinpoche. *Enlightened Courage: An Explanation of the Seven-Point Mind Training*. Ithaca, N.Y.: Snow Lion Publications, 2006.

First Dalai Lama, Gyalwa Gendun Druppa. *Training the Mind in the Great Way*. Translated by Glenn H. Mullin. Ithaca, N.Y.: Snow Lion Publications, 1997.

Gampopa. *The Jewel Ornament of Liberation: The Wish-fulfilling Gem of the Noble Teachings*. Translated by Khenpo Konchog Gyaltsen. Ithaca, N.Y.: Snow Lion Publications, 1998.

Gyeltsen, Geshe Tsultim. *Mirror of Wisdom: Teachings on Emptiness.* Long Beach, Calif.: Thubten Dhargye Ling Publications, 2000.

Gyatso, Lobsang. *The Harmony of Emptiness and Dependent-Arising.* Dharamsala, India: Library of Tibetan Works and Archives, 1992.

H. H. Tenzin Gyatso, the Fourteenth Dalai Lama. *The Buddhism of Tibet.* Ithaca, N.Y.: Snow Lion Publications, 2002.

———. *Cultivating a Daily Meditation.* Dharamsala, India: Library of Tibetan Works and Archives, 1991.

———. *The Dalai Lama at Harvard.* Ithaca, N.Y.: Snow Lion Publications, 1989.

———. *Healing Anger: The Power of Patience from a Buddhist Perspective.* Ithaca, N.Y.: Snow Lion Publications, 1997.

———. *Kindness, Clarity, and Insight.* Rev. ed. Ithaca, N.Y.: Snow Lion Publications, 2006.

———. *The Path to Bliss.* Ithaca, N.Y.: Snow Lion Publications, 2003.

———. *The Path to Enlightenment.* Ithaca, N.Y.: Snow Lion Publications, 1995.

———. *The Way to Freedom.* San Francisco: HarperSanFrancisco, 1994.

Gyatso, Thubten. *Transforming Problems.* Singapore: Amitabha Buddhist Centre, 1999.

Hopkins, Jeffrey. *A Truthful Heart: Buddhist Practices for Connecting with Others.* Ithaca, N.Y.: Snow Lion Publications, 2008.

Jinpa, Thupten, trans. *Mind Training: The Great Collection.* Boston: Wisdom Publications, 2006.

Khandro Rinpoche. *This Precious Life: Tibetan Buddhist Teachings on the Path to Enlightenment.* Boston: Shambhala, 2005.

Lhundrub, Ngorchen Konchog. *The Three Visions: Fundamental Teachings of the Sakya Lineage of Tibetan Buddhism.* Ithaca, N.Y.: Snow Lion Publications, 2002.

Loden, Geshe Acharya Thubten. *Path to Enlightenment in Tibetan Buddhism.* Melbourne, Australia: Tushita Publications, 1993.

McDonald, Kathleen. *How to Meditate: A Practical Guide.* Rev. ed. Boston: Wisdom Publications, 2005.

Patrul Rinpoche. *The Words of My Perfect Teacher.* Rev. ed. Translated by the Padmakara Translation Group. Boston: Shambhala, 1998.

Rabten, Geshe. *The Essential Nectar: Meditations on the Buddhist Path.* Boston: Wisdom Publications, 1992.

Rabten, Geshe, and Geshe Ngawang Dhargyey. *Advice from a Spiritual Friend.* Rev. ed. Boston: Wisdom Publications, 2001.

Rinchen, Geshe Sonam. *Atisha's Lamp for the Path to Enlightenment.* Ithaca, N.Y.: Snow Lion Publications, 1997.

———. *The Six Perfections.* Ithaca, N.Y.: Snow Lion Publications, 1998.

———. *The Thirty-seven Practices of Bodhisattvas.* Ithaca, N.Y.: Snow Lion Publications, 1997.

Sopa, Geshe Lhundub. *Peacock in the Poison Grove: Two Buddhist Texts on Training the Mind.* Boston: Wisdom Publications, 2001.

———. *Steps on the Path to Enlightenment: A Commentary on Tsongkhapa's Lamrim Chenmo.* 5 volumes. Boston: Wisdom Publications, 2004.

Tegchok, Geshe Jampa. *The Kindness of Others: A Commentary on the Seven-Point Mind Training.* Weston, Mass.: Lama Yeshe Wisdom Archive, 2006.

———. *Transforming Adversity into Joy and Courage: An Explanation of the Thirty-seven Practices of Bodhisattvas.* Ithaca, N.Y.: Snow Lion Publications, 2005.

Thubten Zopa Rinpoche, Lama. *The Door to Satisfaction: The Heart Advice of a Tibetan Buddhist Master.* Boston: Wisdom Publications, 1994.

———. *Kadampa Teachings.* Boston: Lama Yeshe Wisdom Archive, 2010.

———. *Transforming Problems into Happiness.* Boston: Wisdom Publications, 2001.

Tsering, Geshe Tashi. *The Awakening Mind: The Foundation of Buddhist Thought.* Boston: Wisdom Publications, 2008.

Tsong-kha-pa. *The Great Treatise on the Stages of the Path to Enlightenment.* 3 volumes. Ithaca, N.Y.: Snow Lion Publications, 2000-2004.

Tsongkhapa, Je. *The Three Principal Aspects of the Path.* Howell, N.J.: Mahayana Sutra and Tantra Press, 1988.

Tsulga, Geshe. *How to Practice the Buddhadharma.* Boston: Wisdom Publications, 2002.

Wangchen, Geshe Namgyal. *Awakening the Mind of Enlightenment.* Boston: Wisdom Publications, 1988.

Yangsi Rinpoche. *Practicing the Path: A Commentary on the Lamrim Chenmo.* Boston: Wisdom Publications, 2005.

Also see:

www.thubtenchdron.org

www.sravastiabbey.org